JANUA LINGUARUM

STUDIA MEMORIAE
NICOLAI VAN WIJK DEDICATA

edenda curat

C. H. VAN SCHOONEVELD

Indiana University

Series Minor, 125

THE ARTICLE
AND THE CONCEPT OF
DEFINITENESS IN LANGUAGE

by

JIŘÍ KRÁMSKÝ

1972

MOUTON

THE HAGUE · PARIS

LIBRARY OF CONGRESS CATALOG CARD NUMBER: 73-190726

Printed in Belgium by NICI printers, Ghent.

TABLE OF CONTENTS

INTRODUCTION

Though it is true that there are many papers dealing with articles in languages such as English, German, French, as well as other Germanic and Romance languages, very rare are papers discussing the essence of articles or their diffusion in different languages of the world, in other words a certain typology of languages classified according to a different kind of the formal expression of articles, or, on a wider scale, of the category of determinedness vs. indeterminedness. Among such broadly conceived works we will quote at least the works of Paul Christophersen[1], further A. Biard[2], R. Brandstetter[3], and R. de la Grasserie[4]. The first of them deals with articles in English, the second with the definite article in principal European languages, the third with articles in Indonesian languages. However, most extensively conceived is the work of Raoul de la Grasserie which presents a sort of typology of various kinds of article in different languages of the world. Today this work, however, isolated as it was in its time, does not answer the purpose, as its data on some languages, especially the non-European ones, are not quite reliable. The author often ascribes the function of articles to formal means that have a different function. Further, R. de la Grasserie does not sufficiently differ-

---

[1] Paul Christophersen, *The Articles. A study of their theory and use in English.* (Copenhagen — London, 1939).
[2] A. Biard, *L'article défini dans les principales langues européennes* (Bordeaux, 1908).
[3] Renward Brandstetter, *Der Artikel des Indonesischen verglichen mit dem des Indogermanischen* (= *Monographien zur Indonesischen Sprachforschung* X) (Lucerne, 1913).
[4] Raoul de la Grasserie, "De l'article", *Mémoires de la Société de linguistique de Paris* IX (1896), 285-322, 381-394.

entiate the demonstrative and the determinative function. In many cases given by R. de la Grasserie only demonstratives and not articles are concerned. This, of course, distorts the overall picture of the diffusion of articles in the languages of the world. Similar shortcomings may be pointed to in the rather extensively conceived monograph by R. Brandstetter which in many cases also does not make a careful distinction between the demonstrative and determinative function. In our opinion, there are two reasons for the inaccuracy and unreliability of many of the works dealing with articles. In the first place it is the fact that linguists did not devote a closer attention to the essence of articles in comparison to other indicaters such as demonstratives. Another reason concerns, in a number of cases, insufficient information on the grammatical structure of some non-European languages in older linguistic literature.

It is therefore the aim of our work to attempt at an elucidation of some basic problems concerning the essence of the category of determinedness vs. indeterminedness and to try to draft a typology of languages using the criteria of a different expression of the category of determinedness vs. indeterminedness by means of articles and other formal grammatical expedients.

It is quite natural that our work could neither include all languages expressing, by some formal means, the category of determinedness vs. indeterminedness, nor devote equal attention to each language as there do not exist equally adequate descriptions of grammatical systems of all languages, even if today we have an incomparably better knowledge of many languages, especially the non-European ones, than we had at the beginning of this century or even before the second World War. We therefore claim the indulgence of our readers in judging a certain disproportion in the degree of information on the occurrence of the category of determinedness vs. indeterminedness in particular languages. On the whole, it is natural that we have devoted most of the space to those European languages for which the use of articles is very typical and considerably interferes in their grammatical structure (e.g. English, French, German, Italian, Spanish, Rumanian, etc.).

The information we could get about some less explored languages is often very insufficient and fragmentary and not always quite reliable. We have therefore tried, so far as more information about the same language was accessible, to confront various pieces of information in view of our problem and in a number of cases we have found disagreement between them. Thus in disputable cases we cannot but wait till more competent descriptions of languages in question are available. Last but not least we meet with fairly detailed descriptions of languages that miss any mention of the category of determinedness vs. indeterminedness though other categories are dealt with. Most regrettable it is in those cases when the described language has no formally expressed article but the category of determinedness vs. indeterminedness is expressed in it in another way. As a matter of fact, it is peculiar how often it is just this category to which grammatical descriptions of languages devote the least attention. Even if it does not belong among basic categories, yet in grammatical respect it is a very interesting phenomenon, as we do not find any other grammatical category that would be characterized by such a diversity of formation and semantic prominence as the category of determinedness vs. indeterminedness undoubtedly is.

Finally we must explain why we have not limited this monograph to articles only. Though originally this was our intention, a thorough consideration of the essence of articles has brought us to the conviction that the article is only one of the means of expressing a broader category, that is to say the category of determinedness vs. indeterminedness. If we were concerned with articles only, we should examine only a part of the problem and that would be a distortion undesirable in a work aiming at a most extensive and exhausting survey of the examined phenomenon in typological respect. Incompleteness would be most damaging just for the typological point of view. It was our aim to try to get hold of this extraordinarily interesting language phenomenon in all its diversity, variety and profundity.

PART ONE

THE CATEGORY OF DETERMINEDNESS
VS. INDETERMINEDNESS

1. ON THE PROBLEM OF WORD CATEGORIES

The concept of grammatical category has its origin as early as in the Old Grecian time. Aristotle stated two "parts of speech": noun and verb. The Stoics distinguished at first four, later five "parts of speech": noun, verb, syndesmos, and arthron, which they stated on a mixed basis of form and meaning. Nouns were defined morphologically, as they had case inflexion and were further divided in semantic respect into proper and common names. The verb was defined as "a part of a sentence that states something when not in construction". Syndesmos is defined as "a part of a sentence without case endings which links up the parts of the sentence", and arthron as "an element of a sentence with case endings which distinguishes gender and number of nouns, such as *ho, he, to* and *hoi, hai, ta*" (the masculine, feminine, and neuter nominative articles, singular and plural, respectively). Thus the Stoics included into the class of arthron articles and relative pronouns. Dionysius Thrax (born about 166 B.C.) was the first to distinguish eight "parts of speech", that means grammatical (word) not logical categories: nouns, verbs, participles, articles, pronouns, prepositions, adverbs, and conjunctions. The classification of Dionysius Thrax has been preserved with minor modifications up to the present day. Similarly Apollonius Dyscolus (2nd cent. A.D., Alexandria). The view of Dionysius Thrax was applied to Latin by Remnius Palaemon (1st cent. A.D.) who keeps to eight categories but instead of article places interjection. Priscian (6th cent. A.D.) who based his grammar on the work of Apollonius Dyscolus defines the "parts of speech" as follows[1]:

[1] Quoted from Francis P. Dinneen, *An Introduction to General Linguistics* (New York, 1967), 115.

1. The noun is a part of speech that assigns to each of its subjects, bodies, or things a common or proper quality.
2. The verb is a part of speech with tenses and moods, but without case, that signifies acting or being acted upon.
3. The participles share case with the noun and voice and tense with the verbs; however, they are not explicitly defined.
4. The pronoun is a part of speech that can substitute for the proper name of anyone and that indicates a definite person. (The forms like *quis, qualis, qui* and *talis* are regarded to be nouns, since they are indefinite as to person).
5. The preposition is an indeclinable part of speech that is put before others, either next to them or forming a composite with them.
6. The adverb is an indeclinable part of speech whose meaning is added to the verb.
7. The interjection is distinguished from the adverb by its syntactic independence and its emotive meaning.
8. The conjunction is an indeclinable part of speech that links other parts of speech, in company with which it has significance, by clarifying their meaning or relations.

Of course, Priscian's definitions of the "parts of speech" are insufficient as they are predominantly based on the concept of "meaning" instead of on morphological and syntactic criteria. Lindley Murray in his grammar from 1798 gives nine "parts of speech": articles, nouns, pronouns, adjectives, verbs, adverbs, prepositions, conjunctions, and interjections. In the 19th century under the influence of historical orientation of linguistics article ceased to be regarded as a "part of speech" and was added to the class of adjectives. In the 20th century mostly eight but also less "parts of speech" are recognized.

There are various views on the substance of word categories; we will mention two main views. According to one, word categories correspond to categories of things, that means to categories of extralinguistic reality. According to this view nouns are names of substances, things; adjectives are names of qualities conceived as invariable, verbs are names of transient qualities. In agreement with the view of H. Paul[2], B. Trnka[3] regards this classification as incorrect, because it is based on semantic criteria. According to Trnka the division into "parts of speech" is a morphological division, as it is based on the participation of words in morphological categories which need not be identical in different languages. In English Trnka regards as "parts of speech" nouns, verbs and uninflected words. Nouns in English are such words as take part in the opposition countability vs. uncountability, in the opposition of number (singular vs. plural) and in the opposition general case vs. adnominal case *(the king — the king's)*. Verbs in English are, according to Trnka, such words as take part in the opposition present tense vs. preterite, further in modal oppositions and in the concord as to number and person of the subject. All other words belong in English to one category which, from the point of view of syntagmatic morphology, can be divided into words subordinate to nouns only which they determine (the so-called adjectives), further into words that are subordinated to verbs and adjectives as their determinants (the so-called adverbs), and finally into words that express determination between words and sentences (prepositions and conjunctions) by themselves. Uninflected words that never determine any words are interjections. As far as pronouns and numerals are concerned which the traditional grammar includes into the "parts of speech", Trnka points partly to the fact that from the semantic point of view these categories are undefinable, partly to the fact that this differentiation is based on a criterion other than that on which the classification into nouns, adjectives, verbs, adverbs, etc. is based, as both pronouns and numerals can be in English partly nouns *(the, three, who)*, partly adjectives *(firstly, secondly*, etc., *wherefrom)*, partly also verbs *(to treble, to thou)*. According to Trnka both categories cannot be precisely delimited even by schematic criteria and, consequently,

---

[2] H. Paul, *Prinzipien der Sprachgeschichte*, 4th ed., 352.
[3] B. Trnka, *Rozbor nynější spisovné angličtiny, II /Morfologie slovních druhů/* [An Analysis of Present-Day Literary English, II, Morphology of Word Classes] (Praha, 1962), mimeographed, 13-14.

there is a considerable variance as to which words belong to pronouns and numerals.

According to another view[4] word categories correspond to syntactic categories. In this view nouns are words that may be used as subject or object, adjectives are words that may be used as coordinate attribute and verbs are words that express predicate. Vilém Mathesius[5] inclines to the opinion that word categories do neither express material categories nor syntactic categories only, but that both criteria interpenetrate them.

2. THE ASPECT MODIFICATION AND THE CATEGORY OF DETERMINEDNESS VS. INDETERMINEDNESS

Let us now turn to the category of determinedness vs. indeterminedness which is predominantly a category of nouns. In some languages, however, it is also a category of other classes of words, e.g. adjectives or verbs as well. Vilém Mathesius regards determinedness vs. indeterminedness not as a category but as an aspect modification, that is a secondary category. Aspect modification is, according to Mathesius, such alteration of the meaning of the word in which the basic meaning remains intact, whereas in categorial differences the change fully affects the meaning of the word. Thus, for example, transitiveness vs. intransitiveness of verbs in Czech is a categorial change, whereas determinedness vs. indeterminedness in English is, in Mathesius's view, an aspect modification. The same aspect modification can in one language be a substantial part of the system of grammar whereas in another language it is only an occasional means of an exact qualification of the meaning. According to Mathesius the existence of articles in Germanic and Romance languages gives evidence of the fact that in them the category of determinedness vs. indeterminedness is a substantial part of their system of grammar whereas the lack

[4] Cf., e.g., Eduard Hermann, *Die Wortarten* (Berlin, 1928).
[5] Vilém Mathesius, *Obsahový rozbor současné angličtiny na základě obecně lingvistickém* [A Functional Analysis of Present-Day English on a General Linguistic Basis] (Praha, 1961), 40-41.

of article in most Slavic languages shows that the determinedness vs. indeterminedness of nouns is something occasional with them.[6] However, Mathesius's classing the determinedness vs. indeterminedness with aspect modifications does not seem quite convincing. In our opinion, the category or aspect modification of determinedness vs. indeterminedness cannot be put on the same level as, for instance, the aspect modification of number. In the case of the number of nouns the change of the word does not affect the basic meaning of the word. On the other hand, determinedness definitely represents a greater interference with the meaning of the word than the aspect modification of number. It is at least disputable what kind of change it must be that it may fully affect the basic meaning of the word. After all, even the term "the basic meaning of the word" is rather vague. As to the opposition determinedness vs. indeterminedness it may be admitted that the basic meaning of the word is not affected; however, that which is added to the noun is of a quite different kind from that which is the essence of the other aspect modifications. We even do not hesitate to speak here about a certain degree of semantic differentiation. Further explanation will be given in our discussion of the essence of article. In any way the opposition determinedness vs. indeterminedness is closer, for example to the opposition transitiveness vs. intransitiveness with Czech verbs which Mathesius regards as a category, than to the aspect modification of number. After all, if, according to Mathesius, the category of determinedness vs. indeterminedness in Germanic and Romance languages is a substantial part of the system of grammar of these languages, it is not in accord with the fact that the opposition determinedness vs. indeterminedness is ascribed the statute of only a secondary category or aspect modification.

In order to be able to state with the possibly greatest exactness whether to regard determinedness vs. indeterminedness as a category or as an aspect modification it is necessary to penetrate deeper into its essence than it has been done so far. We will try

[6] Cf. V. Mathesius, *Čeština a obecný jazykozpyt* [The Czech Language and General Linguistics] (Praha, 1947), 166.

that in the following two chapters of which the first will be devoted to a survey of various theories of article and the following will discuss our own theory of the essence of the category of determinedness vs. indeterminedness.

3. SOME DEFINITIONS AND THEORIES OF ARTICLE

The term 'article' is a translation of the Latin term *articulus* which again is a rendering of the Greek word *arthron* (ἄρθρον) known as a grammatical term since the 4th century B.C. For the Stoics it was one of the five "parts of speech" and was defined, as we have already mentioned, as an element of a sentence with case endings which distinguishes gender and number of nouns. The later articles and relative pronouns were included into the same class. Dionysius Thrax distinguished as one of eight parts of speech the article which "is a case-forming part of a sentence that precedes or follows nouns. The one that precedes is *ho* (and so, implicitly, *he* and *to*) and the one that follows is *hos* (hence implicitly, the other relatives, *he*, *ho*). Its simultaneous features are gender, number, and case".[7] In imitation of the Greeks, the Romans declared their pronouns *hic*, *haec*, and *hoc* to be articles. Donatus and some other grammarians distinguished the dependent *hic*, an article, from the independent demonstrative pronoun *hic*. The Latin grammarian Varro (116-27 B.C.) took over the Stoic terminology in which both pronouns and articles were included in the pronomen articulare which was either finite (the pronoun) or infinite (the article). *Hic* being a demonstrative pronoun (articulus finitus), the term finite or definite article was used for the German *der* and French *le*. The other article was close in its meaning to the definite pronoun (Varro's article) *aliquis*, and hence got its name of indefinite article.[8]

---

[7] Cf. Francis P. Dinneen, *An Introduction to General Linguistics* (New York, 1967), 93, 101.

[8] Cf. Ivan Poldauf, "On the History of Some Problems of English Grammar Before 1800", *Práce z vědeckých ústavů* (= *Příspěvky k dějinám řeči a literatury anglické* LV. Prague Studies in English 7) (Prague, 1948).

However, the article is not present in all languages; it is, according to R. de la Grasserie,[9] "... un organe complémentaire qui s'ajoute en présence de certains besoins psychiques d'expression, lesquels sinon le créent, du moins le développent et lui donnent seuls une existence personnelle autonome". On the other hand, we must keep in mind that the category of determinedness vs. indeterminedness, which is most frequently expressed just by the article, is a universal category and in many languages it is expressed by non-formal means, the article in the usual sense of the word being absent in them. Later we will discuss even these cases.

Before presenting our own opinion of articles and explaining the essence of the category of determinedness vs. indeterminedness we will make the reader acquainted with at least the most important theories of article.

In our opinion, the best survey of important theories of articles is contained in chapter III of Paul Christophersen's book, whereas chapter IV of the same book presents the author's own theory of articles. Our discussion makes full use of Christophersen's comments.

First we will mention some basic definitions of article. The most simple definition states that the role of the article is to designate an object as familiar.[10] According to J. Haas,[11] "das sprachliche Korrelat der Determinationsvorstellung wird als bestimmter Artikel, und das sprachliche Korrelat der Indeterminationsvorstellung wird als unbestimmter Artikel bezeichnet". According to G. Guillaume[12]

---

[9] "De l'article", *Mémoires de la Société de linguistique de Paris* IX (1896), 285.

[10] Cf. F. Miklosich, *Vergleichende Grammatik der slavischen Sprachen* IV (Wien, 1868-1874), 124. Similarly Henry Sweet (*A New English Grammar, Logical and Historical* II, *Syntax* [Oxford, 1898] 55): "... the definite article is put before a noun to show that the idea expressed by the noun has already been stated, and to refer back to that statement." The same idea is expressed by the Czech linguist J. Zubatý (*Naše řeč* 1 [1917], 289): "The definite article indicates that the person or thing that is spoken of is in a way known or familiar ... It is just only the familiarity of the subject in the broadest sense of the word which is indicated by the article."

[11] Cf. J. Haas, *Französische Syntax* (Halle a. S., 1916), 162.

[12] Cf. G. Guillaume, *Le problème de l'article et sa solution dans la langue française* (Paris, 1919), 305.

the article is "un simple signe de relation entre une idée et un fonds d'idées".

Raoul de la Grasserie[13] regards as the principal function of the article the fact that the article individualizes the given subject. He links this fact with the generic meaning of article. On the other hand, A. J. Carnoy[14] regards as the main meaning of the article not the individualization of the subject but the presentative meaning; the article presents the subject to the hearer's mind. Hence the development of both the discriminative and the generic meaning.

According to Karel Horálek[15] the article is a formal (grammatical) word by means of which the subject which is spoken of is closely defined (determined). This close determination may concern either one representative of the genus and this is the case of the so-called individualizing function of article or the determination has a generalizing meaning (i.e. an individual stands for a whole genus) and this is the case of the so-called generic article. Apart from this basic function the article may also have some other functions, for instance the anaphoric function and thus it borders on demonstrative and anaphoric pronouns.

Louis Hjelmslev[16] asserts that the genuine nature of the article is the morpheme of concretization: the article is the morpheme of concretization which indicates that the subject (or its nature) is probably known to the hearer.

E. Schwyzer[17] writes that the definite article determines or individualizes the noun in opposition to another noun.

E. Gamillscheg[18] designates the article as a language "signal".

---

[13] R. de la Grasserie, "De l'article", *Mémoires de la Société de linguistique de Paris* IX (1896), 286, 388-391.

[14] A. J. Carnoy, *Symbolae grammaticae* I (1927), 143, 147-8, 152.

[15] Karel Horálek, *Úvod do studia slovanských jazyků* [Introduction to the Study of Slavic Languages] (Praha, 1955), 241.

[16] Louis Hjelmslev, *Principes de grammaire générale* (København, 1928), 335 f.

[17] Cf. *Zeitschrift für vergleichende Sprachforschung* 63 (1936), 146.

[18] E. Gamillscheg, "Zum romanischen Artikel und Possessivpronomen", *Supplementheft XV der Zeitschrift für französische Sprache und Literatur* (1937), 5.

It is a signalizing means which indicates the familiarity or un-familiarity of the announced noun.

J. Marouzeau[19] has the following definition of article: "Mot accessoire, joint au nom pour indiquer qu'un objet (p.e. *pain*) est conçu comme réel, soit dans un cas donné (article défini: *le paine que voici*), soit comme représentant de l'espèce (article indéfini: *un pain*) soit dans une partie de son extension (article partitif: *du pain*). Dans certaines langues on distingue des articles collectifs, personnels, de parenté, etc."

J. Kurz assumes[20] that having in mind the basic function of the article, that is to say the designation of the determinedness of the notion concerned with the subject as a unit (the individualizing meaning of the article) or the whole class, the genus of the subjects in opposition to the class, or another group (the generic meaning of the article), we can say that the article is a language element which is regularly added to nouns when the notion expressed by the respective noun concerned with a particular subject or with the whole category of subjects is to be designated as familiar.

The so-called anaphoric article can, according to Kurz, be included into the individualizing use but we must not forget to emphasize obligation, regularity of the use of this article, whereas the anaphoric pronoun is used only in case of a matter-of-fact need of reference.

According to Kurz, generic article should be conceived either as indicating an individual taken from a whole genus or from a class of individuals as their representative, or rather as individualizing a certain kind of individual in opposition to other kinds of individuals.[21]

The indefinite article and its relation to the definite article is very realistically characterized by E. Gamillscheg:[22]

[19] J. Marouzeau, *Lexique de la terminologie linguistique* (Paris, 1951), 32.
[20] J. Kurz, "K otázce členu v jazycích slovanských, se zvláštním zřetelem k staroslověnštině" [On the problem of article in Slavic languages with a special regard to Old Slavic], *Byzantinoslavica* VII (1938), 249.
[21] R. de la Grasserie ("De l'article", p. 385) writes that *l'homme* with a generic article is indeterminate so far as individuals of a genus are concerned but determinate in relation to other genera.
[22] E. Gamillscheg, "Zum romanischen Artikel und Possessivpronomen", 45.

Der unbestimmte Artikel *ein*, dazu im Französischen heute der partitive Artikel *du*, *des*, bringt dem Hörenden zum Bewusstsein, dass eine ihm neue oder unerwartete Vorstellung erweckt werden soll. Ist dies geschehen, dann geht "ein" in "der" über, frz. "des" in "les" usf. So wird der Artikel, "bestimmt" oder "unbestimmt", zum sprachlichen Signal und kann in analytisch aufbauenden Sprachen als echtes Signalmittel gar nicht anders als dem Nomen vorangehen. Der Artikel ist daher (nach Kalepki) "präsentierend". Es gibt aber Vorstellungen, die zum Allgemeinbesitz unseres Bewusstseins gehören, die jederzeit aktiviert werden können. Das Auftreten "eines Fremden" ist nichts von selbst Gegebenes. Wohl aber die Tatsache des Vorhandenseins einer "Sonne" oder der "Hände" im Zusammenhang mit dem menschlichen Körper. Man sagt daher nicht "eine Sonne" geht auf oder Il a "des mains" dans la poche, sondern "die Sonne", "les mains". "Die", "les" weist darauf hin: Was nun folgt, ist dir, dem Hörenden, in seinem Wesen bekannt. So kann der Artikel, namentlich in einer Zeit, zu der die Artikelsetzung noch nicht sprachliche Notwendigkeit ist, suggerierend wirken.

E. Schwyzer[23] is of the opinion that the difference between the definite and indefinite article is more terminological than actual. He suggests that it would be better to call the indefinite article relatively definite in contrast to absolutely definite article. Likewise R. de la Grasserie (p. 294) labels the indefinite article "article de détermination imparfaite".

Definite article has various names. Christopherson quotes the following English terms: definite, determinative, defining, individualizing, particularizing, specializing, descriptive, familiarizing, actualizing, concretizing, substantivizing, etc. The term "definite" apparently means that the noun to which the article is added, stands for something definite; it is nearly equivalent to the terms "determinative" and "defining". This is the most common theory held by R. de la Grasserie, Geijer, Behaghel, Jespersen, Poutsma, Heymann, Deutschbein, and others.[24] Some name the article

[23] E. Schwyzer, *Zeitschrift für vergleichende Sprachforschung* 63 (1936), 146, 160.
[24] Cf.: P. A. Geijer, "On artikeln, dess ursprung och uppgift särskildt i franskan och andra romanska sprak", *Studier i modern Sprakvetenskap* I (Upsala, 1898).
O. Behaghel, *Deutsche Syntax* I (Heidelberg, 1923).

"individualizing". According to Poutsma the primary function of both articles is determination but the definite article has also the secondary function of individualization, specialization or particularization. Deutschbein distinguishes beside the determinative article also the "descriptive" article. Geijer uses, without distinction, the terms "actualization" and "individualization". K. Bühler[25] uses the term "substantivization", L. Hjelmslev[26] "concretization".

As we have already mentioned, the most common theory of article is the determinative theory. According to this theory the difference between the zero form of the article and the definite article is in a different degree of determination. That which is indicated by a zero form is of an indefinite extent whereas the form of the noun with a definite article expresses something that is of a smaller extent than the whole genus and is limited by fixed boundaries. Determination usually indicates a contrast not to the corresponding indefinite article but to all other individuals belonging to the same genus. This is true, according to Christophersen, when "unit-words" but not "uniques" are concerned.[27] In these words

---

O. Jespersen, *Essentials of English Grammar* (London, 1933); *Language* (London, 1922); *A Modern English Grammar* I-III (Heidelberg, 1909-27); *The Philosophy of Grammar* (London, 1924).

H. Poutsma, *A Grammar of Late Modern English* II (Groningen, 1914).

W. Heymann, "Über die Lehre vom bestimmten Artikel im Englischen", *Englische Studien* XII, 270 ff.

M. Deutschbein, *System der neuenglischen Syntax* (Göthen, 1917).

[25] K. Bühler, *Sprachtheorie* (Jena, 1934), 310 ff.

[26] L. Hjelmslev, *Principes de Grammaire Générale*. Vidsk. Selsk. hist.-filol. Medd. XVI: 1 (Copenhagen, 1928), 335-7.

[27] Christophersen distinguishes, that is to say, four classes of nouns:

1. Continuate-words and plurals which are connected only either with the zero article or with the definite article *the*. Continuate-words are nouns that indicate something connected and spread in space and time. A part of the subject can be described as having certain limits and a definite form, but the subject as such is regarded as continuative. Continuate-words are either material, e.g. *butter, water, iron, clay,* or immaterial, e.g. *music, leisure, hunger, constancy.*

2. Singular unit-words which may have either definite or indefinite article. They are words indicating something individual and complete in itself, an individual or a unit belonging to a class of similar subjects; they are either material such as *girl, house, flower, pen,* or immaterial such as *day, hour, system, event.*

no contrast exists to other subjects of the same genus and yet article is often used in this case. This is why Caro's theory[28] extends the contrast to all other species. However, if we applied the principle of contrast so consistently then the article would have to be used with every noun, as Christophersen rightly points out. Consequently, this theory is not in agreement with psychological reality. Deutschbein solves this problem by presuming two kinds of article:[29] "a) der definierende, determinierende Artikel, die Deutlichkeit einer Vorstellung hervorhebend, b) der deskriptive oder präsentierende Artikel, die Anschaulichkeit und Klarheit einer Vorstellung andeutend". The latter case is evidently destined for unique nouns. The only cases belonging to this kind of article are (a) the generic article (uniques), (b) *the sun, the moon,* etc., and (c) some proper names which have article. According to Christophersen the theory of this kind can be equally difficult both to rebut and to prove and Deutschbein's theory is allegedly too vague than to be applicable without any difficulty to all cases of the use of article.

G. Guillaume[30] distinguishes between potential and effectual meaning of a noun; the former concerns "language", the latter "speech". In languages a noun can, according to Guillaume, potentially mean an infinite number of different things whereas a noun in speech means only one of these potential meanings. In the latter case a word with a particular sense has an article.[31]

Proper names can be explained by certain theories which are close to each other, be it the theory of actualization (Geijer as

---

3. Uniques, which have only the definite article, are unique nouns that is their class contains only one member (e.g. *the world, the universe*).

4. Proper names which have a zero article.

[28] G. Caro, "Zur Syntax des bestimmten Artikels im Englischen", *Die Neueren Sprachen* IV, 4.

[29] M. Deutschbein, *System der neuenglischen Syntax,* 238.

[30] G. Guillaume, *Le Problème de l'Article et sa Solution dans la Langue Française* (Paris, 1919).

[31] For a more detailed exposition and criticism of Guillaume's theory cf. Christophersen, op. cit. pp. 55-58.

well as Deutschbein),[32] or the theory of concretization (Hjelmslev[33]) and especially the theory of substantivization (Bühler regards this theory not as the only but as the most important). These theories presume that articles add to the naked noun, which by itself is abstract, a concretizing element (with the exception of proper names which are always concrete), that is to say the element of substance in the case of the theory of substantivization. This theory explains proper names by presuming that they contain only substance but not description and therefore they do not need any article. Christophersen tries to solve this problem by his theory of familiarity and unity.[34] According to this theory the definite

[32] According to this theory the noun which without article is the name of a mere idea, by adding article becomes something topical and real. Thus, e.g., the word *house* is a mere concept, a name of a class of individuals, it is an abstract concept or idea without any reality. However, a real house includes, apart from generic features, a number of individual features, it possesses reality and topicality. In other words, the article (definite or indefinite, according to circumstances) "actualizes" the noun.

[33] According to Hjelmslev the grammatical role of articles is to concretize semantemes. Accordingly, the so-called definite article is a concretization-morpheme which indicates that the object in question is supposed to be known to the interlocutor, whereas the so-called indefinite article is a concretization-morpheme indicating that the object is assumed to be unknown to the interlocutor (cf. Christophersen, *The Articles*, pp. 57-58).

[34] Cf. also Jespersen's theory of articles (in *A Modern English Grammar on Historical Principles* VII, *Syntax* [London, 1954] 437) distinguishing the following stages:

Stage I. Complete unfamiliarity.
1. Unit word (singular). Indefinite article *(an apple)*.
2. Mass word. Zero article *(He drinks milk)*.
3. Unit word (plural). *(He eats apples every day)*.
Stage II. Nearly complete familiarity. The article *the*.
1. The necessary determination is given by the context.
2. The necessary determination is given by the whole situation.
Stage III. Complete familiarity. No article needed.
1. Direct address *(Come along, boy)*   4. *Father, uncle, baby, nurse*, etc.
2. Proper names *(John, Mr. Brown)*   5. *Dinner* and other regular meals.
3. *God*.   6. *Church, prison, town*, etc.
A. A. Hill (in "A Re-Examination of the English Articles", *17th Annual Round Table*, ed. F. P. Dinneen, S. J. [= *Monograph Series on Languages and Linguistics* 19] 1966, 217-231) presents a modified version of Jespersen's theory, distinguishing:

article causes that to the potential meaning of a unit-word a certain association with the earlier knowledge is added from which it can be concluded that only one individual is meant. Sometimes, of course, we are acquainted only indirectly with that which is indicated by the word. When speaking about a certain book it is quite correct to say *The author is unknown*, as the familiarity which is here pointed to, is the book. And as each book has its author, the knowledge of the book automatically implies a certain author. The definite article *the* gives through its association with previous experience a peculiar feature to the general meaning of the word. The explicit reference to external knowledge (not contained in the meaning of the new word) gives us to feel that the word stands for a certain individual, having thus something of the character of the proper name. Our familiarity with the indicated subject may be quite small but important is that we feel that the word stands for a certain individual. Likewise the familiarity with the individual designated by a proper name may be very little, but we know that only one definite person or thing is meant.

According to Christophersen, the indefinite article *a* needs no previous knowledge, there is no relation to previous experience outside the idea of the word itself and the modification of the potential meaning of the word is therefore small. With unit-words the function of the indefinite article consists in an emphasis of the unity already inherent in the word itself. The article *a* is, according to Christophersen, neutral so far as familiarity is concerned; it does not indicate it but also does not exclude it. For example *I wonder if you have come across a fellow called James Birch. We were at*

I. Two-article nouns, e.g. *a book — the book*
      books — the books

II. One-article nouns (uncountables or mass-nouns and abstracts). They typically lack plurals and indefinite article, but in the use of the definite article they are nearly normal. For example, *We want money — we want the money for a good cause. Man pursues happiness, but the happiness he gets, is little enough.*

III. Fixed usage nouns: they either never take an article or always take a definite article (place and proper names, the nouns for one-member classes, like *the sun, the moon*, and the generic use of *man* which is always without article).

Eton together. This is about a certain person who is assumed to be known to the hearer. As it is only an assumption, it is necessary to use here a neutral form but it is not possible to say that *a* means indefiniteness here. Another example: *His father is an M.P.* This presupposes definiteness and familiarity. The statement is about a definite M.P. but among such persons none was in the centre of attention before; unity is the only quality which is to be indicated. *His father is the M.P.* would mean an identity between "his father" and a definite M.P. who was already spoken of before.

The function of the definite article with continuate-words and plurals is the same as with unit-words. *The* refers to some knowledge already won by the hearer which explains that only one definite part of a coherent whole is meant. This, however, does not make that part an individual member of the class of similar subjects. The indication of this kind of unity is outside the sphere of the article *the* though it contains the idea of definite limits.

The definite article changes the term from general to particular. Only when *the* precedes a unique-word it can express genericness because it unites in itself both individual and genus; both is here one and the same thing. Familiarity presupposes delimitation and definiteness. Both these qualities are present in unique nouns.

Christophersen continues by asking whether the indefinite article is possible with unique nouns. It is evident that it cannot be used with absolute "uniques". Of course, there are only very few genuine "uniques". It is quite possible to say *a sun* but this deprives the word of its uniqueness. It is likewise possible to say *a universe* but it means that there are still other members of this class. Therefore it is doubtful whether it is reasonable to recognize the group of "uniques". The reason why Christophersen recognizes this category is the fact that these words are very close to proper names. If a word is associated with one and the same individual, it can gradually assume the character of a proper name. The element of familiarity which is originally contained in the article, gradually passes to the word itself, the article is finally felt as redundant and is often dropped. The proper name includes both the element of unity and familiarity. To be understood it must evoke in the mind of the hearer a similar condition of familiarity as is required for the understanding of the form with the definite article *the*. If it is not so, then the word leaves in the hearer the impression that a definite individual is concerned and nothing more. From the point of view of language nothing else is contained in the proper noun.

Christophersen elaborates his theory into further details all of which we cannot deal with here. In fact, his theory is a complementation of the theory of substantivization advocated — among others — by Bühler, Brøndal[35] and Hammerich[36]. According to this theory one of the functions of the definite and perhaps also indefinite article is to denote substance. This substance is that which differentiates nouns from verbs and adjectives. According to Christophersen the theory of substantivization seems to be closest to truth but cannot explain continuate words and plurals; this is why Christophersen complements it with his theory of familiarity and unity. There is no doubt that Christophersen's theory is a certain asset for the problems of the article and in most cases, even if not in all, it can satisfactorily explain the use of articles in English. However, it is valid in English but not quite in French or in other languages. As a matter of fact, it can hardly be decided which of the above discussed theories is the most correct. Undoubtedly a certain theory cannot completely explain ALL cases of the use or omission of articles. And if one theory is suitable for one language — every theory of article is usually elaborated in such a way as to fit to a certain language — it is not suitable for the other. Sometimes there is only a small correspondence between what the article designates in different languages. Languages that do not possess an article of the same kind as English or German does, can express the same concept by means of other grammatical categories. Some Asian languages possess an objective case which corresponds with the definite article of let us say English. The difference between the nominative and

[35] V. Brøndal, *Ordklasserne* (Copenhagen, 1928) 166, 169.
[36] L. L. Hammerich, *Indledning til tysk grammatik* (Copenhagen, 1935), §§ 60, 70.

partitive case in Finnish resembles in a way the function of articles. Similarly the article in French is not precisely the same as the article in other languages. This can lie in an insignificant semantic difference but also in the fact that the article in French has, besides its principle function, also some secondary functions: it indicates gender and number; the article in French is often the only distinction between two numbers, e.g. *une maison, des maisons, la maison, les maisons.* A secondary function can also be found with the German article. In the sentence *Ich ziehe Bier dem Wein vor* the article is used only to indicate dative, as is proved by the alternative phrase *Ich trinke lieber Bier als Wein.*[37] The German article preceding personal names indicates case: *der Tod des Sokrates* but *Sokrates Leben.* The modern English article does not possess similar functions, as stated by Christophersen, but has a secondary function of a rather different character: it substantivizes the adjective (e.g. *the poor* — a whole closed class is designated).

The differences in the function of articles are greater in some non-Indo-European languages. We must be very cautious here so that we may not regard as article something that designates, for example, gender, number, or person or some other category. If we are to compare the occurrence of articles in different languages we must first examine the very essence of the article, its function, and we must find some, at least rough criterion of the article, something that would overarch or at least diminish the differences in the function of the article in various languages. However, to give a precise definition of article which would be valid for all languages that possess an article in some or other form, would be, in the present state of research on this problem, a very difficult if not impossible task. We must agree with W. Hodler[38] that the investigation of articles is still in its beginnings.

---

[37] Cf. L. Edman, "Über den Gebrauch des Artikels im Neuhochdeutschen" (dissertation) (Upsala, 1862).
[38] W. Hodler, *Grundzüge einer germanischen Artikellehre* (Heidelberg, 1954), 10.

4. ON THE ESSENCE OF THE CATEGORY OF DETERMINEDNESS VS. INDETERMINEDNESS

If we want to present in this book a certain typology of the occurrence of articles as well as of expressing the category of determinedness vs. indeterminedness even by means other than articles, none of the theories mentioned above will be satisfactory. Such a broadly conceived investigation requires a more generally based insight into the essence of the category of determinedness vs. indeterminedness.

There is nothing unusual in the fact that many linguistic concepts are difficult to define in such a manner that they might be applied to as many languages as possible. The concept of the category of determinedness vs. indeterminedness is no exception in that line. However, it is necessary to determine the content and extent of this category, the more so as we are treating very diverse means of expressing it in a considerable number of different languages.

By the term "determinedness" we understand the fact that nouns are classified according to whether the content expressed by the noun is clear and identifiable in a concrete way or not. In topical utterances this category is realized in the positive case by "determinedness", in the negative case by "indeterminedness".

If we try to find out the essence of the category of determinedness vs. indeterminedness it is necessary to realize that this category is based on the opposition of individual and genus; it is an opposition inherent to our thinking. Most nouns express both genus and individual. Semantic differentiation is then formed by the article or by other formal means, in some languages determinedness or indeterminedness is inherent in the noun itself, without formal differentiation, as will be mentioned later. The categorial difference individual vs. genus must be understood similarly as e.g. the categorial difference perfectiveness vs. imperfectiveness of verbs which is based on the fact that a certain action affected by the verb passes in a definite way.

There is still another element that is added to that basic difference: determination. According to R. de la Grasserie[39] determination consists in individualization, that is in marking out several beings with respect to others or one class of beings with respect to another group. De la Grasserie distinguishes a number of degrees of determination beginning with the so-called "surindetermination" up to the so-called "surdetermination". Determination is allegedly an indirect and conscious consequence of the primitive stage, that is of the effort to express oneself in a concrete manner. Man originally grasped only individual subjects whereas abstraction was alien to him. J. Haas[40] defines determination as follows: "Wenn ein Sprechender einem Hörenden eine Gegenstandsvorstellung zum Bewusstsein bringen will, so kann er diese als dem von ihm Angeredeten bekannt oder unbekannt voraussetzen. Diese Auffassung der Gegenstandsvorstellung ist die Determination, bezw. ihr Gegenteil, die Indetermination. Die Determinationsvorstellung ist demnach keine selbständige, sondern eine Begleitvorstellung der Gegenstandsvorstellung ... Das sprachliche Korrelat der Determinationsvorstellung wird als bestimmter Artikel, und das sprachliche Korrelat der Indeterminationsvorstellung wird als unbestimmter Artikel bezeichnet". However, not all linguists limit determination to articles only. Included into this category are often, besides articles, also demonstrative pronouns, words indicating the relation of appurtenance (e.g. possessive pronouns, possessive genitive, various periphrases, etc.), words indicating place, order of the subject (ordinal numerals), various attributes (nouns, adjectives, participles and even complete sentences), apposition to a noun, word order and other means.[41] They are usually called "determinatives". A thorough study of this problem is presented by Holger Steen Sørensen[42] who argues that "the class of determinatives and the class of articles are identical". Among deter-

---

[39] R. de la Grasserie, "De l'article", 384-386.

[40] J. Haas, *Französische Syntax* (Halle a. S., 1916) 161-162.

[41] Cf. Josef Kurz, "K otázce členu v jazycích slovanských, se zvláštním zřetelem k staroslověnštině" [On the problem of article in Slavic languages with a special regard to Old Slavonic] *Byzantinoslavica* VII (1938), 238-241.

[42] Holger Steen Sørensen, *Word-Classes in Modern English* (Copenhagen, 1958), 138 ff.

minatives Sørensen numbers the following words: *the, this, these, that, those, my, your, his, her, its, one, their, which, either, neither, each, a, one, some, any, no, every, what,* and the sign whose designator is zero with the word *milk* in such a sentence as e.g. *milk is better than beer* and any sign that is semantically identical with the sign whose designator is zero with the word *milk* in the sentence *milk is better than beer*. Sørensen quotes from Christophersen (p. 81): "That the words (= *a, the*) belong together and constitute a group apart is obvious. They mutually exclude each other, and a great number of substantives (unit-words) must always be accompanied by one or other of them. Their relation to the substantive is as close as that between 'to' and infinitive. The shifting between zero-form, 'a'-form and 'the'-form is as regular as case distortion." Sørensen shows that Christophersen's statement is true only when it is interpreted as concerning the above-mentioned entities. He demonstrates this on many definitions of the articles *a* and *the*. We admit that *a* and *the* indicate "substance" (Christophersen, Hammerich), a transition from "le nom en puissance" to "le nom en effet" (Guillaume), that they "concretize" (Hjelmslev), etc., that the same is valid also about the other determinatives or "indicaters", as Collinson[43] calls them, but all that are only partial qualities of articles. We must search for that which is the essence of articles, that in which articles basically differ from other determinatives or indicaters. Between the article and other determinatives or indicaters there is, in our opinion, an important qualitative difference which imposes restraint upon us to include into our typology of languages according to different ways of expressing the category of determinedness vs. indeterminedness even such "indicaters" as demonstrative and possessive pronouns as well as all other determinatives mentioned above. Of course, it is true that in most languages possessing article the definite article originated in a demonstrative pronoun and the indefinite article in the numeral 'one'. Consequently, of basic importance for us is the problem how to determine when a de-

[43] William Edward Collinson, *Indication* (= *Language Monographs* 17) (Baltimore, 1937).

monstrative pronoun becomes GENUINE article. And here we come to the conclusion that we can speak about an article only when the definite article indicates a noun in a GENERAL function (e.g. *the horse is an animal*); an individual stands here for a whole class. If the pronoun has this meaning it becomes article. Let us mention another difference between the article and the pronoun: the pronoun is only FACULTATIVE whereas the article is OBLIGATORY, it is a constant quality of the noun.[44] Moreover, the article is not a mere determination: this results even from the theories which we have discussed above. The fact that the article adds a definite element (be it a concretizing, substantivizing, actualizing element, the element of familiarity, etc.) to the noun is another important factor of the distinction between articles and demonstratives. In contrast to demonstratives, the article is always determination plus something else, some other element which modifies the meaning of the word. It seems that the article influences the noun somehow from the inside, that is to say it influences the noun directly in its very essence,[45] whereas the demonstrative pronoun merely points from the outside without substantially affecting the noun. The demonstrative pronoun does not insert anything into the noun to which it belongs.

[44] Cf. Pavel Trost, "Německé vlivy na slovanské jazyky" [German influence upon Slavic languages], *Československé přednášky pro V. mezinárodní sjezd slavistů v Sofii* (Praha, 1963), 30: "The article principally does not admit facultative use only but is always obligatory in given conditions; this is just that by which the genuine article is differentiated from the pronominal predecessor of the article". It was already Karl Brugmann (*Die Demonstrativpronomina der indogermanischen Sprachen. XXII. Band der Abhandlungen der philologisch-historischen Klasse der König* [= *Sächsischen Gesellschaft der Wiss.*, No. VI] [Leipzig, 1904], § 11, p. 20) who wrote that when the demonstrative pronoun precedes a word which indicates a known subject regularly and obligatorily, it is called article. In his *Kurze vergleichende Grammatik* (p. 400) he states that the definite article arises from a demonstrative pronoun only when it is added to a substantive concept by a permanent habit; the substantive concept is designated as familiar, that is to say as just present in the mind both of the speaker and the hearer.

[45] Cf. Vilém Mathesius, *Naše řeč* (1926), p. 41: "A genuine article may be spoken of only when its use results from the meaning of the noun itself, may the determination be singular (individualizing article) or general (generic article)".

Further it is necessary to determine the relation between the definite and the indefinite article. Even when the opposition of general and individual plays an important part here, it is not only this opposition which is of concern. It is necessary to determine what is marked and what is unmarked. The indefinite article indicates an unidentified particular term, whereas the definite article indicates, as we have already shown, a particular or general term; for example *der Hund* means 1. *dog* (as a class) — generalness, 2. *the dog* (a definite individual) — particularness.

Ivan Poldauf[46] upholds the semantic-stylistic criterion. In his opinion the use of articles is prevented by the semantic character of the noun (uncountables, i.e. proper names, material nouns, abstract nouns) or by the stylistic isolation of the noun in the sentence (vocative, exclamation, quotation, some of the predicative uses, "telegraphese" and "headlinese"). Poldauf (op. cit. p. 183) points out to the fact that "nouns which are used to build up new semantic units (e.g. *catch sight of, catch a glimpse of, give him a thought, give him the lie, in town, in the country*) lose the independent character of sentence members and the use of one of the articles or the omission of any article is with them a matter of tradition". We must agree with Poldauf's emphasis on the role of the context in marking or unmarking the noun by means of articles. "In English", he writes (op. cit. p. 184), "the form of a noun in a certain context does not make it clear whether it is 'countable' or not, but its context value, and, occasionally, its clash with the categories of number and determination, marked by one of the two articles, leave no doubt about it ... In the category of determination, the formal marks being the articles, only semantic and stylistic considerations can 'neutralize' the opposition known from such couples as *a river : the river*". There is no doubt, in our opinion, that Poldauf's semantic and stylistic criterion holds not only for English but generally for other languages as well. Moreover, it is close to the principle of the functional sentence perspec-

[46] Cf. Ivan Poldauf, *On the History of Some Problems of English Grammar Before 1800* (= *Práce z vědeckých ústavů*, LV. Prague Studies in English, vol. 7) (Praha ,1948), 183-198.

tive which we regard as a very important factor capable of throwing light on the problem of the nature of the category of determinedness vs. indeterminedness in general. As we ascribe key importance to the criterion of functional sentence perspective, we will devote major attention to it in the following lines.

By functional sentence perspective V. Mathesius[47] meant the division of sentence into theme and rheme. The theme is that about which we affirm something, the rheme is that which we affirm about the theme. The theme and the rheme are not the same as grammatical subject and predicate. It is indisputable that in languages there is often disagreement between the functional sentence perspective and the formal principle. This disagreement is solved in different languages in different ways. Thus for instance in Czech, which has a free word order, which means that the theme is placed in the first part of the sentence be it expressed by any sentence member, and the rheme is placed in the other part of the sentence. According to the topical validity of the sentence members the functional sentence perspective and consequently the word order as well, are changed in Czech. In the sentence *Tatínek napsal tenhle dopis (Pa wrote this letter)* the theme is the word *tatínek (= pa)*, whereas *napsal tenhle dopis* 'wrote this letter' is the rheme. If we want to say that he who wrote the letter is *pa* (rheme), we express this sentence with a different word order: *Tenhle dopis napsal tatínek*. In English which has a fixed, grammaticalized word order, the theme is usually expressed by grammatical subject and the rheme by grammatical predicate. As, in principle, subject must not stand at the end of an English sentence, following the predicative verb, it is necessary to overarch this contradiction in the grammatical and functional sentence perspective in English in the second sentence by using the passive voice: *This letter was written by Pa*, or by using a periphrasis: *It was Pa who wrote this letter*.[48]

---

[47] V. Mathesius, *Obsahový rozbor současné angličtiny na základě obecně lingvistickém* [An analysis of Contemporary English on the general linguistic basis] (Praha, 1961), 93.

[48] The principles of the functional sentence perspective have been further developed by Jan Firbas. We quote at least his English written papers: "Some Thoughts on the Function of Word Order in Old English and Modern

It was B. A. Il'jiš[49] who pointed out the possibility of explaining the category of determination in dependence on the functional sentence perspective, critically followed by J. Firbas.[50] B. A. Il'jiš gives (§ 363) two clauses: *The door opened, and the young girl came in* and *The door opened and a young girl came in*, which differ solely by the use of the article with the expression *young girl* and comes to the conclusion that the sentence following *and* in the first clause (with the definite article preceding the expression *young girl*) gives as the rheme the fact that the young girl came in, whereas in the other clause (with the indefinite article preceding the expression *young girl*) is presented as new the fact that it was a young girl who came and Il'jiš attributes this difference to the working of articles. According to his opinion the indefinite article makes the noun, which it precedes, the semantic predicate of the sentence, whereas the definite article deprives the noun of this possibility. Consequently, he sees in the definite and indefinite article the means of functional sentence perspective. Firbas tries to make this thesis more precise and analyzes in detail the occurrence of the definite and indefinite article and the opposition between both articles from the point of view of functional sentence perspective.

According to Firbas the subject *a young girl* in the above-mentioned sentence is a non-thematic subject expressing the centre of the rheme itself. In a quotation from Galsworthy

---

English", *Sborník prací filosofické fakulty brněnské university* (1957), A 5, 72-100; "Thoughts on the Communicative Function of the Verb in English, German and Czech", *Brno Studies in English* I (Praha, 1959), 39-68; "More Thoughts on the Communicative Function of the English Verb", *Sborník prací filosofické fakulty brněnské university* (1959), A 7, 74-98; "On the Communicative Value of the Modern English Finite Verb", *Brno Studies in English* III (Praha, 1961), 79-104; "From Comparative Word-Order Studies", *Brno Studies in English* IV (Praha, 1964), 111-128; "On Defining the Theme in Functional Sentence Analysis", *TLP* 1 (Praha, 1964), 267-280; "Non-thematic Subjects in Contemporary English", *TLP* 2 (Praha, 1966), 239-256.
[49] B. A. Il'jiš, *Sovremennyj anglijskij jazyk*, 2nd ed. (Moskva, 1948).
[50] J. Firbas, "K otázce nezákladových podmětů v současné angličtině" [On the problem of non-thematic subjects in Contemporary English], *Časopis pro moderní filologii* 39 (1957), 22-42, 165-173. Cf. also the same author, "Non-thematic Subjects in English", *TLP* 2 (Prague, 1966), 241 ff.

[*And not for the first time during those fourteen years old Jolyon wondered whether he had been a little to blame in the matter of his son.*] *An unfortunate love-affair with that precious flirt Danäe Thornworthy, now Danäe Pellew, Anthony Thornworthy's daughter, had thrown him on the rebound into the arms of June's mother.*

the expression *an unfortunate affair* is a non-thematic component (it communicates something new), but the proper rheme of the given sentence are, according to Firbas, the words *into the arms of June's mother.* In the sentence

    An "At Home" at Stanhope Gate was a great rarity, ...

the expression *"At Home" at Stanhope Gate* is even purely thematic, it is the proper theme. Similar are the examples with a zero article in the plural subject. When quoting these examples Firbas does not want to negate the ability of the indefinite article and its plural zero variant to signal non-thematic components, he wants only to show that this ability can assert itself only in a favourable interplay of this member or its plural zero variant with other means of functional sentence perspective. A favourable condition of basic importance is, according to Firbas, the semantic content of the indefinite article itself in the case when the indefinite article actually intensively expresses that lack of determinedness of the noun that is given by the newness[51] of the idea. Thus, thanks to this semantic content, the indefinite article is able to signal newness directly and, consequently, as a means of functional sentence perspective to

---

[51] Cf. I. Poldauf, *Mluvnice současné angličtiny* I. [Grammar of Contemporary English], 60-61. According to Josef Vachek (*Obecný zápor v angličtině a v češtině* [General negation in English and in Czech] [= *Práce z vědeckých ústavů, LI. Příspěvky k dějinám řeči a literatury anglické* 6] [Praha, 1947], 31, 34-35) the indefinite article in English means fortuity connected with situational newness but besides there is still in it a considerably strong semantic numerical component. Therefore, as is well known, the indefinite article has still sometimes the meaning of the numeral 'one' (e.g. *one at a time, not a bit*), and, consequently, it does not possess the plural too. Close to the use and meaning of the indefinite article is, as Vachek emphasizes, the original use and meaning of the pronoun *any*. Sometimes it is possible to substitute the pronoun *any* by indefinite article without any relevant semantic disorder. However, the indefinite article lacks the semantic component of arbitrary replaceability of a particular term by another particular term, which is an important feature of the pronoun *any*.

make those parts of the sentence more dynamic whose basic dynamism is weak. If the indefinite generic article (i.e. such as accompanies the noun that does not indicate a concrete particular term but on the contrary any occurrence of that which is indicated by the given noun) is concerned, Firbas is of the opinion that in those cases the indefinite article loses its ability to signal newness and is by itself not able to make the dynamically weak parts of the sentence more dynamic. The newness signalled by the indefinite article is especially prominent in those cases in which thanks to favourable conditions the other components of the sentence show a weak dynamism of statement. In the case of non-thematic subjects, of concern are, according to Firbas, in the first place verbs or verbal expressions such as *come, come into view, come on the scene, come in, come up, appear, to present oneself, to place, to arise*, etc., which imply or directly express a sort of "appearing on the scene" (i.e. appearing on the scene formed by the given word or situational context), a sort of "coming into existence" (within the frame of the given context) or simply the presence (existence) on this scene. Under favourable conditions, for instance in connection with a noun subject preceded by the indefinite article, the meaning rendered by these verbs or verbal expressions can recede into background so that attention is transferred to a person or thing which just appears on the scene. Such a subject then becomes even the proper theme, when no further sentence component follows the verb or verbal expression of the described type, or when the following sentence components have a very weak dynamism of statement. In the example *A young girl broke a vase* we can see, according to Firbas, quite another complex of the means of functional sentence perspective, that is to say a complex that is not favourable for regarding the subject *a girl* as the proper rheme. The rheme is here the expression *a vase*; its proper rhematicity is supported not only by its final position in the sentence but also by the presence of indefinite article. The indefinite article with the subject signals of course, even in this sentence, newness: however, under the constraint of the given distribution of the dynamicity of statement it becomes theme, though it is characterized by a considerable dynamicity of statement.

Firbas further shows that the verbs that are able to express the meaning of "appearing on the scene" need not render it equally distinctly. It may be said that the more indistinctly the meaning is contained in the verb the smaller is also the ability of the verb or of the verb and expressions connected with it respectively to relieve the sentence position of its dynamicity, and the less favourable are the conditions for the subject preceded by a non-generic indefinite article to be able to become a proper rheme.

As far as the definite article is concerned, Firbas criticizes Il'jiš that similarly as in the case of indefinite article he neglects the relations of the definite article to other means of the functional sentence perspective. Above all, it is necessary to say that unlike the indefinite article, the definite article cannot by itself contribute to the dynamic character of the noun which it precedes. However, there are other means that are capable of doing so. Thus, e.g., in the sentence *Dombey sat in the corner of the darkened room in the great arm-chair by the bedside* (Dickens, *Dombey and Son*, Chapter I) all nouns with definite article stand in the rheme. Here the basic distribution of sentence dynamism can be realized undisturbedly. It is possible to speak about a gradual dynamicizing within the rheme so that the most rhematic components become the words *in the great arm-chair by the bedside*. In the sentence *In the passage was standing the girl with the veil, pressing the parcel to her breast and panting for breath...* the subject expression *the girl* is doubtless a thematic component. In spite of the presence of the definite article the basic distribution of sentence dynamism is realized here undisturbedly. On the contrary, in the sentence *The girl came in, brushing him with her shoulder as she went past,* "*the girl*" is a thematic component as it clearly functions as a repeated and familiar component.

It is well known that the definite article expresses a sufficient determination of the noun which presupposes the hearer's FAMILIARITY with that what the noun designates. This is extremely important for the theory of the functional sentence perspective which works with the concepts of familiarity and unfamiliarity. By means of this familiarity contained in the semantic content of the definite article Firbas explains why the definite article, in contradistinction to the indefinite article, cannot contribute by itself to the dynamicity of the noun it precedes, that is to say why it is not able in itself to signal the non-thematicity, unfamiliarity. The scale of familiarity expressed by the definite article is, however, considerably extensive. On its one end there are the nouns with definite article that, admittedly, in view of the general atmosphere between the originator and addressee of the statement express things sufficiently known but which from the view of a narrow "scene", to which the functional sentence perspective reacts, can interpret even non-thematic components, that is to say even purely rhematic ones. On the other end of the scale there are those nouns with definite article which are characterized by their familiarity in the fullest sense of the word, that is to say by familiarity even from the view of that narrow scene to which the functional sentence perspective reacts. This is a familiarity which is identical with the thematicity and which is supported by that which is called word and situation context. It is only in these cases — under the necessary condition of a favourable combination of the other means of the functional sentence perspective — that the definite article can fully assert its ability of stripping the sentence positions of their dynamicity.

The possibility of the opposition of the definite and indefinite article as a means of functional sentence perspective considerably contributes, in Firbas's opinion, to attaining a change in functional sentence perspective without any cooperation of the word order. It is again conditioned by the favourable working of the other means of the functional sentence perspective. Let us compare the following examples:

1. *A brooding look came instantly on Irene's face, ...*
2. *The brooding look darkened on her face, ...*

In the first case the proper rheme is *a brooding look*, in the second case *darkened*. The role of the definite and indefinite article and of the verb *come* is obvious here. The components *on Irene's/her face* are stripped of their dynamicity by the situational context; *instantly* is a rhematic component but not the rheme proper.

Further, Firbas mentions two types of sentence we can meet with at the beginning of a narration, that is to say a type containing in the subject a non-generic definite article

1. *The Picton boat was due to leave at half-past eleven*
2. *The week after was one of the busiest weeks of their lives*

and a type containing in the subject a non-generic indefinite article:

3. *A stout man with a pink face wears dingy white flannel trousers, a blue coat with a pink handkerchief showing, and a straw hat much too small for him, perched at the back of his head. [He plays the guitar]. A little chap in white canvas shoes, his face hidden under a felt hat like a broken wing, breathes into a flute; and a tall thin fellow, with bursting over-ripe button boots, draws ribbons — long, twisted, streaming ribbons — of tune out of a fiddle [They stand, unsmiting, but not serious, in the broad sunlight opposite the fruit-shop, ...]*
4. *A brilliant and obscure young Czech engineer makes a tremendous discovery.*

These sentences have no preceding homogeneous word context, they do not even come out of any situational context, they simply stand at the very beginning of a narration. It is interesting to observe how different the working of the definite and indefinite article in the subjects of the above quoted sentences is from the angle of the functional sentence perspective. Though the subjects express here mostly new ideas, the definite articles, occurring in the subjects of sentences (1) and (2), through the working of their semantic contents evidently strip of its dynamicity the idea with the name of which they are connected and thus call forth an atmosphere of "pseudo-familiarity" about their subjects. On the other hand, the indefinite articles in sentences (3) and (4) directly dynamicize the quoted ideas and present them, in fact, as new ones. The ability of the indefinite article to indicate incoherence, the colligation with the previous context asserts itself quite in agreement with objective linguistic reality.

We have not quoted here all the examples Firbas presents in order to make more precise the use of definite and indefinite article as the means of functional sentence perspective. In our opinion, Firbas has succeeded in showing that under certain circumstances that can reliably be ascertained the articles work as relevant means of functional sentence perspective. In his opinion, under certain circumstances articles are in a definite degree of a dynamic tension of the statement to the preceding context and thus become the signals of a certain degree of the dynamicity of statement. It is for this ability that these articles together with other words mentioned above differ from those words that do not show the ability of signalling the degrees of the dynamicity of statement and therefore from this point of view they are neutral and cannot work as means of functional sentence perspective either.

The fact that the definite and indefinite article can function as important means of the functional sentence perspective, may be applied to other languages too. Let us now turn our attention to a language which does not express the category of determinedness vs. indeterminedness by any formal means but where an important role is played by the principle of functional sentence perspective. It is Czech that differs from such languages as e.g. English not only by not possessing any articles but also by possessing a free word order which enables it just to make use of the functional sentence perspective to the highest degree. Moreover, there is a relation between the functional sentence perspective and the expression of the category of determinedness vs. indeterminedness as can be seen in the following examples:

1. *Kniha je na stole. (The book is on the table) — Na stole je kniha. (On the table [there] is a book)*
   In the first sentence the theme is the word *kniha (book)* and in this function it implies determinedness, whereas in the

second sentence the theme is the expression *na stole je (on the table [there] is)* and the word *kniha* is the rheme and in this position it implies indeterminedness.

As the second example we are quoting the Czech translation of English clauses as given by B. A. Il'jiš and mentioned above:

2. *Otevřely se dveře a mladá dívka vešla. (The door opened and the young girl came in.) — Otevřely se dveře a vešla mladá dívka. (The door opened and a young girl came in.)*

In the first sentence the expression *mladá dívka* is again the theme and implies determinedness, in the second sentence the same expression is the rheme and implies indeterminedness. What matters is, of course, the situation. If we modify the first sentence of the clause so that we say *Dveře se otevřely a ...*, then the contrast to the sentence *Otevřely se dveře a ...* consists only in the emphasis of either the noun or the verb but this does not influence the noun *dveře*, as the situation is such that the speaker is sure to have in mind a definite door, that is to say the door of a definite room which was entered by a (certain) girl.

The next example is again a translation of the above quoted English sentence *A young girl broke a vase*. In this case, according to Firbas, the indefinite article with the subject *A young girl* signals newness but under the pressure of the given distribution of the dynamicity of statement it becomes the theme in spite of the use of the indefinite article which is normally used for the rheme. We will now observe the Czech rendering:

3. *Mladá dívka rozbila vázu. (The young girl broke a vase.) — Vázu rozbila mladá dívka. (The vase was broken by a young girl)*. Though in the first case the expression *mladá dívka* is the theme, it is not quite certain whether it implies determinedness or indeterminedness. Decisive will be here the preceding context. If a sentence precedes in which the young girl is already spoken of then in the above-mentioned sentence a certain young girl is concerned and therefore we should translate the sentence into English *The young girl*

broke a vase. In this case the word *vázu* (*a vase* [acc.]) implies indeterminedness. In the second sentence, however, the word *vázu* explicitly implies determinedness as it is a theme whereas the expression *mladá dívka* belongs to the rheme and implies indeterminedness.

The given examples show that in Czech there is a certain relation between the category of determinedness vs. indeterminedness and the functional sentence perspective unless the influence of context is working here. A similar relation may be assumed in other languages which do not possess a formally expressed article but have a free word order.

Summing up all that we have written about the essence of the category of determinedness vs. indeterminedness we can make the following conclusions:

1. The category of determinedness vs. indeterminedness is based on the opposition of individual and genus which is inherent in our thinking.
2. As the second basic feature of the category of determinedness vs. indeterminedness may be regarded the fact that determinedness is something more than a mere determination (as it is in determinatives) and that it need not be expressed by formal means only.
3. The third basic feature which concerns the essence of the category of determinedness vs. indeterminedness is its close relation to the functional sentence perspective.

However, the category of determinedness vs. indeterminedness is not manifested equally, in the same extent and in equal depth in all languages. We often meet with overlapping with other categories. It is a phenomenon of a considerable variety of forms which can only very roughly be typologically compartmentalized. More than in other language categories there is manifested vagueness in very diverse degrees. If, in spite of all this, we attempt at a typology of languages according to the way of expressing the category of determinedness vs. indeterminedness our reasons for doing so spring rather out of our effort to attain a clearly arranged classification than an inner typology.

5. THE PSYCHOLOGICAL FUNCTION OF ARTICLE

Like any grammatical category, the category of determinedness vs. indeterminedness has certain psychological foundations which depend on the character of the given language. In explaining the origin, working and extension of the category of determinedness vs. indeterminedness in languages we cannot neglect other factors than the grammatical ones, especially the psychological factors. A very detailed discussion of the psychological functions of articles is contained in the paper of Raoul de la Grasserie. In spite of many reservations to his work which we have expressed above, we must admit that his account of psychological functions of articles is very interesting and stimulative not only in his time but that even today it supplies arguments for reflection. This is why we will give here a rather detailed account of his ideas.

Grasserie distinguishes[52] four psychological functions of article: 1. the function of concretism or "surdeterminism"; 2. the function of normal determination; 3. the function of an auxiliary word; 4. the relational function. Further he adds a fifth function, that of abstraction resulting from the function of an auxiliary word. This ranking of functions is, according to Grasserie, chronological.

1. *The function of concretism*

At the beginning of his development man knew only individuality, concreteness, whereas abstraction, systemization, was unknown to him. If he wanted to designate a being, a not individual, particular person, he had to change it, first of all, by special procedures into an individual being. Sometimes he expresses the concepts he wants to approximate by means of quite different derivatives. Sometimes he changes an objective concept into a subjec-

[52] R. de la Grasserie, "De l'article", 388 ff.

tive one capable of being grasped by senses. To attain this objective he uses pronouns and articles. It was just to attain concretism which, in Grasserie's opinion, article was originally used for. Even the possessive pronoun serves concretization as it serves individual designation but it is always a transformed pronoun, not an article. The speaker's objective was not determination — no difference was made between determination and indetermination. In many languages, even in the very developed ones, such as Latin, determination is missing and so is the article. It was the idea of concreteness that seemed indispensable to the mind of primitive people as it were just the ideas of abstractness that were inaccessible to them. According to Grasserie a concrete idea leads to determination just on account of "surdetermination" brought with it by concretism. When we say *homme-toi (man-you)* instead of *l'homme (the man)*, the concept *l'homme* is concretized but at the same time also "surdetermined", completely individualized. The same result may be attained by means of a possessive pronoun (when we say *sa lèvre "his lip"* instead of *la lèvre "the lip"*). Thus the concrete expression and "surdetermination" are identified. Concretism was primary; determination is only an indirect result, more conscious, intended.

2. *The function of determination*

Determination can have many degrees. R. de la Grasserie gives the following degrees:[53]

1. *Homme, hommes,* ἄνθρωπος, e.g. in the sentence *il est homme*. This is the highest degree of indetermination.
2. *Du bœuf, du cheval.* Here the determination is smaller but still considerable. It is the case of the partitive article.
3. *Un homme, des hommes.* This is a normal indetermination. In Greek it is expressed either by ἄνθρωπος or ἄνθρωπός τις. It is the individual that is concerned here, not the genus.
4. *Un homme* in opposition to *deux hommes, trois hommes.*

[53] R. de la Grasserie, "De l'article", 384-386.

Indetermination is the same, only a little reduced by the numerical determination.

5. *L'homme*, generally in opposition to *bœuf*, *cheval*, etc. Here the genus is concerned. This is an indetermination between individual and genus but a perfect determination as far as the other genera are concerned.

6. *L'homme* (*aimable*, *cruel*, *bon*, etc.). Here we have a limitation to one category of people; it is indetermination, but a limited one.

7. *L'homme d'Europe*; the meaning is narrowed here and, moreover, determined.

8. *Le fils de Primus*. If Primus has only one son, the determination is perfect, if he has more sons, the determination is imperfect as it can be applied to any of the sons.

9. *L'homme qui est venu chez moi hier*.

10. *Cet homme* or *l'homme celui-ci*.

11. *Homme-moi, homme-toi, homme-il*. The determination is greater here but at the same time anormal; it shifts the nearer determination to the personality, is subjective and predicative.

12. *Son fils, son père*. Here we meet "surdetermination". The words *fils* and *père* cannot be used independently, they must be individualized.

13. *Primus, Secundus*. The determination is not only complete but also absolute, as we come to the designation of a unique individual.

All the above given degrees of determination or indetermination are, of course, formed not only by article but also by other means. The article has sometimes the function of indetermination and determination (e.g. if the article *un* or *le* is concerned). In fact, these are already different degrees of determination; a total absence of determination is expressed by the absence of the marker. According to Grasserie the most remarkable fact is that what later became functional, be it from instinctive or volitional motives, originally was quite mechanical. The function is often changed in this way; the function of concretism has changed into the function of determination.

3. *The function of auxiliary word*

According to Grasserie the function of determination has changed into the function of auxiliary word. As the pronoun which has become article and agglutinated towards noun did not cease to decline (inflective languages) as a pronoun and as the noun itself was also declined, it came about that the same relation and the same categories of gender and number were expressed dually, pleonastically. That was the case in Old Greek (ὁ ἄνθρωπος, τὸν ἄνθρωπον, οἱ ἄνθρωποι), where, in this way, the expression of all grammatical categories was strengthened by article. The result was a certain monotony but there was also a number of advantages, for example the impression as if the same note were repeated twice in succession and moreover a certain rhyme attained through the fact that morphological means were identical (cf. τοῖς ἀνθρώποις, τοὺς ἀνθρώπους); consequently, it is a pleonastic declension.

Another auxiliary function of the article consists in dropping the pleonastic, non-functional forms from language. There are also phonetic causes that contribute to this phenomenon. The accent with nouns, if it is not oxytone (not falling on the ultimate syllable), tends to suppression, dropping of the last syllable. The unaccented article, on the other hand, standing in the position of an enclitic, is preserved with respect to its grammatical function and also just to recompense the dropped noun endings. That is the case of Modern French where the noun is invariable as it does not express in a clean-cut way either the genus or the number or the case; all that is expressed by the article preceding the noun. Consequently, it is a word that has fully become an auxiliary word. It does not tend any more to the strengthening of the noun neither does it help to carry grammatical categories but itself assumes this task. The role of the auxiliary word becomes still more important if the written form is not considered, for example in the words *l'homme*, *les hommes*, where the pronunciation of the word *homme* is identical in both cases except when a following word beginning with a vowel makes the final *s* of the word *hommes* to sound.

On the other hand, in languages such as Latin which have no article, the situation is different: if the case endings of nouns disappear, owing to an instinctive effort to preserve the desirable distinctness of the declination there is put before the noun a demonstrative pronoun with its endings which have been more easily preserved owing to the absence of stress; the demonstrative pronoun expresses gender, number, and case of the noun. This occurs in Romance languages.

The function of article as an auxiliary word leads, according to Grasserie, to a deeper analysis and to a more abstract characterization of language. As already mentioned, the accessory categories of number, gender and relation are separated from the noun, being separately expressed before it. It is, as if we, before pronouncing the words *homme, hommes, de l'homme,* said: genitive, masculine, singular, *hommes,* setting apart all the accessory categories. This leads us to the abstracting function of article.

4. *Abstracting function*

This function is the result of the function of auxiliary word. The noun appears naked, as if all parts of its dressing were represented by article. These are number, gender, and case. These categories are abstract categories. If, according to Grasserie, they are merged with the noun, the abstraction will cease to be apparent. The noun will absorb them in its substance but if we set them apart, if we specify them outside the noun, the abstraction will appear very clearly, the formal and grammatical element will be isolated before the ontological element. According to Grasserie this role of article substantially contributes to the prominence of this feature in modern languages: it brings about that preciseness which is the goal of the writer and especially of the scientist in scientific prose. Grasserie writes that article is the soul of the languages that are stripped of flexion similarly as the pronoun is the soul of the so-called primitive languages, whereas languages standing from the point of view of evolution in the midst, that is to say the flexive languages, can do without it.

In Grasserie's opinion, if it were necessary to suppress article and replace it by quite distinct endings in a post-tonic position, the language would be hampered in its working. The article loosens the language, strips the words of their grammatical burdening and as it is very light it carries this burdening very effectively and without fatigue. Article is, in Grasserie's view, one of the most flexible springs and it could not be removed without the economy of expression being unfavourably affected and the speed of expression retarded.

5. *The function expressing relation*

Exceptionally and only in some languages the article fulfils, according to Grasserie, a much more limited task: it fulfils, either alone or with the help of a pronoun, the functions of relations. That means that article has not only the function of determination and classification but also the function expressing the genitive relation and the relation of the relative pronoun and in its pronominal form the relation of the accusative and dative case. This is, for example, in Bantu and Caucasian languages. The article which expresses, as a noun prefix, the gender and number of the noun, is repeated in its full or shortened form with the noun that is dependent on it and in genitive relation. It is also repeated with the adjective which it determines. Thus we meet with a concatenation built up by means completely unknown to European languages. By the same repetition the article expresses, this time without being linked to some noun, relative pronouns and various oblique cases. Something analogical with this repetition may be observed in German as far as the relative pronoun is concerned: it is the superposition of two articles. For example, in the genitive relation the word which in European languages would be in genitive is accompanied by an article which belongs to it by gender and number. As, however, that noun is not independent, it must also receive an article which belongs to the directing noun upon which the mentioned noun is dependent. Thus it will have two articles: the nearer, that means its own, and the farther, that is the article of the directing noun. The basis of this system is a double article: *in-kosi i-aba-ntu* 'chieftains of the people'; *in* is the article of the first noun, *aba* is the article of the other noun; but the article of the first noun is repeated before the other noun in the form of *i*.

According to Grasserie, both from the psychological and morphological point of view the article gives the language, according to the scope of its use, a quite specific feature: it is one of the most effective instruments of analysis, of abstraction and clarity in developed languages. On the other hand it can be found in ancient languages in which it fulfils quite a different role, that is that of concretism, and it fulfils that role with the same efficacy, though it is a role of quite a contrary character.

Even if Grasserie's comments are sometimes disputable, there is no doubt that in principle he characterized quite correctly the development of the functions of the article in psychological respect. On the other hand, he somewhat overestimates some of its functions, especially in those passages where he writes about article as loosening the language, making its working easier, serving the economy of expression, etc.[54] However, Grasserie is quite right in adjudging to article a refinement and precision of expression. In our opinion the existence of article in some languages and its non-existence in other languages as well as various ways of expressing the category of determinedness vs. indeterminedness put questions which are hard to answer but which, nevertheless, have to be put and solved, even if sometimes in a speculative way only.

First of all, there is the question of the universality of the cate-

---

[54] He writes, p. 392: "... l'article le [langage] dégage à son tour, décharge les mots de substance de leur poids, et comme il est très léger, il le porte allègrement et sans fatigue. L'article est un des ressorts les plus souples du langage, et l'on ne saurait le supprimer sans en altérer l'économie et en retarder la vitesse." Page 394: "... ce petit mot ... donne à un langage, suivant l'extension de son emploi, un aspect tout particulier; il se développe avec la civilisation elle-même, domine les langues dérivées, est un des plus puissants instruments d'analyse, d'abstraction et de clarté tout à la fois."

gory of determinedness vs. indeterminedness in languages. From the lack of formal expression of this category in some languages one cannot infer the non-existence of this category in those languages. The category of determinedness vs. indeterminedness is, in our opinion, a category of thinking which is given in mind to all people. We know that it is expressed in very different ways such as no other grammatical category. It only testifies to the fact that the ways of thinking are very diverse with different nations and that of the same diversity are also the means of language expression. A. Biard writes:[55] "La question de l'emploi de l'article dans des diverses langues est donc, avant tout, une question de mentalité comparative, et c'est précisément ce qui en fait la difficulté." It is well known that in most languages the article has arisen from a demonstrative and that its original role was to designate real objects (cp. Grasserie's concretism) existing on a definite place. Later the use of article was transferred from the realm of matter into the realm of intellect (e.g. *Le roi s'empara de la ville*). According to Biard (p. 6), the basic characteristic of the use of article is the idea of integrity and conceptual universality. It is well known that in English, contrary to other languages, without article are abstract nouns, rational, intangible and unintelligible concepts, unlimited substances ("substances partitives") and indeterminate pluralities. Cf. the following examples (according to Biard, p. 4):

> *Truth is the daughter of time. — Die Wahrheit ist die Tochter der Zeit. — La vérité est la fille du temps.*
> *One must love justice before everything. — Man soll vor allem die Gerechtigkeit lieben. — On doit aimer la justice avant tout.*
> *One must yield to necessity. — Man muss der Notwendigkeit gehorchen. — Il faut obéir à la nécessité.*
> *One ought to despise danger and death. — Man soll der Gefahr und dem Tod trotzen. — Il faut mépriser le danger et la mort.*

---

[55]   A. Biard, *L'article "the"* (Bordeaux, 1908), 1.

On the other hand, when a concrete object is concerned, that means a distinct and individual object in its form and material physiognomy, or limited and delimited in its intellectual expression, i.e. in its extent, degree, or duration, as, for example, "*la toise, le pied, le pouce, l'année, le mois, le jour, l'heure, la minute*, etc.", English agrees with other languages in acknowledging a "détermination intrinsèque et spontanée" and a specific identity which represents a genus, class, or category of objects in an apparently non-fixed number. For example,

> The *horse is our noblest helpmate.* — Le *cheval est notre plus noble auxiliaire.* — Das *Pferd ist unser edelster Gehülfe.*

But:

> *Horses are our noblest helpmates.* — Les *chevaux sont nos plus nobles auxiliaires.* — Die *Pferde sind unsere edelsten Gehülfen.*

These divergencies in the use of article show, according to Biard, the working of the idea of "d'intégralité ou d'universalité notionnelle", which is the basic characteristic of the use of article when we pass from any language to English and, *vice versa*, from English to the principal languages of Europe.

On the other hand, in English the idea of conceptual integrity remains indeterminate and this is why it so often comes across different shades, more or less delicate and remote, which admit the idea of determination similarly as in other languages. In the following cases, where the article is absent in English, it is present in other languages:

> *The water is bad in Venice.* — *Water is an article of trade in Venice.*
> *One must always speak the truth.* — *One must always adhere to truth.*
> *I dislike to walk in the snow.* — *I dislike snow.*
> *The snow keeps the seed warm in the ground.* — *Snow is the vapour of the atmosphere frozen by a current of cold air.*

I like to lie on the grass. — Cattle are fond of fresh grass.
I like to rise early in the morning. — Morning is the best
time for intellectual work.
Spring is the sweetest time of the year. — I generally spend
the spring in the country.
The weather is generally fine in this country. — I do not
like to walk in hot weather.

Similar examples could be quoted in countless quantity. Nearly all may be explained by the principles of determination in English. There are, of course, cases which so far have not been satisfactorily explained. Thus, for example, 'the stars' means an unlimited set of stars. The idea of collectiveness is said to justify here the use of article. On the other hand, however, the most evident and most general collectives such as *mankind, posterity, society* have no article. According to Biard, the set of stars, though by itself not determinate, is spontaneously determined in our thinking owing to the idea of implicit localization which is inseparable. In spite of the generality of thinking article can therefore be used in English like in other languages, that is to say owing to the idea of a genuinely demonstrative and localizatory determination, the idea which is an implicit and spontaneous nuance of the idea of determination.

According to Biard it is possible to say that the idea of a demonstrative meaning, spontaneously expressed by the English article, is more actual and effective than in the other languages. In French and in other Continental languages the idea of determination, necessary for expressing the demonstrative meaning, is so fully developed that any thing, even an abstract one, appears to be determined by itself. In English, on the contrary, the idea of determination is, according to Biard, strictly limited to various shades which contain its original and etymological interpretation and it is just this limitation of the idea of determination that is the cause of differentiation of English usage.

Biard's analysis of the character of the article is still more complicated than we have shown here. However, even if it may be very deep, and perhaps just because of it, it appears that when we compare several languages, any deep analysis cannot find the common principle that would link at least some of the compared languages. Biard gets entangled into more and more complicated relations between various kinds and shades of determination and indetermination, proving thus in fact that a unified explanation of the psychological substance of article is not possible.

However, we will once more return to the universality of the category of determinedness vs. indeterminedness. There may arise the question, whether there really exist languages in which this category is not manifested at all. As we have already suggested, the category of the definite and the indefinite, of the familiar and unfamiliar, is a universal, indispensable part of any reality in the same way as the positive and the negative, the black and the white, etc. It can be hardly assumed that it has no influence upon language. The category of determinedness vs. indeterminedness must have been originally connected very closely or have been part of the category of demonstrativeness. Without any doubt, demonstrativeness may be regarded as universal. This connection of the category of determinedness vs. indeterminedness with the category of demonstrativeness proves the fact that article usually arose from a demonstrative. However, it is difficult to answer the question why some languages developed, besides the category of demonstrativeness, the category of determinedness vs. indeterminedness, why besides demonstratives or from them there developed articles which must be something completely different from demonstratives. If some languages, in order to express determinedness, use demonstratives (having therefore no articles), it means only a smaller sharpness, smaller precision of thinking in the language in question. No other reason can be given for it as really decisive? is here the way of thinking which may be different in different languages. And as thinking is closely connected with language and speech, any deviation in the way of thinking means a deviation in the way of language expression as well.

6. DETERMINATION AND INDICATION

A concept seemingly very close to that of determination is the concept of indication. To this concept William Edward Collinson[56] devotes a thorough monograph and as he includes among the so-called "indicaters" also the definite and indefinite article, it is necessary to direct a close attention to this work.

"Indication" is described by Collinson (pp. 24-25) as "the use of a word or gesture whose function it is to direct attention either towards or away from a given item or items ... An 'indicater' is an expression whose sole function is to direct attention toward or away from an item or items". Further he distinguishes a "definite" and an "indefinite" indication. Let us consider the words *Arab* and *negro*. Both are class-terms: *Arab* relates to all persons that possess certain attributes, as well as *negro* relates to all persons that possess certain other attributes. Some classes have only one member, for example the class of those reigning over England is at the present moment represented by one member only, by the present Queen, but the class "English sovereign at any time" may have more than a single member, e.g. William and Mary. We will, however, return to the words *Arab* and *negro*. Imagine there is a group of ten boys including three negroes and one Arab. It is our task to select one boy from this group. If it is the Arab, then solely the word *Arab* would be a complete indication. The word *Arab* normally indicates many individuals; here, however, it is used for a single or unique representative and therefore we indicate this fact by calling him *the Arab*, just as we speak of *the Queen*, if only one is on the throne at the time. If we want to select one of the negroes and say *a negro*, all the possibilities of indication are not exhausted. As both *a* and *the* indicate a class, we may call them, according to Collinson, "classifying indefinite (or definite, respectively) indicater". "Classifying indefinite" can then be defined as an expression indicating by directing attention to a class within which a further indication may be made, whereas

---

[56] William Edward Collinson, *Indication. A Study of Demonstratives, Articles, And Other "Indicaters"*, edited by Alice V. Morris (= *Language Monographs* 17) April-June 1937, (Baltimore).

"classifying definite" directs attention to a class represented, in the given context, by one member only. "*The negro*" would be of no sense if it were not accompanied by a further specification. We can say, for instance (p. 29) "I want *a certain* negro or *a particular* negro, who was with us last time". Even this answer is still indefinite, but we hope it may be possible to give a definite indication.

Because *a certain* (p. 29) "merely alludes to the fact that a particular item is known to fulfil a given condition without definitely indicating the item in question", Collinson calls it an "allusive indicater". When *a certain* is used as a provisional indication in the case that a more specific indication will eventually be made, he speaks of an "allusive indicater of unknown specificity". He then continues: "*A certain* occupies from one point of view an intermediate position between definite and indefinite indication. To the speaker the indication is definite either because he knows the particular item but will not say or because he at least knows that there is a particular item which fulfils his condition. To him, then, it is a 'provisional demonstrative': '*This*, if only I could tell you'. To the hearer *a certain* is indefinite, for he must at once ask: 'Which?' ".

We will now abandon Collinson's further discussion of the sense of other indicaters such as *some, any, someone, any one, that*, etc., and will pass to his discussion of articles. He sees here the matter complicated by the treatment of plurals and mass-concepts (continua), in which cases English and German may use "zero-indication", e.g. "We drank tea", i.e. "some tea", in German "Wir tranken Tee", whereas in French we must say "Nous avons bu *du* thé". He rightly points to the fact that even languages which do not use articles are often able to make a distinction between uniqueness and non-uniqueness. Finnish uses the nominative and accusative cases for a unique specimen or group of specimens, but the partitive case "for both the alternative and instantial indefinite".

Collinson proposes to distinguish between zero-indication which occurs in a context in which indication can be made explicit by a word like *some* and the absence of indication in a word-grouping which does not require any indicater. As Collinson writes (p. 36), "In such groups the name of an object is so closely associated with that of an activity that the two form a unit in the mind which is not concerned with the question of uniqueness, e.g. "to sweat blood", "suer sang et eau", "Blut schwitzen". Cf., in English at least, "to take horse" (= ride), "draw bridle" (= stop), "by land", "by sea", "by car" (also the German "per Auto", "per Rad", "zu Wasser", etc.). The distinction is well seen in "to shut up shop" compared with "to shut up the shop". Much depends upon the standpoint. We say "to lay and clear *the* table", because it is usually one particular table used for meals. The use of *the* in both "the shop" and "the table" in the phrases just quoted raises an important point, viz. the use of *the* for that which is so well-known to speaker and partner that no further specification is required. Thus in London *the* River is the Thames, *the* Abbey is Westminster Abbey, *the* Tower is the Tower of London, etc. These, indeed, are cases in which the reference is so obvious that even the definite article might be disposed with. In this connection, Kalepky, in an article in the *Zeitschrift für Französische Sprache und Literatur* (vol. LV, p. 440 ff) has made an interesting distinction between what he calls "apperceptive" and "presentative" expressions. If a father sees his son slouching along, he says: "Boy, how on earth are you walking? Head up, chest out!"... Such an utterance is to Kalepky "apperceptive". A not dissimilar case occurs in rapid enumerations where the mind hurries through an accumulation of miscellaneous objects and does not stop to "indicate" them, e.g. "All left the stricken city — king, queen, princes, nobles and commoners". French and German show parallels here ... A "presentative" utterance: "My boy, you are walking very badly — keep your head (the head — den Kopf, la tête!) higher and your chest out". "This is more objective than zero-indication; it is more like a special application of a general rule ... and comes near generic indication ..."

A zero indication may further appear with nouns indicating a single object which has no fellows and is therefore equivalent to a proper noun. Thus in English we have — unlike French and German — *Heaven, Hell,* and even *Council, Parliament, Convo-*

cation, etc. with a capital letter showing that the feeling of a proper noun is prevalent. Further, English, French and German can omit the article before a day of the week clearly individualized to both speaker and hearer, e.g. *Come (next) Tuesday,* French *mardi (prochain),* German *(nächsten) Dienstag.* The indefinite article may be used in instances such as "He came on *a* Tuesday" (Tuesday alone would signify a definite Tuesday). Definite article is used for a unique possibility: "He was buried on *the* Tuesday" (= next following his death). Similarly, "He came on *the* Easter Tuesday" means a special day. In French "*le* mardi" is used of customary or repetitive occurrence and means the English "of a Tuesday" or "on Tuesdays", German "Dienstags" (or "des Dienstags" as against "den Dienstag" of a single definite day). In the same way English treats the names of months, whereas with the names of seasons we use the definite article for a particular season and when it is regarded only as one of the four seasons we use either, e.g., "in spring" or "in *the* spring".

With proper names of places and persons we use either the zero-indication or the indefinite or definite article. For example (cf. Collinson, p. 38):

> He returned to London, not indeed *a* London he could remember (out of various ensemble-impressions) and certainly not *the* London of his youth (that particular impression he had gained then).

Similarly, "She is married to Mr. Smith" or "*a* Mr. Smith" (used when the hearer does not know the particular Mr. Smith), or *the* Mr. Smith (= whom we met last year). If we use the indefinite article before a family name, the indefinite article can have both the alternative and the instantial force, e.g. "He wants to marry *a* Courthope and make his fortune" (= some one or the other member of the Courthope family), and "He married *a* Courthope" (= a certain member of the Courthope family). "The Courthopes" means either the whole family or a particular family-group of Courthopes ("I was at *the* C's'", in German "bei Courthopes", without article). Used in singular with the definite article "*the*

Courthope" means the best-known of the family, the use being now archaic. In English and French the definite article is attached to the family name cf a famous actress or singer, e.g. "*The* Duse", in French also before the names of well-known modistes or coiffeures or women like "*La* Pompadour".

Similar is the use of articles or of zero-indication with other proper names (cf. Collinson, pp. 38-39). Fundamental for the problem of indication is the distinction between the individual and the generic. The most appropriate way of indicating the generic is, according to Collinson (p. 40), the zero-indication, i.e. the omission of the indicater. It is justified in so far as we want to predicate of the whole class and do not need to direct attention to its separate members and do not want to mark the contrast of whole and part. However, in the use of zero-indication we are much restricted by the conventions of each language. We can use *man* and *men*, *woman* and *women* with zero-indication but only *children*, *animals*, etc. Zero-indication with mass-words may be generic, e.g. "*Water* is the best thirst-quencher" or alternative, e.g. "We hope to find *water*", or instantial, e.g. "We drank *water*". In French and German and occasionally in English the definite article is used in cases like "*The* lion is a noble animal" (French "*le* lion", German "*der* Löwe"). According to Collinson, this use springs from type-indication, type being "an ideal or imaginative embodiment of certain predominant characteristics conceived to be raised to their highest power and to be untrammeled and undisturbed. Type is vague, more diffuse than class". Cf., e.g., "to act *the* gentleman", "to play *the* fool"; the definite article is also used of typical stage-parts, e.g. "*the* hero", "*the* villain", "*la* jeune ingénue", etc.

Collinson ends the chapter discussing the use of articles or zero-indication by giving the following diagram showing the relation of articles to pronominal indicators:

/I/   *This That*   /II/   *This/That*   *Every*

─────────   ──────────────────────
The   The
(definite particular)   (genus type)

/III/ *Some*   *Any*
——————————
A
zero-singular
zero-plural
(instantial)

The question now arises: is Collinson right in including articles among indicaters? To be able to solve this problem we must decide whether there is any difference between the concepts of indication and determination or, to be accurate, determinedness. At the first sight, both terms are evidently not identical. They may partially overlap, but they do not coalesce, they are not identical.

We will again quote Collinson (p. 17): "The simplest and most universal form of communication is gesture and the simplest kind of gesture is the act of pointing ... In any case the standpoint taken here is "notional", not grammatical, and our business is to deal with those cases in which a speaker uses various linguistic devices either to *point* to (or away from) some item with a view to making his partner deal with that item, or to *mark* some item already presented with a view to retaining his partner's interest in it". In the definite article, however, pointing is not implied in the sense it is implied in the demonstrative pronouns *this, that*. Only in some special cases the article may be said to imply pointing but it is in a rather weaker sense than it is in *this, that*. There are cases where the definite article does not imply pointing at all, for example in the sentence "*The* horse is an animal". Unlike English, German and some other languages, Czech has three demonstrative pronouns: *ten, tento, onen* as compared for example with the English *this, that* and the German *dieser, jener* which may be identified with the Czech demonstrative pronouns *tento, onen*. The Czech pronoun *ten* is a demonstrative pronoun too, but it has much in common with the English article *the* or the German *der*. Therefore, when translating from Czech into English it is usual to put the definite article in English in those cases where in Czech it is possible to use the pronouns *ten* (masc.), *ta* (fem.), and *to* (neuter).

According to J. Zubatý[57] the transition from a proper demonstrative to the definite article is so gradual and continual that it is difficult to say where the pronoun ceases to be a demonstrative and becomes definite article. As we have shown in the preceding chapter, we can speak about a definite article only when it marks a noun in a general function, when an individual stands for a whole class. Only in that case the pronoun becomes article. The Czech pronoun *ten* has, in fact, a position which is nearer to that of the article, even when it does not cease to be a demonstrative: we cannot translate the English "*The* horse is an animal" into Czech as "*Ten* kůň je zvíře", but only "Kůň je zvíře". However, when we say in Czech "Dej mi *tu* knihu" (= "Give me *the* book"), we feel that we are not pointing to a book but only expressing familiarity with a certain book.

To sum up: the definite article has a qualitatively different function than the "indicaters" given by Collinson. It never possesses SOLELY the indicative and marking functions as the other "indicaters" do. In spite of overlapping of these functions in some cases the definite article possesses some qualities and functions, as discussed in this and the preceding chapter, which clearly exclude it from the class of Collinson's "indicaters". Consequently, the "indicaters", with the exception of the definite and indefinite article, do not belong to the sphere of determination or determinedness and we shall exclude them from our discussion.

By substantially differentiating the article from the demonstrative we have proved that it is not possible to put on one and the same level the function of articles and the function of demonstratives and the other means possessing the same function.[58] Both are

[57] Jan Zubatý, "Ten", *Naše řeč* 1 (1917) 10: 289-294.
[58] We will still mention the opinion of Paul M. Postal "On the So-called 'Pronouns' in English", *17th Annual Round Table* [= *Monograph Series on Languages and Linguistics* 19] [1966], 177-206) who regards the pronouns *I*, *our*, *they*, *this*, *that*, *these*, *those*, etc., as types of definite article, as syntactic features of nouns. He asserts (p. 179) that "English NP, that is, the elements which function as subjects, objects, etc., must be categorized into definite vs. indefinite in order for their distributional possibilities to be described properly." In our opinion, categorization on the basis of distributional criteria does not

clearly separated. In the chapter on determination and indication we have shown that articles cannot be classed with "indicaters" as their function is different from all the other means expressing "pointing" and "marking". As there is a clear separation of two distinct kinds of grammatical expedients that influence nomina or other parts of speech they belong to in a different way, a possibility is offering to distinguish the category of determinedness vs. indeterminedness on one hand and the category of indication on the other hand. The correlates of the category of determinedness vs. indeterminedness are articles or other grammatical means of identical function respectively, whereas the correlates of the category of indication are demonstratives and other words of identical or similar function.

To sum up the basic characteristics of articles as correlates of the category of determinedness vs. indeterminedness in contrast to the characteristics of demonstratives and other indicaters as correlates of the category of indication:

1. The definite article indicates particular or general term, the indefinite article indicates an unidentified particular term. The demonstrative only points and indicates, its primary function being that of pointing.
2. The article is a constant quality of the noun whereas the pronoun is merely facultative.
3. The article is determination plus some element that modifies the meaning of the word, whereas the demonstrative does not innerly modify the meaning of the word.

The article influences the noun directly in its substance whereas the demonstrative points merely from the outside inserting nothing into the noun it belongs to.

7. LOGICAL THEORIES OF ARTICLE AND TRANSFORMATIONAL GRAMMAR

After we have discussed some psychological functions of article, the reader may be interested in the ideas of the latest linguistic

get to the bottom of the problem. We must categorize on the basis of qualities, not on the basis of distribution which is a purely formal criterion.

trend, the transformational grammar. So far there is only one monograph, that of Beverly L. Robbins,[59] which treats the article from the point of view of transformational grammar and which is also our principle source of information (especially chapter 1). The transformational conception of article comes from logical theories of definite article. According to Robbins (p. 12), in the last hundred years the role of the definite article has concerned philosophers and logicians more urgently than grammarians. "Philosophers have emphasized the use of the definite article as a symbol by which a predicative expression can be converted into a name of a single thing, and therefore their contributions to the understanding of the definite article can only be approached through their theories of predication". It is the theory of John Stuart Mill, the theory of Gottlob Frege, and the theory of B. Russell, which fall within the context of the theory of transformational grammar, more definitely the theory of noun-phrase formation.

We will now briefly discuss Mill's view of the so-called connotative individual names. Proper names (e.g. *John*, *York*) are not connotative, according to Mill; they are not given because of any qualities, attributes, of the individuals. However, there are genuinely connotative individual names formed from concrete general names. According to Mill, a strictly individual name is formed from a general name so that the general name is limited by adding other words to it. He quotes the example *The present Prime Minister of England* as containing the general name *Prime Minister of England*. This general name is in the first case limited by the article and by the word *present* so that it is applicable to one individual only. Further examples: *the king who succeeded William the Conqueror*; *the only son of John Stiles*; *the first emperor of Rome*; *the father of Socrates*. The collective name *the 76th regiment of foot in the British Army* is, according to Mill, not a general name but a collective one denoting a collection of individuals. On the other hand, *a regiment* is both a collective and a general name.

Individuality of otherwise general names may be expressed

[59] Beverly L. Robbins, *The Definite Article in English Transformations* (The Hague, 1968).

by the preceding definite article or some other definite determiner, e.g. *the author of the Iliad, the murderer of Henri Quatre*. A general name can also be changed into an individual one by using definite article when it is clear from the context which individual is to be understood.

According to Robbins, however, the examples such as *the only son of Stiles* also admit the indefinite article. This problem seems to be solved by G. Frege for whom an expression beginning with indefinite article is not a name of an object but stands for a concept.

Frege distinguishes two grammatical categories: proper names and predicates. A proper name is, according to Frege, any expression that denotes an object. Thus proper names are, for example, such words as *Caesar* and *zero*, the phrases *the capital of Germany, the number four, the direction of the Earth's axis*, and whole sentences. A proper name is never a predicate but it may be a part of it. Predicate denotes a concept. Against the objection that sentences like *The morning star is Venus* refute the assertion that a name of an object cannot be a predicate Frege points out to the use of *is* as a copula, or sign of predication, and to its use as a sign of identity and therefore an essential part of the predicate. In the paraphrases of this sentence *The morning star is no other than Venus* or *The morning star is identical with Venus* "is" is a copula and *no other than Venus* and *identical with Venus* are the predicates. Nouns are either concept-words or proper names. A noun which is preceded by the definite article or a demonstrative adjective is a proper name which designates an object and not a concept whereas when it is used with the indefinite article or in plural without an article, it is a concept-word. Also the nouns preceded by the quantifiers *all, every, any, no, some*, are concept-words. In his *Principles of Mathematics* B. Russell stresses the importance of *a, the, some, any, every* and *all*, but does not regard the difference between *the* and *a, some, all*, etc. as the central distinction. Each of the six words with a noun form is, according to Russell, a denoting phrase. A noun can stand for a concept, but most sentences are not about the concept but about a term which in a certain way is connected with the concept. A phrase containing a noun is a denoting phrase in such sentences. A denoting phrase consists of the class-concept preceded by an article or a quantifier. According to Russell (p. 62) "the word *the*, in singular, is correctly employed only in relation to a class-concept of which there is only one instance". In Robbins's argument (p. 37) the definite article, unlike the indefinite article and the quantifiers, "provides a method of denoting one single term by means of a concept. In a sense definite descriptions are less problematic than other denoting phrases, which denote many terms combined in a certain way".

We will now give a brief sketch of how transformational grammar views the articles. The transformational grammar includes articles in a separate category of determiners.[60] There are three major subclasses of determiners: regular determiners, postdeterminers, and predeterminers. The subclass of regular determiners includes articles, demonstratives, and genitives. Articles and demonstratives are further subdivided into those occurring with plural nouns, whereas the genitives can occur with either singular or plural nouns. To articles belong, according to transformationalists, the following words: *a (an)*, Ø, *the, any, every, each, some*, to demonstratives belong *this, that, these, those*, to genitives *my, our, your, his, her, its, their*, and Nom + Z_3 (= the genitive morpheme). The Nom + Z_3 stands for the genitive form, e.g. *my poem*, or *Phil's poem*, or *boy's poem*, etc.

Regular determiners stand before nouns. Every noun in English must be preceded by one regular determiner (including the zero article Ø). The determiners are mutually exclusive, that is to say, no more than one regular determiner can be used with a noun. Sentences in which the noun is preceded by more than one regular determiner (e.g. *a this boy, this your girl*) are ungrammatical. This mutual exclusiveness is a very important feature that distinguishes regular determiners from adjectives. To regular determiners belong the so-called prearticles which precede articles or demonstratives or genitives or the zero article. The most important prearticles are:

[60] The following exposition is mostly based on Owen Thomas, *Transformational Grammar and the Teacher of English* (New York, 1967), 79-87.

all, only, both, just, (e.g. *all the boys, only that boy, both those girls, just my speed, all Ø boys*).

Postdeterminers are a class of words which precede the adjectives and can co-occur with themselves but only in a fixed order. They are different from regular determiners in that there can be two postdeterminers before any noun in a sentence whereas there can be only one regular determiner before any noun. The order of the postdeterminers is fixed in opposition to almost free order of adjectives. There are the following kinds of postdeterminers: 1. ordinals (e.g. *first, second, third* etc., *next, last, final*), 2. cardinals *(one, two, three* etc., *several, many, few)*, and 3. superlatives and comparatives *(more, most, fewer, fewest, less, least)*.

The postdeterminers can co-occur (a) with determiners (e.g. *the first orange, those three statues, some more gravy*), (b) with each other but only in a fixed order *(the first two azaleas, the last several months)*.

Predeterminers are such determiners as precede both the regular determiners and the postdeterminers. Their characteristic feature is that they are invariably separated from the regular determiners by the word *of*. The predeterminers include most of the regular determiners and postdeterminers and some nouns of quantity that function with *of* as predeterminers. Examples:

all of *the emperors*, some of *those owls*, the first of *those three bubbles*, just the last two of *my first five children*, a quart of *molasses*, a mile of *spaghetti*, only the first two barrels of *oil*.

A relatively systematic, though not exhaustive description of the transformational decomposition of English sentences containing definite noun-phrases consisting of a noun preceded by the definite article and followed by a closely appositive adjunct is contained in the above-mentioned monograph by Beverly L. Robbins. In chapters 3 - 8 of that book Robbins tries to prove that *the* preceding N + Right Adjunct (*N* being primitive or derived *Xxn*; $X = V, A,$ or *N*) has the status of a constant which is introduced by transformations producing the *N*-phrase. According to Robbins this use of the definite article reinforces and is reinforced by the limitation imposed on the centre of the phrase by the adjunct. A singular count noun can have either the indefinite or definite article. The occurrence of the definite article before a noun followed by an adjunct is regarded as depending on the presence of the adjunct. Certain syntactic relations can be stated between the article and various adjunct structures.

Robbins further shows that the definite article is a transformational constant in the analysis of sentence structure of the form S *(the N + Right Adjunct)*, *S (the Xxn + Right Adjunct)* and S_L *(N_1) C S_R (the N_1)*. Of other uses of the definite article Robbins mentions as the most prominent the use of *the* with a noun to which a pre-nominal adjective is adjoined. There is a problem of the use of the definite article with an adjective forming a noun term, for example *The rich prosper, The beautiful is different from the sublime, The old gives way to the new*. Such sentences have paraphrases without article: *Rich people prosper, Beauty is different from sublimity, What is old gives way to what is new*. Robbins explains these cases as serving for stating corresponding *the*-introducing transformations. Another construction with the definite article is that joining the definite article with the comparative degree of adjectives or adverbs, e.g. *Your rug looks the prettier because it has slight imperfections* and *The longer Mary waits, the harder her task will become*. Robbins thinks that the former example in which the article has the function of a determinative in connection with an explanatory clause of cause, might be derived from *Your rug looks pretty* and *Your rug has slight imperfections* if we regard *the ...er because* as the connective.

Likewise Robbins explains the generic use of the definite article as (p. 239) "generalizing in the direction of what is normal or typical for members of a class, which only sometimes coincides with what is true of all the members". The sentence *The cheetah attains great speed* is equivalent to *Cheetahs attain great speeds* when the former sentence is not about a particular cheetah but is not equivalent to *All cheetahs attain great speeds* or *Any cheetah attains great speeds*.

Apart from the fact that so far the transformational grammar has tried to solve only a few of the problems of article, some of them, moreover, being controversial,[61] the transformational view of the article does not contribute to our knowledge of the SUB- STANCE of the article. On the other hand it must be admitted that transformational rules concerning article throw new light upon the formal aspect of its occurrence.

[61] For example, the above-mentioned construction of the definite article with the comparative degree of adjectives or adverbs. Has *the* in this case the function of the definite article at all? In our opinion, *the* in this construction is no article as article in its basic function is essentially connected with noun and there is no noun in this construction. The article *the* does not fully comply here with the criteria valid for the function of the article. It does not determine the comparative of the adjective or adverb in the same way as it does the noun, neither does it modify it as it does the noun, nor does it influence it in its substance as it does the noun.

Similarly, the function of *the* in the sentences *The rich prosper, The beautiful is different from the sublime,* and *The old gives way to the new* cannot be regarded as determination which is the principle function of article, as in these cases *the* does not determine anything. That it is so, is manifested by the para- phrases *Rich people prosper, Beauty is different from sublimity, What is old gives way to what is new,* quoted by Robbins. No determination is expressed in these paraphrases.

PART TWO

A TYPOLOGY OF LANGUAGES BASED
ON THE OCCURRENCE OF THE CATEGORY
OF DETERMINEDNESS VS. INDETERMINEDNESS

In this part of the book we will give a survey of the distribution of the category of determinedness vs. indeterminedness in various languages of the world. Though this survey cannot comprise all the languages of the world, it strives after representativeness as large as possible[1] so that it may render the distribution of this important language phenomenon.

In our typology we classify languages into seven main groups indicated by capital letters A to G. The languages are classified by formal means expressing the category of determinedness vs. indeterminedness. Thus type A includes languages expressing the category of determinedness vs. indeterminedness by independent words, type B includes languages expressing one member of the category by an independent word and the other member by an enclitic or proclitic. Type C comprises languages expressing both members of the category by enclitics or proclitics. Type D takes in languages in which the category of determinedness vs. indeterminedness is inherent in the noun itself. To type E belong languages in which the category is expressed by flexion, in type F by prosodic means (accent or intonation), and languages of type G have a zero category of determinedness vs. indeterminedness. Most of these types are divided into subtypes.

---

[1] In spite of a certain incompleteness there will appear some differences in the representation of languages in particular types so that in addition to the qualitative aspect of the typology the quantitative aspect will be represented, to a considerable extent, too.

A. LANGUAGES EXPRESSING THE CATEGORY OF DETERMINEDNESS VS. INDETERMINEDNESS BY MEANS OF INDEPENDENT WORDS

I. Languages Possessing Definite and Indefinite Article

1. *The definite article is in singular and plural, the indefinite article is only in singular*

Typical representatives of this subtype are Germanic languages: English, German, and Dutch.

As the function of the English articles has sufficiently been treated above, we will turn our attention to the other Germanic languages. In German the definite article is *der*, (masc.), *die* (femin.), *das* (neuter) in singular, and *die* (for all genders) in plural, whereas the indefinite article *ein* (masc., neuter) and *eine* (femin.) is only in singular.[2] Beside the categories of gender and number the German article also takes part in the category of case (the definite article: sing. *der, des, dem, den; die, der, der, die; das, des, dem, das*; plural: *die, der, den, die* for all genders. The indefinite article: *ein, eines, einem, einen; eine, einer, einer, eine; ein, eines, einem, ein*). The indefinite article has no plural and therefore the indefinite article in singular is confronted with zero article in plural, e.g. sing. *ein Haus* — pl. *Häuser*. The article is usually unstressed and therefore it is often added to the preceding stressed prepositions and is fused with some, e.g.

(a) dative masc.: *am, im, vom, beim, zum*;
(b) dative femin.: *zur*;
(c) accusative neuter: *ans, ins, aufs, fürs, durchs*.

Similar to English the definite article in German points to familiar items, whether they are explicitly named or made familiar by the

---

[2] On articles in German cf., e.g., Johannes Erben, *Abriss der deutschen Grammatik* (Berlin, 1959), 149-151; O. Moskal'skaja, *Grammatika nemeckogo jazyka* (Moskva, 1958), 113-153; K. G. Krušel'nickaja, "Smyslovaja funkcija porjadka slov v sovremennom nemeckom jazyke", diss. (Moskva, 1948). The so-called theory of individualization was elaborated by O. Behaghel (*Deutsche Syntax*, Bd. I) and H. Paul (*Deutsche Grammatik*, Bd. III).

preceding or directly following parts of speech, or given in a certain situation or in memory. Some examples of the use of the definite article in German[3]:

1. *Der Hund trägt ein breites Halsbund* (realizing meaning).
2. *Der Hund ist ein Säugetier* (generalizing meaning).
3. *Ein Schwan kam ihnen entgegen. Der Schwan und ihr Boot glitten lautlos aneinander vorüber.* (H. Mann, Der Untertan.)

The indefinite article indicates an indefinite object, e.g. *Hat ihn ein Hund gebissen?* (= any dog). Or: *Vor der Haustür liegt ein Hund.*

In using the zero article any individualization or exemplification is, according to Erben (p. 149), disregarded, for instance *Sie leben wie Hund und Katze.* Or *Hunde fressen gern Fleisch.*

Close to the use of the zero article are the cases with indefinite article where any specimen is concerned, or the cases with a generalizing definite article:

> *Der (ein) Hund kann schwimmen = (die) Hunde können schwimmen. (Die) Elektrizität treibt Maschinen. (Der) Fleiss ist eine löbliche Eigenschaft.*

According to Erben's argumentation, the relative equivalence of the zero, indefinite, and generalizing article enables the definite article *der, die, das* to function as a guide of the noun even in cases in which not a demonstrative meaning but simply the designation of class and function (genus, casus, numerus) is concerned. Therefore we say *der Ruhe bedürfen*, not because a definite measure or a certain way of rest might be concerned but because *Ruhe* is here an adverbal genitive (in contradistinction to *Ruhe brauchen*). Similarly *Zeichen der Ungeduld* (= *Zeichen von Ungeduld*, the preposition *von* having taken here the role of designating the word *Ungeduld* as adnominal complementary determination [Ergänzungsbestimmung]). In these cases the

---

[3] Cf. J. Erben, *Abriss der deutschen Grammatik*, and O. Moskal'skaja, *Grammatika nemeckogo jazyka*, sub (1).

definite article is, according to Erben, less "Bestimmtheitspartikel" than "Gelenkwort" (articulus).

O. I. Moskal'skaja[4] states the following characteristic features of the category of determinedness vs. indeterminedness in German:

1. The article is part of the noun as a part of speech and expresses determinedness or indeterminedness proper to the noun. This significance appears most fully when the noun is used in a sentence (within it the category of determinedness vs. indeterminedness is concordant with the category of case).

2. The characterization of an object as definite or indefinite is not connected with the qualities of the object itself (no object by itself can exist as indefinite) but is determined by the relation assumed by the speaker and hearer in the process of communication. A decisive moment is the degree of familiarity of the hearer with the respective object.

O. I. Moskal'skaja brings some new, interesting elements to the elucidation of the essence of the category of determinedness vs. indeterminedness in German. To grasp the essence of this category, it is necessary, in her opinion, to register the co-working, the relation between the use of article on one hand and the word order and intonation in sentence on the other hand. The article expresses the communicative role of the noun within the sentence, that is to say it points, together with the word order and intonation, to whether the noun belongs to the system of the starting point of communication or to the system of the communicated, i.e. of the new[5]. Cf.:

> *Die junge Frau brachte einen Brief.*
> *Den Brief brachte eine junge Frau.*

A different communicative content of these sentences is realized, according to Moskal'skaja, by means of the word order, the definite

---

[4] Cf. O. Moskal'skaja, *Grammatika nemeckogo jazyka*, sub (1), 121 f.
[5] We see that here Moskal'skaja clearly applies the theory of functional sentence perspective, though explicitly she does not mention it.

and indefinite article, and in oral utterance, moreover, by means of intonation.

The noun which is new is used with indefinite article, is put nearer to the end of the sentence and is stressed. The noun that serves as the starting point of communication stands at the beginning of the sentence and has a secondary stress.[6]

The significance of determinedness and indeterminedness is closely connected with the communicative charge of the noun in the sentence as a starting point of communication or as an expression of something new. Both are given by a concrete situation. This is why, according to Moskal'skaja, the function of the expression of determinedness and indeterminedness and the function of the expression of the communicative charge are often identical. That is the case of the already mentioned sentences.

> Ein Schwan *kam ihnen entgegen*. Der Schwan *und ihr Boot glitten lautlos aneinander vorüber*.

The definite article with the noun *Schwan* expresses partly the determinedness, partly the starting point of action.

The relation of the function of determinedness and indeterminedness of nouns and the communicative function can, according to Moskal'skaja, be expressed as follows:

1. The article expresses determinedness vs. indeterminedness of the noun and its use in the sentence as a starting point of communication or as something new.
2. The article expresses only the communicative function of the noun in the sentence; the meaning of determinedness vs. indeterminedness is lacking with respect to the character of the use of the noun.
3. The article cannot simultaneously express determinedness or indeterminedness of the noun and its use in the sentence in the quality of something new so that these two meanings cannot

---

[6] In the terminology of functional sentence perspective the indefinite article with a noun is, similarly as in English, the signal of the rheme, whereas the definite article with a noun is the signal of the theme. However, the problems concerned are not simple and deserve a more thorough elaboration.

be fused in the form of one and the same article. Therefore (a) the article expresses only the determinedness of the noun and its communicative role in the sentence is expressed by other language expedients, (b) the article expresses only the use of the noun in the quality of the new, in spite of the situational determinedness of the noun.

We turn now to Dutch where the definite article in singular is *de* for masculines and feminines, *het* for neuters, in plural it is *de* for all three genders. The indefinite article has a single form for all genders: *een*. The use of articles is substantially analogical to that in other Germanic languages. Proper names of persons, towns, villages, and lands, as well as collective and abstract nouns, when they are not further determined by an attributive adjective or noun, are without article. Personal names in plural have the article *(de Willems)*. Without article are further the names of months, days in a week, plurals of further not determined nouns and common names standing for proper names (e.g. *moeder* 'mother'). However, when these nouns have further determination, they have the article, e.g. *de kleine Jan, de brave vader, het oude Utrecht, de eerste Januarie, de tweede Maandag*, etc. The definite article is before the names of cardinal points, even if they indicate direction: *naar het Westen* 'to the west'; further after the word *al*: *al het Geld* 'all gold', before *een*, if it stands in contrast to *ander*, e.g. *de eene hand wast de andere* 'one hand washes the other' and before superlative: *in de grootste nood* 'in the greatest need'.

In Portuguese the definite article in singular is *o* (masc.) and *a* (femin.), in plural *os* (masc.) and *as* (femin.), e.g. *o pai* 'the father' — pl. *os pais* 'the fathers'; *a mãe* 'the mother' — pl. *as mães* 'the mothers'. The indefinite article in singular is *um* (masc.) and *uma* (femin.), e.g. *um livro* 'a book', *uma cadeira* 'a chair'. The forms *um, uma* have also plurals *(uns, umas)*; these, however, have no more the function of article but of the indefinite numeral "several".

In Portuguese the article merges with some prepositions, for example with the preposition *em* 'in', e.g. *em + o = no, em* + *a* = *na*, *em* + *um* = *num* (beside *em um*), *em* + *uma* = *numa* (beside *em uma*).

The definite article in Portuguese is used mainly in the following cases:[7]

1. With nouns designating persons or things already familiar or mentioned before.
2. Very often with nouns accompanied by possessive pronouns, when designation of relationship, addressing, or title are not concerned.
3. With the names of all continents *(a Europa)* and of many countries *(a Alemanha, o Brasil)*.
4. With the names of rivers, mountains and seas, e.g. *o Elba, o Etna, o Atlântico*.
5. With geographical names in plural: *os Estados Unidos da América do Norte, os Cárpatos, as Canárias*.
6. If the name of a town is determined: *a Praga de hoje* 'the present-day Prague'.
7. To indicate certain qualities of human body: *Ela tinha os olhos azuis e os cabelos louros* 'She has blue eyes and fair hair'.
8. To designate languages, e.g. *o italiano* 'Italian', but *Êle falou francês comigo* 'He spoke French with me'. Similarly there is no article after a preposition *(de inglês em alemão* 'from English into German').
9. With the names of cardinal points *(o Norte* 'north').
10. With proper names preceded by an attribute *(o grande Santos Dumont* 'the great Santos Dumont').
11. With the epithets of proper names: *Alexandre o Grande*, but *Carlos Magno*.
12. With the indication of time *(as oito horas* 'at eight o'clock', *pela tarde* 'in the afternoon').
13. With substantivized adjectives, infinitives, prepositions, adverbs, etc., e.g. *Admiramos todo o belo* 'We admire all beautiful'; *O comer é necessário para o viver* 'To eat is necessary for

---

[7] According to Zdeněk Hample and Jaroslav Holbík, *Učebnice portugalštiny* [Textbook of Portuguese] (Praha, 1965), 369-371.

living'; *Meu irmão defendia o contra* 'My brother defended the reverse'.

14. In cases like *todos os homens* 'all people', *ambos os países* 'both countries', *dar os bons dias* 'to wish good day', *dar os parabéns* 'to congratulate', *dar os pêsames* 'to present condolence'; *dar os boas vindas* 'to welcome', etc.

The article is not used:

1. With proper names that have no nearer determination: *Meu cunhado chama-se João Pereira* 'My brother-in-law's name is João Pereira'.

2. With non-determined abstracts, especially after prepositions (*sem dúvida* 'without doubt', *com licença* 'with permission'), and in predicate (*Não perca coragem* 'don't lose courage').

3. In expressing an indefinite quantity, e.g. *João tem trabalho* 'John is busy'.

4. In a partitive indication of quantity, e.g. *Tenho un quilo de pão* 'I have one kilo bread'. Similarly with the expressions of quantity: *número, porção, quantidade.*

5. With titles and in addressing (*bon dia, senhor*: 'good day, sir').

6. In inscriptions and headings: *Entrada* 'Way in', *História de Portugal.*

7. In the date: *7 de junho 1971.*

8. Before *tão, tal* 'such', *somelhante* 'similar', *meio* 'half' /adj./, *certo* 'certain', etc.: *tão alto preço* 'such a high price', *semelhante coisa* 'a similar thing', *meia libra* 'half a pound', *certo dia* 'on a certain day'.

9. After the forms of the verb *ser* with nouns expressing nationality and profession. Likewise after the verbs *crer, considerar, julgar* 'consider as', *nomear* 'to name', *eleger* 'to elect'. For example, *Eu sou português* 'I am a Portuguese'. *Crê-me (considera-me, julga-me) professor* 'He considers me a professor'. *Foi nomeado ministro* 'He was appointed minister'. *Foi eleito deputado* 'He was elected deputy'.

10. Mostly in apposition: *O Conselho Nacional de Estatistica, orgão do Instituto Brasileiro de Geografia e Estatistica* 'National Council of Statistics, the organ of the Geographical and Statistical Institute of Brazil'.
Exception is the superlative of adjectives: *O café, a mais preciosa mercadoria* 'Coffee, the most valuable goods'.

11. When two or more nouns follow, the article is used only with the first noun: *Compro o livro, caderno, papel e penas* 'I buy a book, an exercise-book, a paper and pens.'

12. In expressions such as *correr risco* 'to risk', *lançar (levar) âncora* 'to drop (weigh) anchor', *perder de vista* 'to lose sight of', *ir a casa* 'to go home', *viajar de trem (de automóvel, de navio)* 'to travel by train (car, ship)', *ir a pé* 'to go on foot', *fazer sinal* 'to give signal', *dar graças* 'to thank', etc.

Modern Greek[8] has a declined definite article which agrees with its noun in gender, number, and case:

Sg.	masc.	fem.	neut.
Nom.	ὁ	ἡ	τό
Gen.	τοῦ	τῆς	τοῦ
Acc.	τό(ν)	τή(ν)	τό

Pl.	masc.	fem.	neut.
Nom.	οἱ	οἱ	τά
Gen.	τῶν	τῶν	τῶν
Acc.	τούς	τίς	τά

[8] Cf. Fred W. Householder, Kostas Kazazis, Andreas Koutsoudas, "Reference Grammar of Literary Dhimotiki", *IJAL* 30: 2, Part II (Bloomington — The Hague, 1964) 29-30, 80f., 92, 95 f.

If the noun has no inflexion, the article may be the only indicator of gender, number, and case. Contrary to English, the definite article in Modern Greek is used before proper names (both the first name and the family name), before abstracts, before a class of objects or people, before possessive pronouns and after demonstrative adjectives, e.g. ὁ Γιῶργος 'George', ὁ Πέτρος ὁ Νομικὸς 'Peter Nomikos', ἡ εἰλικρίνεια 'sincerity', οἱ ἄνθρωποι εἶναι μυστήριοι 'people are funny', ὁ ἄνθρωπος εἶναι μυστήριο ζῶο 'man is a strong animal', τὸ σπίτι μου 'my house', τὸ σπίτι τοῦ πέτρου 'Peter's house', αὐτὸ σπίτι 'this house'.

In some cases, especially in the language of poetry, the accusative femin. pl. is τὲς instead of τίς. Sometimes the forms of nominative and accusative plural femin. are substituted by the forms αἱ (instead of οἱ) and τάς (instead of τίς). In the older language of poetry it is sometimes possible to find the definite article in the function of a relative pronoun.

As indefinite article serves in Modern Greek the word ἕνας (masc.), μιά (μία) (femin.), ἕνα (neut.) 'one' with a weak stress in attributive use. The indefinite article is not so frequent in Modern Greek as it is in English. It is not used for example with predicative nouns, it is often not used with indefinite direct objects and generally it is not used in proverbs and folk sayings, when an entire class and not a specific member of this class is concerned.

In Finno-Ugric languages this type is represented by Hungarian which possesses the definite article a, az (preceding a vowel), and the indefinite article egy which, contrary to its function as a numeral 'one', is unstressed, e.g. a bor 'the wine', az állat 'the animal', egy ember 'a man'. In contradistinction to the demonstrative az 'that', the article az is always used attributively and is invariable. It is necessary to point out to the fact that demonstratives requiring grammatical concord must be followed by the definite article a, az when used adjectively, attributively, except in exclamations and addresses, such as in én istenem, én istenem 'my God, my God'.[9] It could be compared, according to Robert

---

[9] Cf. John Lotz, "Grammatical Derivability", *In Honour of Anton Reichling*, *Lingua* 21 (Amsterdam, 1968), 630.

A. Hall Jr.[10], to the apposition to the pronoun: 'this, the book', 'to these, to the books', etc. For example, *ez a könyv* 'this book'; *ez a könyvem* 'this book of mine'; *ezek a könyvek* 'these books'; *ezek a könyveim* 'these books of mine'; *ezeknek a könyveknek* 'to these books', etc.

In Hungarian the article is used approximately in the same way as in English. It is never used before proper names or names of continents, countries, towns or villages (except when a qualificative adjective precedes), even when in the original language the article is used, e.g. *Hága* 'den Haag' (cf. the English *the Hague*). With the names of rivers, seas, mountains, and certain regions article is used, e.g. *a Tisza*, *a Duna* ('the Danube'), *a Fekete tenger* 'the Black Sea', *a Karpátok* 'Carpathians', *az Alföld* 'the lower plain of Hungary'. Besides, however, determinedness and indeterminedness in Hungarian is also expressed in verbal flexion so that Hungarian also belongs to Group E, type III. (cf. pp. 183-5).

In Old Egyptian the definite article is *pa*, *pe*, feminine gender *ta*, *te*, plural *na*, *ne*, *nan*, *nen*, the indefinite article is *ua*, e.g. *pa nuter* 'the god', *ta nuter-t-a* 'the goddess', *na nuteru* 'the gods', *ua atef* 'a father'.

This type also includes a number of Iranian languages. For instance, in Yazghulami[11] the function of the definite article is expressed by the demonstrative pronoun *du* 'the' and the function of indefinite article is expressed by the numeral *wŭ* 'one', e.g. *du ni bəčkén anəz əm xod?* 'My children are still on the shore?' or *Du Damdóri kāl-u xasá mad?* 'Has Damdor no more headache?' Further we will mention the Central Dardic languages Gavar, Xovar, and Torwalī[12]. In Gavar the category of determinedness vs. indeterminedness is expressed in two ways: 1. by the use of the indefinite article *ya* (< *yak* 'one'), e.g. *ya mānuš* 'a man' and by the use of the demonstrative pronoun *se* which loses its independent meaning and becomes definite article, e.g. *se mānuš*

[10] Robert A. Hall Jr., *An Analytical Grammar of the Hungarian Language* (= *Language Monograph* 18) (Baltimore, 1938), 46.
[11] Cf. *Jazyky narodov SSSR* I (Moskva, 1966), 346.
[12] Cf. D. I. Edel'man, *Dardskije jazyki* (Moskva, 1965), 83, 127, 134.

'the man'; 2. by the difference in the case forms of the direct object expressing a definite and indefinite object. In Xovar the category of determinedness vs. indeterminedness is expressed by means of the indefinite article *ī* 'one' and the definite article whose function is taken on by demonstrative pronouns. In addition to this, the category of determinedness vs. indeterminedness is expressed by different flexion of the direct object. Also Torwalī uses the numeral *ē* 'one' in the function of independent article and demonstrative pronouns in the function of definite article. However, we are not quite sure whether genuine articles may be assumed here. A similar situation is in the Tatar language[13] which expresses indefiniteness by the preceding numeral *ber* 'one' and definiteness by the demonstrative pronoun *tege* 'the'. Besides, nouns expressing indefinite objects are used in indefinite case and definite objects are indicated by accusative. The so-called indefinite case has no affix.

Of Polynesian languages, Maori has the definite article *te*, plural *nga*, the indefinite article *he* (e.g. *he hoiho* 'a horse', *he wairere* 'a waterfall', *te pouaru* 'the widow', *te taɲata* 'the man', *te raakau* 'the tree'), Tahitian has the definite article *te*, plural *na*, the indefinite article *e*, Moiki (Moava) has the definite article *te*, plural *na*, indefinite article *he*. Nuguria has the definite article *te*, plural *na-*, indefinite article *he*. All these languages possess, moreover, the personal article (Tahitian *'o*, the other languages *ko*).

The Melanesian language Nengoné has the definite article *re*, indefinite *se* (e.g. *re ngome* 'the man', *se ngome* 'a man').

The Indonesian language Masaretian (of an island opposite New Guinea) uses as definite article the demonstrative *di* and as indefinite article the numeral *emsian* 'one', the language of Bazee, spoken in Celebes, has a definite (personal) article *i* and indefinite *on*.[14]

---

[13] Cf. M. Z. Zakijev, "Tatarskij jazyk", *Jazyki narodov SSSR* II (Moskva, 1966), 143.

[14] Our information on Indonesian languages is predominantly based on Renward Brandstetter's monograph *Der Artikel des Indonesischen verglichen mit dem des Indogermanischen* (= *Monographien zur Indonesischen Sprachforschung* X) (Lucerne 1913), which is the only monograph devoted to this

When writing about Polynesian and Indonesian languages, we regard it necessary to discuss the character of articles in these languages. As stated by W. K. Matthews[15], articles in these languages are personal or deictic (demonstrative). They classify nouns into proper and common. The deictic articles have more or less the character of definite and indefinite article, even when they do not always correspond to the general Indo-European usage: the distinction between "definite" and "indefinite" in these languages is not identical with that in English and is sometimes obscured.

Very extensively used in these languages is the so-called personal article. Its form is usually *ko* (*'o*) and it precedes proper names in nominative (cf. the Tahitian *'o Tahiti*, Tongan *ko Paulo*, Marquesan *'o Wapu*, etc.). It may also be emphatic (e.g. the Hawaian *'o Louo*, Rapanai *ko vau* 'I', Tahitian *'o vai te haere i Tahiti?* 'Who went to Tahiti?' etc.). In many Polynesian languages the alternative personal article is *a* which may also be used in nominative before proper names (e.g. in Rarotongan *a Makea*, in Tongan *a Tonga*) and before pronouns (e.g. the Tongan *ahai?* 'who?', the Fakaofo *ko ai?* 'who?', East Uvea *aia* 'he', etc.).

In our opinion the personal article cannot be compared with the definite article, as it stands with proper nouns or pronouns which by themselves are definite, expressing a definite individual. Thus it does not comply with our criterion of article. Of course, neither can we include into our typology the ligative article which has quite a different function from that of the other articles. The ligative article is a bond or 'tie' (according to MacKinley) between

---

special subject. However, Brandstetter's statements must be taken with reservation; it is often uncertain whether articles or demonstratives are concerned. Even E. M. Uhlenbeck's excellent bibliography (in: *Current Trends in Linguistics*, 2, *Linguistics in East Asia and South East Asia*, The Hague, 1967, 847-898) does not give any work dealing with articles. There are, of course, mentions of articles in some books and papers describing particular Indonesian languages. Thanks to the kind help of Professor Uhlenbeck the author had opportunity to get materials from some of those papers otherwise inaccessible for him so that he was not entirely dependent on Brandstetter's monograph.

[15] W. K. Matthews, "The Polynesian Articles", *Lingua* 2, 14-31.

noun and adjective, the substance and the selected quantity. According to H. Kun[16] the ligatives are form-words like the articles and prepositions. In the Philippine language Tagalog (in Luzon) the ligative *(ng, n, na)* follows the definite article, e.g. *ang tavo* 'human being', *nang lalaki* 'of the man'. Further it is used with attributive adjectives (e.g. *ibang bayan* 'another town') and with the forms of decade numerals (e.g. *limang povo* 'fifty').

2. *The definite article is only in singular, the indefinite article is both in singular and in plural.*

The representatives of this group are the Polynesian languages Samoan (the definite article *le*, indefinite singular *se*, indefinite plural *ni*), East Futuna (the definite article *le*, indefinite sing. *se*, pl. *niiki*), Fakaofo and Vaitupu (the definite article *te*, indefinite sing. *se* or *he*, pl. *ni*).

3. *Both articles are in singular and in plural.*

This subtype is not a very frequent one. Of Romance languages it is especially Spanish which belongs to this subtype. In Spanish the definite article in singular is *el* (masc.), *le* (femin.), and *lo* (neuter), in plural *los* (masc., neut.) and *las* (femin.); e.g. *el vino* 'the wine' — pl. *los vinos, el hombre* 'the man' — pl. *los hombres, la mujer* 'the woman' — pl. *las mujeres.*
The definite article is used:[17]

1. Before personal names with an attribute, e.g. *La pequeña Elvira* 'the small Elvira', *Luis el Grande.*
2. Before feminine Christian names in familiar use: *He visto a la Dolores en el teatro* 'I saw Dolores in the theatre'.

---

[16] H. Kun, "Over zoogenaamde Verbindingsklanken in het Tagata en wat daarmee overeenkomt in 't Kawi", *Verspreide Geschriften* XIII, (The Hague 1927).
[17] According to C. M. Sauer and H. Ruppert, *Spanische Konversations-grammatik* (Heidelberg, 1941), 297-305.

3. If a proper name is used in generic sense, e.g. *el César de su siglo* 'the Caesar of his century'.

4. Before the names of some older Italian artists: *el Ticiano, el Veronés*.

5. Before titles: *El señor Figueras*. In addressing a person no article is used before the title: *Sí, señor, Vd. tiene razón*.

6. If the personal name designates not a person but a work: *He comprado el Quijote* 'I have bought a Quijote' (= the novel).

7. Before the names of days (except after *en*), with temporal expressions (excluding the date) and with the names of grammatical tenses, before the names of seasons of the year (except after *en*), with the majority of the names of ecclesiastical festivals, and with the names of cardinal points. Cf. *el martes* 'Monday', *a las ocho* 'at 8 o'clock', *la primavera* 'spring', *la Conception* 'Conception', *el este* 'east'.

No article is used with the names of months, further with the names of days and seasons of the year in connection with the preposition *en*, before numerals indicating the date by means of a preposition (e.g. *Miércoles, a diez y nueve de octubre* 'on Wednesday the 19th October'), and before temporal expressions *fines, mediados, principios* (e.g. *a fines de abril* 'at the end of April', *a mediados del mes que viene* 'in the middle of the next month').

8. With generic, material, and abstract names.

When a generic name concerns only an individual, no article is used: *Le han dado gato por liebre* 'He was given a tom-cat instead of hare'.

With material names no article is used when parts of wholes are concerned, e.g. *Un travajo incrustado en oro* 'a work set in gold'.

Abstracts are without article after prepositions, e.g. *No hay que hablar por vanidad* 'One shouldn't speak from vanity'.

9. After the verb *tener* 'to have', if a description of bodily qualities or states is concerned, e.g. *El niño tiene los cabellos negros* 'The child has black hair'.

10. After the names of singular things, e.g. *el sol y la tierra* 'the Sun and the Earth'.

11. After *nos otros* 'we' and *vosotros* 'you (thou)' when followed by a collective concept without numeral, e.g. *nosotros los españoles* 'We Spaniards'.

12. After the verb *dar* having the meaning 'to wish' in certain phrases: *Dar las buenas noches* 'to say good night'.

13. After *todo*, if the following word is concrete: *todo el dinero* 'all the money'. When the following word is an abstract, the article is not used: *con toda consideración* 'with all regards' but *con toda la consideración* 'with the best regards'.

14. After *tocar* and *jugar* with a following noun: *tocar el piano* 'to play piano', *jugar a los naipes* 'to play at cards'.

15. With the names of languages when they are conceived as wholes. When a language is meant in opposition to another language, the article is omitted: *Estas señoras hablan (en) castellano yo no en italiano* 'These ladies speak (just) Spanish, not Italian'.

The indefinite article in Spanish is *un* or *uno* (masc.), *una* (fem.) in singular, *unos* (masc., neut.) and *unas* (fem.) in plural, e.g. *un hombre* 'a man', pl. *unos hombres*; *una mujer* 'a woman', pl. *unas mujeres*.

The indefinite article is used especially when an individual person or thing or a striking characteristic is to be emphasized, or if a predicative noun is complemented by a close modification, e.g. *Es un bobo* 'he is a blockhead', but *es bobo* 'he is stupid'. *El Marqués es un general de mérito* 'The marquis is a general of merit'.

The indefinite article is omitted before predicative nouns designating an office, rank, state, nationality, denomination or some other outstanding attributes, further before the adjectives *tan, tal, otro, semejante, igual, medio, cierto, tanto, tamaño* and before the nouns *número, parte, porción, cantidad, multitud,* in exclamations and questions which are expected to be answered in negative (e.g. *Hay mujer más arrogante?*) as well as in negative sentences and after verbs expressing doubt (e.g. *Dudo que Vd. encuentre mejor calidad* 'I doubt whether you find a better quality' or *Nunca ví hombre más impertinente* 'I have never seen a more impudent man').

Apposition is usually without article but when it is introduced by a cardinal numeral the article is used (e.g. *Carlos, Felix y Juan, los tres discipulos mejores de su clase* 'Charles, Felix, and John, the three best pupils of their class') as well as when it is accompanied by a superlative (e.g. *Shakespeare, el poeta dramático más famoso de Inglaterra* 'Shakespeare, the most famous dramatic poet of England'); the article is also used when a historical name is accompanied by a characteristic attribute (e.g. *Luis el Grande*, but *Carlos Tercero* 'Charles III').

This subtype further includes Coptic which has the definite article *pe, pi* (masc.), *te, ti* (fem.) in singular, *ne, ni* (both genders) in plural, and the indefinite article *u* in singular, *han* in plural. Examples: *pi kahi* 'the earth', *ti šime* 'the woman', *ne taŭ* 'the mountains', *u romi* 'a man'. In Old Egyptian the definite article is *pa* (masc.) and *pa* (fem.), indefinite *ua*, e.g. *pa nuter* 'the god', *ua atef* 'a father'.

Some Polynesian languages also have both articles in singular and plural. For example, Sikayana has the definite article *te* in singular, *na* in plural, the indefinite article *he* in singular, *ni* in plural. Another Polynesian language, Leuangina, has the definite article *he* in singular, *ng(i)* in plural.

4. *Both articles are in singular only.*

This subgroup is rather unproductive. For example, the Polynesian language Rarotongan has both the definite article *te* and the indefinite article *e* in singular only. Similarly East Uvea (the definite article *[ko]*, *te*, the indefinite *he*), Rapanui (the definite article *te [ko]*, the indefinite *he*).

5. *Several kinds of definite article, only one kind of indefinite article.*

This subtype includes some Polynesian and Indonesian languages as well as some American Indian languages.

The Polynesian language Nine has singular definite articles *(ko)e, koe*, plural *na* and indefinite article *ha*. Tongan has the definite articles *koe, ae, 'e he* (only singular) and the indefinite article *ha*. Hawaiian has two forms of the definite article: *ke, ka*, plural *na*, the indefinite article is *he*, plural *na*.

The Philippine language Tagalog has articles with common nouns of things *ang, nang* (graphic form *ng*) and *sa* and personal articles standing with proper names *(si, ni, kay; sina, niná, kiná)*. M. Krus and L. I. Škarban[18] write that functionally the articles *ang, si* and *sina* are in opposition to the other articles approximately in the similar way as the nominative of Indo-European languages to the indirect case. The meaning of the articles *nang, ni* and *niná* may be compared to the genitive of Indo-European languages.

The particle *na(-ng)* expresses a tie between the determined and the determining, both in postposition and in the prepositional determination. By means of this particle determinations are added both to nouns and to verbs, e.g. *gurong matalino* 'a wise teacher', *tumakbóng mabilis* 'to run fast'.

The articles *ang, si, sína* are indicators of independent position of the noun in sentence (they usually indicate subject), e.g. *Si Balagtás ay dakilang makatà ng Pilipinas* 'Balagtas is a great poet of the Philippines'.

On the other hand, the articles *ng, ni, niná, sa kay, kiná* are indicators of a dependent position of the noun in sentence, e.g. *buhók ni Marya* 'Mary's hair'; *sinulat ng gurō* 'written by the teacher'; *pagbabaka sa katahimikan* 'the struggle for peace', etc.

The articles *sína, niná* and *kiná* are syntactically identical with the articles *si, nang* and *kay* but the former three, in contradistinction to the latter three, involve the idea of collective quantity. Together with the proper noun which they precede, they

---

[18]   M. Krus and L. I. Škarban, *Tagal'skij jazyk* (Moskva, 1966), 82-83, 86.

indicate a group of persons connected with the given person either by a family relation or friendly relation, or by some other association (following from the context), e.g. *sina Teresa* means 'Theresy and her family or friends etc.'

In another Indonesian language, Paulohu[19], the function of the definite article is implied in the noun so far as it is used in singular, e.g. *ama i-lepa ue ni-anai* 'The father spoke to his child'.

In cases in which German has no article and French has the partitive article, Paulohi has no article, e.g. *a-tana waele* 'fetch water!'

When there is a need of local fixation of an object the noun is usually used with the adverbs of place *nei* 'here' and *mei* 'there'; however, these adverbs are used even in cases where local fixation appears superfluous so that *nei* and *mei* have something of the function of the definite article. Nouns in plural, without local adverbs, are translated into German or English without definite article so that the adding of *mei* and *nei* equals the use of definite article.

With names of relatives such as *ama* 'father', *ina* 'mother', *waa* 'elder brother', *wari* 'younger brother', *mo* 'uncle', *sau* 'brother-in-law', etc., the prepositive particle *a*, which has also the meaning 'own (der eigene)', is used before the noun, e.g. *a leu manawa i-famata ni-a-leu pipina* 'der (eigene) Bruder tötet seine (eigene) Schwester'. *A ina i-falahia nianaia* 'die (eigene) Mutter ruft ihre Kinder'.

To express the indefinite article the numeral *sae* 'one' is used with nouns in singular.

Bare'e, one of the Celebes languages[20], has the definite article *i*, plural *si* (genitive *ntji*) which is used before proper nouns, e.g. *i Merendo, i Lelajoe*, as well as before names of relatives and before titles, e.g. *i Papa* 'the father', *i Toe'a* 'the grandmother', *i Datoe* 'the prince'. *I* can also be used before personal pronouns for emphasis. The honorific article is *siri*, gen. *ntjiri*.

---

[19] Cf. E. Stresemann, *Die Paulohi-Sprache, Ein Beitrag zur Kenntniss der Amboinischen Sprachengruppe* (The Hague, 1918), 51-52.
[20] N. Adriani, "Spraakkunst der Bare'e-taal", *VBG* 70, 350-352.

The indefinite article is *noe* which gives emphasis to the following noun without making it definite. Adriani includes in articles also the prefixes of titles *la-* and *ra-*.

The Label language[21] spoken in the south of New Mecklenburg in the Bismarck Archipelago has the articles *a, na* which express mostly determinedness, sometimes also indeterminedness. They stand in nominative and accusative, at the beginning as well as inside the sentence and correspond with the articles *a, ra* in Pala (central New Mecklenburg). Examples:

Label: *A kaiko i mutmut; a gĕnĕs i kök.*
Pala: *A kok i buŋbuŋ; a butẽn i palpalān.* 'The crow is black, the pigeon is white'. Or:
Label: *a tnan labíu i lulu.*
Pala: *A tamǎt na kih i pupuh.* 'A strong wind is blowing'.
Label: *Na tagara bĕl i ŋis.*
Pala: *No ra liŋe pa i tahŭt.* 'The thing is not good'.
Label: *J puŋa ha na tuŋ.*
Pala: *J puko ta ra tuŋ.* 'He fell into a pit'.

The indefinite article *ta* means 'one, any, some, something'. Examples:

Label: *Jar tŏl ta nǎt a wǎga.*
Pala: *Ñi pǎkile ta hansik na ŭǎga.* 'I shall make a little boat'.
Label: *Kĕp ta įah!*
Pala: *Kap ta įah!* 'Fetch some fire!'

Before proper nouns as well as before general names as objects when they are used without any limitation, there is no article. For example, *kĕp kiabo* 'To collect shells'.

If a noun is preceded by an adjective, both are connected by means of *a* (after a consonant) or *na* (after a vowel), e.g. *a nat a wǎga* 'a small boat'.

However, if a noun is followed by an adjective, it has no particle: *a ŋas bǎkbak* 'a long way', *a rumai to* 'a new house'.

---

[21] Cf. Gerhard Peekel, "Grammatische Grundzüge und Wörterverzeichnis der Label-Sprache", *Zeitschrift für Eingeborenen-Sprachen* 20 (1929/30), 13-16.

The American Indian language Dakota[22] has the indefinite article wa^n which is postpositive, e.g. *mako'će wa^n* 'a country'[23] and two definite articles ki^n and ko^n. Ki^n (after *a* or a^n it is changed, inclusive of the preceding vowels, into *e ći^n*) expresses the definite article: *wića$^{n'}$hpi ki^n iye'ga wa^n ya'kapi* 'they saw the stars shining' (*wića$^{n'}$hpi* 'star'; *iye'ga* 'to shine'; *wa^{n}ya'ka* 'to see'). Ko^n (after *a* or a^n it is changed into *e ćiko^n*) expresses the definite article in the past: *ni'na iye'je ćiko^n* 'the one aforesaid that shines much'.

Articles in another American language, Ponca, are highly developed. They are differentiated into articles for animate nouns and articles for inanimate nouns. Animate articles are divided into subjective and objective, singular and plural ones:

I. Inanimate articles

    1. *k'ě* horizontal objects
    2. *t'ě* standing objects, collective terms
    3. *ǫa^n* rounded objects
    4. *gě* scattered objects

II. Animate articles

    A. Subject
       1. *ak'á* singular animate object at rest
       2. *amá* singular animate object in motion; plural

    B. Object
       1. *t'an* singular animate object standing
       2. *ǫi^n* singular animate object moving
       3. *ma* plural animate objects
       4. *ǫiňk'é* singular animate object sitting
       5. *ǫaňk'á* plural animate objects sitting

III. Indefinite article: *wi^n*

[22] Cf. Franz Boas, *Handbook of American Indian Languages* (Washington, 1911), 939 f.
[23] This and the following examples are from the Santee dialect.

Examples:

I. 1. *k'ĕ* is regularly used with horizontal objects:
       t'an'de k'ĕ 'the ground'
       man'ge k'ĕ 'the sky'
       pahí k'ĕ 'the neck'
       man k'ĕ 'the arrow'
       pahé k'ĕ 'a long hill'
Some animate nouns have an inanimate article:
wéṣ'a k'ĕ 'the snake'.

   2. *t'ĕ* is used with several classes of nouns and indicates:
       (a) standing objects:
           tí t'ĕ 'the lodge'
           ħeabé t'ĕ 'the tree'
       (b) plurality and collectiveness of inanimate terms.
           According to Dorsey it expresses in this sense a
           rectilinear set of horizontal objects as the following
           examples show:
           kande t'ĕ 'the plums'
           pá t'ĕ 'the heads'
           sihi t'ĕ 'the feet'
           ǥéze t'ĕ 'the tongues'
       (c) abstracts: —
           téṣĕ t'ĕ 'the killing'
           íwaśk'an t'ĕ 'struggle'
           waźin' t'ĕ 'disposition'
           íe t'ĕ 'the word'
           waǥít'an t'ĕ 'work'
       (d) past actions seen by the speaker:
           gáǥe t'ĕ 'he did the (act)'
           wain' t'ĕ 'he wore as a robe'
           hút'an t'ĕ 'he cried out'
           át'ai t'ĕ 'he exceeded'

   3. *ǥan* indicates round objects and parts of objects:
       (a) round objects:
           min ǥan 'the sun'

našk'í ẹa^n 'the eye'
maẑa^n *ẹa*^{n} 'the land'
(b) a part of an object:
baṣa^n *ẹa*^{n} 'the bent part'
índé ẹa^n 'face part'

4. *gĕ* indicates a set of dispersed objects:
waṣi^n*-gĕ* 'pieces of fat'
wahí gĕ 'bones'
na^n*' za gĕ* 'fences'

II. A. 1. *ak'á* indicates an animate object in singular at rest:
a'-biamá Usní ak'á 'the cold said'
With numerals *ak'á* is used in the function of plural:
ẹábẹi^n *ak'á* 'the three';

2. *amá* indicates an animate object in singular in motion
or an animate object in plural, both at rest and in
motion:
(a) animate object in singular in motion:
ẑábe amá miáta aẹá-bi 'beaver went to the water';
(b) animate object in plural, both at rest and in
motion:
e-na^n*' -biamá níaṣi*^{n}*ga amá* 'the people said often,
it is said';
ník' agáhi amá géẹa-baẑíi 'the chiefs are sad'.

B. 1. *t'a*^{n} indicates an animate standing object in singular:
ṣyú ṣét'a^n *k'ída-gă* 'shoot at this prairie-chicken';

2. *ẹi*^{n} indicates an animate moving object in singular:
dáda^n *ẹi*^{n} *píga*^{n} *ẹi*^{n} *áha*^{n}! 'I'll blow that into the air';
ẹi^n is sometimes used with generic or collective terms:
wanít'a ẹi^n 'the quadrupeds'.

3. *ma* indicates an animate object in plural:
tangá-ma áẹut'a^n *waẹizá-bi a*^{n} 'he took the large ones
at once, it is said';

4. *ẹiňk'i* indicates an animate object in singular in a
sitting position: *ẑábe ẹiňk'édi bẹé t'áṣe* 'I must go to
the braver'.

5. *ęańk'á* indicates an animate object in singular in a sitting position: *wágaźí śímedan ęańk 'á* 'he commanded the dogs'.

The last two forms *ęińk'í* and *ęańk'á* are in Boas' opinion not genuine articles, though they seem to perform their function. They are genuine verbal forms.

III. *wiⁿ* is an indefinite article: *máśiⁿga wiⁿ* 'a person', *waᵉ'ú wiⁿ* 'a woman'.

6. One kind of definite article, several kinds of indefinite article

This is also an unproductive subtype. It is represented by the Polynesian languages Marquesan, Mangareva, Fakaofo, and Vaitupu. In Marquesan the definite article is *te* in singular, *na* in plural, whereas the indefinite article has the forms *'e, he, 'a*. Mangareva has the definite article *te* (only in singular) and the indefinite article *he, e*. Fakaofo and Vaitupu have the definite article *te* (only in singular) and the indefinite article *se, he*, plural *ni*.

II. Languages Possessing Only Definite Article

1. Only one kind of definite article

This fairly productive group includes, beside modern languages, several ancient languages. One of them is Old Greek which has the articles ὁ, ἡ, τό for masculine, feminine and neuter genders. These articles are declined both in singular and in plural, e.g. ὁ ἄνθρωπος 'the man' — plural οἱ ἄνθρωποι; ἡ τέχνη 'the art' — plural αἱ τεχναι; τὸ δῶρον 'gift' — plural τὰ δῶρα. The use of articles in Greek corresponds approximately to that in German. However, there is a difference: in Greek the article may be used with noun, adjective, infinitive, and participle as well as with adverb, possessive genitive and a whole sentence. Another difference from German consists in the fact that in Greek the article is used with a possessive pronoun and apposition but not with a predicative noun. With names of persons, nations, towns, rivers, and mountains article is regularly used if they had been named before and are to be pointed at, or if they are to be introduced as commonly known. Kühner[24] writes: "... der eigentliche Artikel ist als eine grammatische Form anzusehen, welche gewohnheitsmässig angewandt wird, um einen Substantivbegriff zu INDIVIDUALISIEREN d.h. ihn aus seiner Allgemeinheit herauszuheben und aus einem allgemeinen zu einem besonderen, aus einem unbestimmten zu einem BESTIMMTEN zu machen. Das Substantiv ohne Artikel bezeichnet entweder irgend ein unbestimmtes Einzelwesen oder giebt den abstrakten Begriff ganz allgemein an". A. J. Carnoy[25] regards the deictic meaning of the article as well as the anaphoric element calling up the feeling of intellectual familiarity as dominant functions of the article. The determining, defining, and individualizing functions of the article are, according to Carnoy, merely secondary and consecutive in their PRESENTATIVE role.

Old Gaelic[26] (or the language of the inhabitants of the Isle of Man) has the definite article *yn* in singular before a vowel of the following word and *y* before a consonant, in plural *ny*. However, *yn* is often used even before consonants. For example, *yn lioar* 'the book' — *ny lioaryn*. Nouns of feminine gender change the root sound after the article, e.g. *ben* '(a) woman' — *y ven* 'the woman'. There is no change with the nouns of masculine gender, e.g. *haink dooinney* 'a man came' — *haink y dooinney* 'the man came'.

Another old language, Old Irish, had the definite article *ind*, e.g. *ind anim* 'the soul'.

In Modern Irish[27] the definite article in all cases singular is *an* with the exception of genitive feminine which is *na*; the plural

[24] *Griechische Grammatik*, § 461.
[25] A. J. Carnoy, "Psychologie de l'article grec", *Symbolae grammaticae in honorem Ioannis Rozwadowski* I (Cracoviae, 1927), 152.
[26] Cf. John Kelly, *A Practical Grammar of the Ancient Gaelic, or Language of the Isle of Man, Usually Called Manks* (London, 1870), 9.
[27] Seán O'Beirne, *Irish Self-Taught* (London), 88-89.

in all cases and both genders (masc. and fem.) is *na*. A peculiar feature of the Irish article is that it influences in a different way the word to which it belongs:

1. In nominative and accusative singular masculine a *t-* is prefixed to the initial vowel after the article, e.g. *an t-arán* 'the head', *an t-athair* 'the father'.
2. In genitive singular masc. and nominative and accusative sing. fem. the initial consonant of the following word is aspirated (e.g. *an bhean* 'the woman', *mac an bhaird* 'the son of the bard') and the initial *s* is preceded by *t* (e.g. *an t-súil* 'the eye', *mac an t-saoir* 'the son of the craftsman').
3. In dative sing. masc. and femin. the article eclipses the initial consonant of the following noun, e.g. *ins an bpaire* 'in the meadow'. In genitive plural there is, in addition to the eclipse (e.g. *mic na mbárd* 'the sons of the bards'), an *n-* prefixed to the initial vowel (e.g. *tír na n-óg* 'the land of the young').
4. In genitive singular fem., further in nominative, dative and accusative plural an *h-* is prefixed to the initial vowel (e.g. *na h-aibhne* 'the rivers'; *sagart na h-eaglaise* 'the priest of the church').

Another Celtic language, Welsh, has the definite article *y*, *yr*, *'r*[28]. Before a consonant of the following word the article is *y* (e.g. *y dyn* 'the man', *y dynion* 'the men'), before a vowel or *h* it is *yr* (e.g. *yr afal* 'the apple', *yr afalan* 'the apples'), after a vowel it is *'r* (e.g. *a'r afal* 'and the apple').

In Welsh, similar to Irish, the article causes some changes of the initial sound of feminine nouns:

c > g : *cadair* 'a chair' — *y gadair* 'the chair'
p > b : *pib* 'a pipe' — *y bib* 'the pipe'
t > d : *traf* 'a town' — *y draf* 'the town'
g is dropped: *gardd* 'garden' — *yr ardd* 'the garden'
b > f : *basged* 'basket' — *y fasged* 'the basket'

[28] Cf. John T. Bowen and T. J. Rhys Jones, *Teach Yourself Welsh* (London, 1960), 16, 19-20, 32, 40-42.

d > dd: *desg* 'a desk' — *y ddesg* 'the desk'
m > f : *mam* 'a mother' — *y fam* 'the mother'.
Words beginning with other sounds remain unchanged.

Feminine nouns do not change the initial consonant in plural after the definite article, e.g. *cadair* 'a chair' — *y cadeiriau* 'the chairs'; *merch* 'a girl' — *y merched* 'the girls'.

If an adjective is added to a feminine noun singular, its initial sound is subject to following changes when article is used: c > g, g > 0, d > dd. Examples (the adjective always follows the noun): *caseg gref* 'a strong mare' — *y gaseg gref* 'the strong mare'; *geneth dlos* 'a pretty girl' — *yr eneth dlos* 'the pretty girl'; *dynes drom* 'a heavy woman' — *y ddynes drom* 'the heavy woman'.

Feminine plural nouns do not cause mutation in the adjectives that follow them, e.g. *merch* 'a girl' — *y ferch dda* 'the good girl' but *y merched da* 'the good girls'.

Determinedness and indeterminedness of nouns is further manifested in sentences with the verb 'to be'. The 3rd person of the verb 'to be' *(bod)* can be expressed in three ways: *y mae*, *yw* *(ydyw)*, and *oes*. The form *y mae* is used in affirmative sentences, whereas the form *oes* is used with indefinite nouns in negative, interrogative and conditional sentences. In affirmative sentences is used *y mae'r*, in negative, interrogative and conditional sentences is used *yw'r* with definite nouns.

Examples:

	Definite noun	Indefinite noun
Affirmative Sentences	*Y mae'r dyn yn yr ardd* 'The man is in the garden'	*Y mae dyn yn yr ardd* 'There is a man in the garden'
Negative Sentences	*Nid yw'r dyn ddim yn yr ardd* 'The man is not in the garden'	*Nid oes dim dyn yn yr ardd* 'There is not a man in the garden'
Interrogative Sentences	*A yw'r dyn yn yr ardd?* 'Is the man in the garden?'	*A oes dyn yn yr ardd?* 'Is there a man in the garden?'

Conditional Sentences	*Os yw'r dyn yn yr ardd ...* 'If the man is in the garden...'	*Os oes dyn yn yr ardd ...* 'If there's a man in the garden...'

In Latvian there are used in the function of definite article the demonstrative pronouns *tas* (masc.), *ta* (fem.), *ter* (plural). It is problematic, whether they can be regarded as genuine article.

In Indonesian, the function of the definite article is performed by the demonstrative pronoun *itu* which is postpositive, e.g. *gula itu manis* 'Sugar is sweet', *emas itu mahal* 'Gold is expensive', *bulan itu bulat* 'The moon is round'. The Indonesian language Atjeh has the personal article *si* which has a very limited use. The Dayak language has the personal article *i* (used with proper names and titles, e.g. *i raja* 'the king') and in the function of article it uses the demonstrative *jetä* (weak form *tä*); however, it is doubtful whether it can be regarded as a genuine article. Madurese has the personal article *se* which substantivizes and ligates adjectives. Example: *se ano* 'the (man)'; *lakeq* 'manly' — *se lakeq* 'the little man'. Rare is *san* as a personal article (only with human beings) e.g. *san pottre* 'the princess'. The Philippine language Tiruray has the article *i* (e.g. *i gedare* 'the love', *i Juan*); in addition to the article there are weak demonstrative adverbs *an, e, o* which are added to the noun. Dative and locative which are formed by prepositions *dob* and *be*, have no article. In plural, *da, de*, or *do* are inserted between the article and the noun, e.g. *i de degu* 'die Donnerschläge (cf. Brandstetter, p. 39). Sawu, the language of one of the islands opposite New Guinea, has a definite article (Sachartikel) *ne* in singular, *he* in plural standing after the noun. Numerals have the ligative article *ñ*.

The Polynesian language Tuamotu (Paumotu) has the definite article *te* (sing.), *a* (plural), Mangaia *te* (only sing.), Tikopia (Ruf Islands) *te* (sing.), *na, a* (plural), Kapingamarangi (Pikiram) *ti*, variant *te* (sing.), *nia* (plural). The Bauan dialect of Fijian[29] has only the definite article *na*, e.g. *sa moce na gone* 'the child is

---

[29] Cf. *Anthropological Linguistics* 6: 9 (December 1964), "Languages of the World: Indo-Pacific fascicle three" (Indiana University), 69 ff.

asleep' (= 'is sleep the child'). The article is also used before nouns with a possessive pronoun, e.g. *e tiko evei na tama-qu* 'where is my father' (= 'is continuative [where] the father-my') or *sa yali na no-qu kato* 'My box is lost' (= 'is lost the classifier-my box'). Or: *e dua na nona cina vou na tamata* 'The man has a new lamp' (= [is one] [the [his] [lamp new] the man]'). Rotuman has also only the definite article *ta* (postpositive), e.g. *vao ta luak* 'The net is short' (= 'net the short'). It is also used after nouns with possessive pronouns, e.g. *(otou kes ta maoana* 'My box is lost' (= 'my box the lost'), but not after nouns with a numeral, e.g. *vak fol* 'There are three canoes' (= 'canoe three').

The Ono language[30] distinguishes "casus indifferens" and "nominativus agentis", e.g. *vesi* 'stone' — *vesi-ŋo* 'the stone'. The determinedness of the noun in the predicative position of the adjective is expressed by personal pronouns, e.g. *ŋei eŋe suaine* 'the man is tall' (= 'man he tall'). They also determine a noun with an attributive adjective, e.g. *ŋei suaine* 'the tall man' (= 'man tall').

Similarly another language of New Guinea, Kâte, distinguishes "casus indifferens", e.g. *qânâ* 'stone', and "nominativus agentis", e.g. *qânâ-zi* 'the stone'. The suffix *-zi* as "nominativus agentis" emphasizes the subject. Where such emphasis is not necessary and no confusion between nominative and accusative is possible, *-zi* may even be omitted, e.g. *ʒoc ʒakac* 'fire burns' — *ʒoczi ʒakac* 'the fire burns (something)'.

2. More kinds of definite article

This subtype includes a number of Indonesian and Polynesian languages. Thus, e.g. Buginese (one of the languages of the island Celebes) has personal articles *la* (for men), *i* (for women) and the definite postpositive Sachartikel *e* (e.g. *aruṅ e* 'the king'). In addition there can be found, especially in poetry, the article *ede*. The ligative article is *ṅ*. Sangirese has a prepositive personal

---

[30] Cf. K. Wacke, "Formenlehre der Ono-Sprache (Neuguinea)", *Zeitschrift für Eingeborenen-Sprachen* 21 (1930/31), 161-208. Ono is spoken north of Huon-Golf on the eastern coast of New Guinea.

article *i* and a postpositive Sachartikel *e*. Bolaang Mongondow
has the personal article *ki* and the Sachartikel *in* which are declined
as follows:

	Personal article	Sachartikel
nominative, accus.	*ki*	*in*
genitive	*i* or *in*	*in*
dative	*koi*	*kon*

New Macassar has personal articles *i* and *pusi* and the definite
article *a* standing after the noun; it is not dropped when a demonstrative is added to the noun. For example, *aṅiṅ a* 'the wind'.
If a word ends in *a* or *o*, a transitional *w* is put before *a*, e.g.
puru-w-a 'the bowl', after *i* and *e* is inserted a *y [j]*, e.g. *bali-y-a*
'the enemy'. By analogy *y* may be put even after *a*, e.g. *mata-y-a*
'the eye'. The definite article is not dropped when a demonstrative
is added to the noun.

Tontemboan has a personal article and a Sachartikel which
are declined as follows:

	Personal article		Sachartikel	
	sing.	plural	sing.	plural
nominative	*si*	*se*	*ĕn*	
genitive	*i*	*e*	*in*	
dative - locative	*a si*	*a se*	*an*	
accusative	*si*	*se*	*in*	

The Philippine language Bisay has the personal article *se* (gen. *ni*,
dat.-loc., accus. *kan*) and the Sachartikel *aṅ* (the other cases *sa*);
ligative articles are *na* and *ṅ*, with numerals *ka*. Cokan has the
personal article *si* (gen. *ni*, dat. *ken*), the definite Sachartikel *ti*
(gen. *ti*, dat. *iti*; nomin. and gen. plural *dagiti*, dative plural *ka
dagiti*). The personal article has in nominative beside *si* also *ni*.

Bontoc has the personal article *si* and Sachartikel *nan*. The
genitive of the personal article has the preposition *n*, the dative
kĕn but the article is dropped, for example *nan kali n ina ca* 'the
word of her mother' (= 'the word of mother her'). The genitive
of the Sachartikel has the preposition *n*, the dative *is* (also *si* or *s*),

but the article remains, e.g. *tomoli is nan apo ca* 'the return to their commanders' (= 'the return to commanders their'). The personal article stands with proper names of persons and with most names of relatives, the Sachartikel in the other cases. The Sachartikel is definite or indefinite or partitive, e.g. *is nan pañuan* 'at the door'; *woda nan sinaki ay mañanub* 'It was a couple of brothers who hunted'; *keceñ yai ca nan finayu* 'Then they bring rice'. Instead of *si* and *nan* also the article *san* can be used but it belongs to a higher style. Thus the Bontoc language is not a typical representative of this type; it could also be classed with type A I. 5 or A IV.

Howa (in Madagascar) has personal articles *i* and *ra*. The article *ra* expresses respect and stands before proper names of persons and sporadically before titles and names of relatives; the article *i* is familiar but it stands even with place-names. Howa possesses also the definite Sachartikel *ni* which stands before the names of things and before those personal designations that do not require either *ra* or *i* (e.g. *ni olona* 'the man, men'). The article *ni* is very regular and frequent; it occurs also with the genitive and possessive cases. Similar is the situation in Betsiles, a language spoken in Madagascar.

This subgroup also includes some languages spoken in the island of Sumatra. Thus Toba Batak has the personal article *si* before the names of persons and places and before personifications. Moreover, the demonstratives *i, on, inon* have the function of article (according to Brandstetter, p. 21). In Karo the personal and personificative article is *si*. In addition, also the demonstrative *ndai (ĕnda, ĕndai)* is used in the function of article but not so frequently as *itu* in Indonesian or *tä* in Dayak. Numerals have the ligative article *ñ*. In Seraway the personal article is *sañ* (very rare) and in the function of article is used the demonstrative *itu*. Sumbawar has the personal article *ña* which in Seraway is a relative pronoun. Similar conditions as in Seraway are also in Bĕsĕmak. Minankaban has the personal article *si* which stands before proper names and occasionally also before designations of persons. The ligative article is *nau* (with adjectives and nu-

merals) which in Bontoc has the function of Sachartikel, in addition
to the personal article *si*. In Lampong the personal article is *san*,
like in Old Javanese; moreover, the demonstrative *sena* is also used
in the function of article. Mentaway has the article *ši*, before
vowels *š* (e.g. *ši anitu* or *š anitu* 'the ghost, demon') which stands
before proper names of persons and places, often also before the
designation of persons and animals in fables, before some names of
plants even in indefinite sense. With *ši* competes the article *tai*
which, however, is not so frequent. The article *ta* stands with the
names of relatives. More scarce is the article *ša* which competes
with the article *ta*. Nias has the article *si* (before vowels *s*) which
has a number of secondary functions. Thus, for instance, it serves
substantivization, forms nomen agentis, and ordinal numerals
(e.g. *tolu* 'three' — *si tolu* 'the third'). It is rarely found with
personal names. Last but not least it has the function of a relative
pronoun and of ligative article with adjectives.

Old Javanese has, according to Brandstetter (p. 26), five personal articles: *ra, sa, pun, saṅ, si*, of which the first three occur
only sporadically; *saṅ* is respectful, *si* is familiar. Moreover, Old
Javanese has the Sachartikel *an* or *n*. The variant *n* either precedes
or follows vowels but in these cases the full form can also occur,
for example *ṅ anak* or *aṅ anak* 'the child'. After case prepositions
ni, i, ri there is used only *si* which is contracted with the prepositions: 'of the child' is translated *niṅ anak*, not *ni aṅ anak*.
The article *aṅ, ṅ* is dropped, if a genitive or a possessive pronoun
is added to the noun, but not always. Thus, for example, according
to the rule: *ri gulû nira* 'on his neck' (= 'am Halse desselben'),
but *iṅ patapan ňa* 'in his cell', with the article *ṅ*.

New Javanese has the familiar article *si*, the respectful article
pun and the ambitious article *saṅ*; in the function of collective
article is used *para*. The Old Javanese article has the only function
of ligation with numerals. According to A. S. Teselkin[31] the
function of the definite article is performed by the suffixes of appurtenance *-e, -ipun* after consonants and *-ne, -nipun* after vowels

---

[31]　Cf. A. S. Teselkin, *Javanskij jazyk* (Moskva, 1961), 37 f.

when the meaning of appurtenance is expressed by means of the juxtaposition of two nouns, for example *omah-e bapak* 'father's house' but here the suffix does not express appurtenance, it expresses determinedness showing that the object is familiar. Consequently, it is used here in the function of the definite article and the original meaning of the suffix is weakened and in many cases completely disappears. This suffix can be used even in the case when it is understood that the object relates to the first or second person. However, A. S. Teselkin observes that the use of this suffix for the expression of determinedness is not so regular as, for example, in English, French, German, etc. The sentence 'the book is gone' can be translated into Javanese *bukune ilaŋ* (= 'book-the-lost')[32]. However, the suffix can also have the function of the possessive pronouns *his, her*. Cf. *turune aŋlər tənan* 'He slept soundly' (= 'sleep-the sound indeed' or 'sleep-his [her] sound indeed').

Chamorro, a language belonging in linguistic respect to Indonesian languages but geographically to Micronesia and spoken in Marianas, has the definite article *i*, e.g. *I taw taw matu* 'the man comes' (= 'the man come'), *Hu paca i hagan* 'I touch the turtle'; it is also used after a noun accompanied by a possessive pronoun, e.g. *hu culi i lepblomu* 'I have your book' (= 'I have the book-your'). Chamorro has also a personal article which is *isa* before a vowel (e.g. *isa Ulama*), *si* before a consonant (e.g. *si Pedro* 'the Pedro', *si hwan* 'the Juan'), under certain conditions (in relative clauses) also *æs*, e.g. *tiniŋu si hwan æs mariya* 'It is Juan who is known to Maria' (= 'rel.-know the Juan the Maria'), or *pinaca si hose æs pedro* 'It is Jose whom Peter touches' (= 'rel.-touch the Jose the Pedro').

Sundanese has two personal articles, the familiar *si* and the respectful *ki*. The relative *nu* serves substantivization, e.g. *boṅkok* 'hunch-backed', *nu boṅkok* 'the hunch-backed (man)'. The numeral *hiji* 'one' serves as indefinite article with expressions of time, place, and acting persons.

---

[32] Cf. *Anthropological Linguistics* 7: 2 (February 1965), 124 f.

Balinese has the personal article *i*, beside *ki* (masc.) and *ni* (femin.). Moreover, there is the definite Sachartikel *e* or *ne*.

Kungeanese has the article *se* which stands before proper names and serves substantivization and ligation; for example, *se Kabasa* 'the Almighty'. In addition to *se* there is the personal article *saṅ* which is, however, very rare; in fables it is also used with the names of animals.

Of languages spoken in the islands opposite New Guinea Bimanese has the personal article *la* (which is also found in Buginese) which is dropped in vocative being replaced by the postpositive particle *e*, e.g. *hai cilaka Baṅs e*! 'Hey, miserable Blockhead!' Further there is the definite Sachartikel *de* or *ede* (e.g. *wai ede* 'the lady'). *De* occurs also in Buginese. Kamberian has the personal article *i* and the definite Sachartikel *na* (in sing.) and *da* (in pl.), e.g. *na lima* 'the hand', *da lima* 'the hands'. The forms *na* and *da* are homophonous with the possessive pronouns *na* and *da* but the latter stands after the noun, e.g. *na lima* 'the hand' — *na lima na* 'his hand' — *da lima na* 'his hands'. The article also serves substantivization, e.g. *mahamu* 'good' — *na mahamu* 'the good'. Kupang has the postpositive definite Sachartikel *lia* with variants *li, la* used irregularly; plural is *lias, las, lis*. The numeral *mesa* 'one' is often used in the function of indefinite article but not so regularly as in Rotinese.

Of languages spoken in the island of Borneo Bolongan has the personal article *si* and in the function of article is also used, according to Brandstetter (p. 34), the demonstrative pronoun *inan*.

The Philippine language Iloko[33] has the definite article *ti* (before nominative and genitive of the noun, in the other cases *iti*), plural *dagiti* (nominative, genitive, oblique case *kadagiti*). Examples: *ti áso* 'the dog', *ti baláy* 'the house', *ti baláy ti táo* 'the house of the man', *matúrog iti datár* 'he sleeps on the floor', *dagiti bábuy* 'the hogs', *dagiti talí* 'the ropes', *ti kabáyo dagiti tás* 'the horse of the man', *addá kadagiti baláy* 'it is in the houses'. The article *ti*

[33] Cf. Morice Vanoverbergh, "Notes on Iloko", *Anthropos* 23 (1928), 1029-1050.

is also used before adjectives and verbs or verbal forms in the function of nouns, e.g. *dagití íma ti natáyag* 'the hands of the tall one', *ti napán* 'the one who went', *ti manála* 'the one who takes'. Iloko has also the personal article *ni* or *si* (nom. and gen. sing.), oblique case *ken*, plural nom., gen. *da*, oblique *káda*, e.g. *ni Juán* 'John', *si Jesus* 'Jesus', *ti baláy ni António* 'the house of Anthony', *tédmo ken Luis* 'give it to Lewis', *da Juán ken Luis* 'John and Lewis', *ti landók da Pédro ken Páblo* 'the iron of Peter and Paul', *yáwatmo káda Luisa ken Ana* 'give it to Louisa and Ann'. If the name does not represent individual persons, the forms *dagití* and *kadagití* are used in plural instead of *da* and *káda*, e.g. *addá dagití gayyémko* 'my friends are there', *ti buláy dagití kasinsinmo* 'the house of your cousins', *da amám kadagití gayyémmo* 'your father and your friends'.

In the Central Dardic language Kaňavali demonstrative pronouns are used independently and in the function of determinedness. Their declension is in this case rather different. There are three forms of distance: near, middle, and distant:

SINGULAR

case	near		middle		distant	
	independ.	definite	independ.	definite	independ.	definite
nominative oblique case factors	*šu*	*šu* *šu, šas*	*so* *tas* /*ī*/ *sě̃, sē̃*	*so, su* *so, su* *tas* *sě̃, sē̃,* *so*	*u, ū̃* *asī, as* *ě̃, ē̃*	*as* *ě̃*

PLURAL

case	near		middle		distant	
	independ.	definite	independ.	definite	independ.	definite
nominative oblique c. factors		*šai*	*saī* *sayõ*	*saī*	*ayõ*	*aī*

Definite forms are used only in the function of prepositive determinants (and articles) which are in accord as to the number and case (if expressed) with the determined: *šu gharĭ dhī* 'the daughter of this woman', *ma šas zaī paisā dašat* 'I'll give money to the village', *so waxta mā* 'to that time', *mi-ge as kitāb dē* 'give me the books'. In the Shina language the demonstrative as well as the interrogative pronoun can be used both independently, in the function of nominal sentence members, and in the function of determinedness. In the latter function they are not declined, only the nominative form is used.

Oriyạ, one of the four languages (together with Bengalī, Bihāṛī, and Assamese) making up the eastern group of the Indo-Aryan languages (according to Grierson, *Linguistic Survey of India*, vol. 5, part 2) uses as definite article the suffixes *ṭā* and *ṭi*, the first one being used with irrational beings and things, the second with rational beings, e.g. *ghōṛā-ṭā* 'the horse', *pilā-ṭi* 'the child'.

Among African languages the Sudan language Fulbe has the personal article and Sachartikel (postpositive) in singular and plural. In the Gola language[34] we find a definite article which is expressed by certain suffixes as well as an emphasizing definite article.

There is also a number of Polynesian languages which belong to this subtype. One of them is Aniwa with the definite articles *ta-*, *te-*, *ti-* in singular and *a-* in plural, e.g. *teriki* 'chief', *tiafi* 'fire', *tamtangi* 'wind'. Many nouns in Aniwa have the prefix *no-* (e.g. *norima* 'hand', *nokawe* 'brother', *nokabisa* 'glory', etc.) which is probably, according to W. K. Matthews and S. H. Ray[35], the Melanesian definite article *na*. This prefix is redundant in *ta nontariki* 'the son' and *a nontariki* 'the sons'. W. Futuna has normally the definite article *ta-* (e.g. *tatangata* 'the man'), plural *a-* (e.g. *atangata* 'the men'); before substantivized adjectives there

[34] Cf. D. Westermann, *Die Gola-Sprache in Liberia* (Hamburg, 1921). The same author: *Nominalklassen in westafrikanischen Klassensprachen und in Bantusprachen*, (= *Mitteilungen des Seminars für Orientalische Sprachen an der Friedrich-Wilhelms-Universität zu Berlin* XXXVIII) (Berlin 1935), 1-53.

[35] S. H. Ray, *Sketch of Aniwa Grammar* (London, 1888).

appears the form *te-* (e.g. *tesore* 'the great one'). Fila has the definite articles *te*, *ti*, *ta* in singular, *a* in plural; sometimes this *a* is singular in meaning, e.g. *a tuai* 'the letter'[36]. The Kapinga-marangi (Pikiram) language has the definite article *ti*, *te*, pl. *nia*; Nukoro has *te*, *ne* (only in singular).

Malgash[37] has three kinds of article: common (l'article commun), personal article and vocative article.

1. The common article is
    (a) *ny* which corresponds with the French article *le*, *la*, *les*, e.g. *ny tany* 'la terre, les terres';
    (b) *ilay*, *iley*, *ilehy* which imply that the object has already been spoken of, e.g. *ilay tany* 'la terre'.
2. Personal articles: *I*, *Andria*, *Ilai*, *Ra*.
    I is used (a) as capital letter before a proper name in the quality of a prefix, e.g. *Imainty* 'Le noir', (b) as small letter before a proper name, e.g. *i Paoly* 'Paul'.
    Andria is prefixed to any word to form a proper name: *Andria-manitra* 'God'.
    Likewise *Ilai*: *Ilaimanjato* 'the rich'.
    Analogical to *Andria* and *Ilai* is *Ra*.
    Further there are special personal articles *Rai* and *Reni*. They are nouns meaning 'father' *(Rai)* and 'mother' *(Reni)* but used as articles. In Madagascar father or mother has the name of the first-born son or daughter with the preceding article *Rai* (for the father) or *Reni* (for the mother). If the baby's name is *Ikoto*, the child's father accepts the name *Rainikoto* 'Ikoto's father'; similarly *Renikoto* is 'Ikoto's mother'.
3. Vocative article is *ry* (sing. and pl.), e.g. *Ry sakaiza*! 'dear friend!' This article is also used with a name of a family, when all its members are meant collectively, e.g. *Tonga ry Raza-fimandimby* 'The Razafimandimbies have arrived'.

---

[36] Cf. A. Capell, "Notes on the Fila language", *Journal of the Polynesian Society* CI (Wellington, 1942).
[37] Cf. Eugène Dupuy and Charles Ranaivo, *Le Malgache simplifié* (Paris, 1903), 9.

III. *Languages Possessing Only Indefinite Article*

Some Iranian languages have only indefinite article, for example in Jagnobi the numeral *ī/i (iy-)* 'one' serves as indefinite article. Of Dardic languages Kati has the indefinite article *e, ev*, e.g. *ev lē ǰuguṛ* 'a pretty woman'; definiteness is expressed by demonstrative pronouns. Aškun, another Dardic language, has the indefinite article *ač* 'one' or a shortened form *a*, e.g. *a mac safar diẽsőnwe* 'a man set out for a journey'. In Votapuri the numeral *yek* 'one' has the function of indefinite article, e.g. *yek šair yek mutabar maniš-aŋgē gā au tasan lao sifat kir* 'a poet went to a noble man and praised him very much'. In the Pašai language the indefinite article is *ēkī* or the numeral *i* 'one' is used in the function of the indefinite article, e.g. *ēkī ādəmis dō puṭhtə hāink* 'a man had two sons', or *i bādšā hāik* 'there was a shāh'. The Falura language has the indefinite article *ǎ*, e.g. *ase moš a cīz aṭu-m* 'the man has brought me a thing', or *ā mīši dū putra hēsila* 'a man had two sons'. Similarly in the Tat language which belongs to the south-western group of Iranian languages and with its lexical system ranges to Persian and Tajik[38], the singular form of nouns indicates, in dependence upon context, both the unique object and the total of all given objects as well as their indefinite quantity. Indeterminedness in singular is indicated by the indefinite *yæ* 'one', e.g. *yæ kitab vægi* 'take a book'. If an indefinite quantity of objects is concerned, the direct form of noun is used, e.g. *kitab vægi* 'take (a) book/books'.

Languages having an enclitic or proclitic indefinite article are classed with group C; they are, e.g., Persian, Tajik, and Pashto which have, in addition to an enclitic indefinite article, also the numeral 'one' in the function of indefinite article.

This type further includes Turkish with the indefinite article *bir* 'one' in singular[39]. However, the position of the article creates

---

[38] Cf. A. L. Gr'unberg, "Tatskij jazyk", in: *Jazyki narodov SSSR* I (Moskva, 1966), 281, 286.

[39] However, Turkish belongs only partially to this type. That is to say, the category of determinedness vs. indeterminedness is manifested in Turkish and in other Turkic languages partially in the declension of nouns: the definite

in Turkish certain differences in meaning which can hardly be expressed in any language. First of all, it is necessary to realize that *bir* has the function of article but also of the numeral 'one' so that the sentence *bir ev yandi* can have the meaning 'one house was burnt' (when it answers the question 'how many?')[40]. Secondly, the non-occurrence of indefinite article with a word makes this word definite. In the plural of nouns the category of determinedness vs. indeterminedness is not expressed. *Evler* can mean both 'indefinite, some, houses' and 'certain, definite, houses'. The suppression of the category of determinedness vs. indeterminedness in plural is partly compensated by the definiteness being also expressed by the affixes of genitive and accusative. As far as singular is concerned, the ambiguity of *bir* is often removed by its position in the izaphat and non-izaphat connection of words.

We will now discuss the position of the article *bir* in non-izaphat constructions.

Büyük ev means 'a certain large house'. *Büyük bir ev* and *bir büyük ev* roughly mean 'a big house' but yet there is a fine distinction that cannot be rendered in any other language. In the expression *büyük bir ev* the *bir* serves not only to point out to the indeterminedness of the house but also to the emphasis of the fact that a large house is spoken of[41]. In the expression *bir büyük ev*, *bir* is used not to emphasize the dimension of the house but to emphasize that some large house is concerned. The other words in both expressions — *büyük bir ev* and *bir büyük ev* — point out to the quality of the house (in each sentence only one house is spoken of), but the first expression emphasizes more the quality of a non-determined object which is called house, whereas the

---

accusative has the ending *-i*, e.g. *babçeyi gördüm* 'I saw the garden', the indefinite accusative has no ending but is used with the indefinite article *bir*, e.g. *bir bahçe gördüm* 'I saw a garden', and in the forms of present, past and future participles, as will be discussed later. Consequently, we meet here with a combination of two very different formal expedients of expressing this category.

40 Cf. S. S. Majzel, *Izafet v tureckom jazyke* (Moskva, 1957), chapter VI.
41 Cf. N. K. Dmitrijev, *Stroj tureckogo jazyka*, 49.

other expression emphasizes more the indefiniteness of the object which is called a large house.

If an adjective and a noun form one concept (a word group), *bir* precedes the word group as a whole; for example, *demir yol* 'railway' — *bir demir yol*. If the word group, due to its relatively recent origin, is not yet fixed as a terminological expression, *bir* can be inserted between the members of the word group, e.g. *uçar kale* 'flying fortress' — *uçar bir kale*. Consequently, there are different degrees of comprehending similar word groups in the sense of their greater or smaller closeness to terminological expressions. In this case the article helps to make clear whether to conceive the word group as stable or occasional. According to Majzel *bir* in the expression *büyük bir ev* is an adjectival indicator of the word preceding the noun and an indicator of substantiveness of the word following it. In this function *bir* assumes the ability of adjectivizing other parts of speech (nouns, adverbs), e.g. *Şaşı Hanife hanım ömür bir kadindir* 'Shashi Hanife is an excellent woman' (the noun *ömür* 'life' is used in colloquial language in the form *ömürdür* 'it is excellent'). Further Majzel points to the rhythmic factor. In the case of the word group *büyük bir ev* a strong emphasis is on *büyük*, whereas *bir* is unaccentuated. In the other case, *bir büyük ev*, a strong accent is on *bir*, if it has the function of a numeral, or the accent is spread uniformly over all three words, if the function of numeral is not emphasized. If *bir* has the function of a numeral but the speaker wants to emphasize not the quantitative but the qualitative aspect of the object, then a strong accent is on the word *büyük* but the proclitic character of *bir* does not permit one to identify it with the indefinite article due to its different position in both expressions. If we want to emphasize both the qualitative aspect of the adjective and the indetermination of the following noun, we use a double *bir*, one before each of both parts of speech: *bir güzel bir kiz* 'a beautiful girl'.

In his book (cf. note 3) S. S. Majzel gives a very keen and thorough analysis of the izaphat construction in Turkish, devoting chapters VI and VII to the expression of the category of determinedness vs. indeterminedness in the izaphat construction.

We regard the function of the article in the izaphat construction as highly interesting and important so that we do not hesitate to give it more space reproducing in essence Majzel's excellent analysis.

Majzel distinguishes three types of izaphat:

1. $C_1 - M_1$ (*kadının şapkası* 'le chapeau de la femme')[42]
2. $C_0 - M_1$ (*kadın şapkası* '*[le]* chapeau de femme')
3. $C_0 - M_0$ (*fötr şapka* 'a felt hat').

C means the first member of the word group, M the second member, number 1 means the presence of the affix, number o means its absence.

We will now give a detailed analysis of these three types:

1. $C_1 - M_1$

Variant A. Here the zero article with the first member of the izaphat makes it definite (as if it were preceded by a demonstrative pronoun). For example, *kadının şapkası* 'le chapeau de la femme'. The word *kadının* means a person known to the speaker and the same may be said about the word *şapkası* which is also definite as if it had a zero article.

Bir kadının şapkası 'le chapeau d'une femme'; *bir* may be here either a numeral or an indefinite article. According to Majzel we meet here with a certain antinomy: on one hand there is *bir* indicating an indefinite woman, on the other hand the genitive affix indicates definiteness as far as genitive in Turkish expresses not only appurtenance and partitiveness but also determinedness. This antinomy can be solved by a compromise: the word *woman* is determined in the sense of non-substitutiveness (as far as the hat belongs to a married woman and not to some other woman) but indetermined in the sense that she is unknown to the participants of the discourse. It can be *kadının bir şapkası* 'un chapeau de la femme' or *bir kadının bir şapkası* 'un chapeau d'une femme'. In both cases *the hat* can be conceived both as 'one' and as 'some' (in the sense of indetermination).

[42] We mostly use French rendering here because it is more adequate than the English one.

Variant B (appurtenance of the indicator to the object). The inseparability of the indicator of the object from the object itself does not permit one to use in this variant the article *bir* so freely as in the preceding variant. The limitation of the use of *bir* lies in the fact that in this variant the izaphat resists interposition, i.e. the position of article between the members of the izaphat construction. The indicator of the object (*şapkanın beyazlığı* 'la blancheur du chapeau') appertains to it as a certain indicator independent of whether the object itself is definite or not. Therefore there are two combinations: 1. *şapkanın beyazlığı* 'la blancheur du chapeau' and 2. *bir şapkanın beyazlığı* 'la blancheur d'un chapeau'. In this case *bir* cannot be differentiated as article and numeral.

Variant C (appurtenance of material to the object made of it). So far as there is a closer connection between the content of the object and its form (between material and object made of it) than between the object and its indicator, then the use of *bir* is made still more difficult in this variant than in variant *B*: *bir bardağın camı iyi öbürünün fena* 'the glass of one glass is good, of the other bad'. This variant has three subvariants:

1. If M_1 of the given izaphat can be only in singular, it does not accept *bir* but C_1 can accept *bir* in the sense of article and in the sense of numeral: *bir aslanın başı* can be translated 'the head of one lion' or 'the head of a certain lion'.
2. If M_1 is possible even in plural, there are (as in variant *A*) four combinations with *bir*:
   a) *sandalyenin ayağı* 'le pied **de la** chaise',
   b) *bir sandalyenin ayağı* 'le pied **d'une** chaise',
   c) *sandalyenin bir ayağı* '**un** pied **de la** chaise',
   d) *bir sandalyenin bir ayağı* '**un** pied **d'une** chaise'.
3. In the type *adamın iyisi*, *bir* is used as indefinite number of the first component of the izaphat. If the first component of the izaphat is in plural, it is possible to use *bir*. For example *çocukların bir haylisi* 'many children' where the first component of the izaphat is in partitive genitive.

Variant E (appurtenance of action to object). In this variant *bir* can precede the first or the second component of the izaphat. There are possible three combinations:

(a) *muallimin okuması*
(b) *bir muallimin okuması* } 'the reading of the teacher'
(c) *muallimin bir okuması*

In (b) *bir* can mean both numeral and article: *bir muallimin okuması* 'la lecture d'une professeur'. In (c) *bir* expresses neither number nor indetermination but mood, gender, the picture of the action symbolizing M_1: *muallimin bir okuması* 'la manière de lecture du professeur'.

Variant F (appurtenance of action to the object of action). The same combinations are possible here as in variant *E*.

Variant G (appurtenance of state to object). The same combinations as in variant *E*.

In the last three variants the interposition of *bir* is possible only when the second component of the izaphat is followed by *var*, *yok*, or *olmak*, e.g. *muallimin bir okuması var idi ki herkes kulak kesilmişti* 'The teacher was reading (= had such a way of reading) so that all may hear'.

2. $C_o - M_1$

Variant A (the relation of a unique object to a general one). The izaphat may be either definite or indefinite; the indicator of determinedness or indeterminedness can relate to M_1 only, not to C_o.

(a) *kadın şapkası* '(le) chapeau de femme',
(b) *bir kadın şapkası* '**un** chapeau de femme'.

Bir cannot stand between the components of the izaphat as the izaphat of this type itself represents a word group.

Variant B (relation to a "unique" object). The use of *bir* with C_o which expresses a "unique" object is limited. In the type *ölüm (bir) tabiat kanunudur* 'death is the law of nature' the article is facultative. Usually the article is not used in this variant, e.g. *karşıda ay vardı* 'Moon was shining in the face'.

Variants C - H. The use of *bir* is the same as in variant *A*.

Variants I and J (relation to place and time). The use of *bir* is limited more strongly than in variant *A*. In variant I *bir* is more often used in the position between the first member of the word group in locative and the second member of the word group *(bir kŏy hayatı — kŏyde bir hayat; bir sokak muharebesi — sokaklarda bir muharebe)*. In variant *J bir* has still rarer use than in variant *I*.

Variant K (the relation to action or state expressed by an infinitive). A characteristic feature: *bir* is never used in this variant. C_0 is regarded as determined and its determination makes even the M_1 determined.

Variants L - P. The use of *bir* is the same as in variant *A*.

Variant R (relation of the object or indicator to a nationality). The use of *bir* is different here. *Bir* is not used if M_1 cannot be the property of a representative of a nation (e.g. *Türk musikisi* 'Turkish music', *Ingiliz donanması* 'English fleet'). The article *bir* is used when M_1 can be an individual property (e.g. *bir Ermeni şivesi* 'Armenian pronunciation').

Variant S (the relation of the object to its own name). In this variant *bir* is used when we meet for the first time with an object bearing proper name: *Bir "Hızlı" vapuru geldi* 'A steamer (called) "Hizli" has come'.

Variant T (the relation to a word in inverted commas). In this case *bir* has a rather limited use.

Variant U (the relation between C_0 and M_1 in which the first member is a logical subject of the second member). Here *bir* is used as an expedient of comparison (*bir çocuk uykusu* 'child's dream') and in sentences pointing to a strong degree of some quality or state (e.g. *bir baş dönmesi idi ki ...* 'It was such a turning the head that ...').

Variant V (the relation between C_0 and M_1 in which the first member is a logical object of the other member). The use of *bir* is different: from the extremely rare use in the izaphat constructions of the type *kitap okunması* and *mektup yazılması* (where C_0 is in indefinite number) to a considerably frequent use in the izaphat constructions of the type *kurtuluş ümidi* (e.g. *kurtuluş ümidi var mı?* 'Is there any hope of rescue?').

Variant W (the relation of an object expressed in numbers to the number designating it). So far as the first member of this variant is a numeral, *bir* having also the sense of a numeral is used. In these cases *bir* is followed by the numerator *tane* 'pieces', e.g. *bir tane 8 rakamını yacınız* 'Write one number 8'.

As we have already seen, in the izaphat of the type $C_0 — M_1$ *bir* has a more limited use than in the izaphat of the type $C_1 — M_1$. At the same time it must be emphasized that the applicability or inapplicability of *bir* and of the izaphat construction $C_0 — M_1$ relates only to the izaphat as a whole, that is to say, *bir* can stand only before the izaphat, never within it.

3. $C_0 — M_0$

This type of izaphat has interesting properties from the point of view of the category of determinedness vs. indeterminedness. In type $C_0 — M_1$ this category does not relate to the first member of the izaphat: determined or indetermined can be only the second member of the izaphat construction. Similarly as in type $C_0 — M_1$ *bir* can never stand within the construction, in type $C_0 — M_0$ it can in many cases stand between C_0 and M_0.

Variant A (C_0 expressing the name of material and M_0 the object made of that material). Names of materials are usually used with a zero article in Turkish but this does not mean that they do not accept *bir*; the latter expresses here not indeterminedness but, on the contrary, such a part of the object that can be represented quantitatively, e.g. *bir demir* 'a piece of iron', *bir su* 'a glass of water', *bir ekmek* 'a loaf of bread', *bir et* 'a portion of meat', *bir kahve* 'a cup of coffee'. As a matter-of-course, in the izaphat of type $C_0 — M_0$ where *bir* can be related to M_0 only but never to C_0, *bir* does not accept the sense of partitiveness when used before C_0. Thus, for example, *bir taş köprü* means 'a stony bridge' or 'one stony bridge.' *Taş* may have the meaning 'stone' in the sense of both a noun and an adjective. *Bir taş köprü* = *taş bir köprü*. The connection of the type *büyük bir ev* suppresses the connection *bir büyük ev*.

Variant B (C_o expressing social condition and M_o personal proper name). In this variant *bir* cannot stand either before C_o or before M_o; to express indetermination of the given type it is necessary to substitute the positions of both members of the izaphat and to interpose the words *adında* or *isminde* 'by name', for example *çoban Hasan* 'shepherd Hasan' but *Hasan isminde bir çoban* 'a shepherd by name of Hasan'.

Variant C (C_o expressing a representative of a nationality, M_o profession). The indefinite article is possible here but only before the izaphat as a whole: *bir Tatar arabacı* 'some Tartar-coachman'.

Variant D (C_o expressing appurtenance to sex or age). In this case *bir* can also stand only before the izaphat as a whole: *bir kadın doktor* 'some lady doctor'.

Variant E (C_o expressing a vocative epithet, M_o a personal proper name). *Bir* can be used here in the function of indefinite article before the izaphat as a whole: *bir müsyü Ribot* 'a Mr. Ribot'.

Variant F (C_o expressing a personal proper name, M_o a vocative epithet). The use of *bir* as in variants *B* and *E*. For expressing indetermination a periphrastic form is often used, e.g. *Hacı kalfa isminde birisi* 'a certain Hadji-Kalfa'.

Variant G (C_o expressing the object of comparison). The use of *bir* is very limited here. *Bir* is inserted between C_o and M_o only in those cases when C_o has also the sense of an adjective, e.g. *şeytan bir çocuk* 'a devilish child' (*şeytan* means 'devil' and 'devilish'). *Bir* is further used with C_o which expresses the name of the thing with which the other object is compared, e.g. *bir altın kalp = altın bir kalp* 'golden heart'.

Variant H (C_o expressing the number by which M_o is measured). The use of *bir* is not possible here.

Variant I (C_o expressing measure, degree, gender, etc., of M_o). In this variant *bir* can be used before the izaphat as a whole. If C_o expresses a numerative, *bir* is conceived as a numeral, not article: *bir nevi hastalık* 'some kind of illness' but *bir litre süt* 'one litre milk'.

Majzel's analysis of izaphat constructions in Turkish has

revealed delicate differences and diversities in the use of *bir* as indefinite article and has contributed, without doubt, to a better elucidation of intricate problems of the category of determinedness vs. indeterminedness.

Analogous to the function of indefinite article is the use in Chinese of the so-called numerative in connection with the numeral *jî* 'one' preceding the noun. Thus, for example, *kūŋřen* means 'worker' (or 'workers'), *jî kᵊ kūŋřen* '(one, some) worker'[43].

IV. *Languages Possessing Definite, Indefinite, and Partitive Articles*

The most outstanding representatives of this type are French and Italian.

French has the definite article *le* (masc.), *la* (femin), *l'* in singular, *les* in plural, the indefinite article *un* (masc.) and *une* (femin.) in singular only, and the partitive article *(du, de l', de la*; pl. *des)*.

The use of articles in French is similar to that in English and German. However, there are certain differences between these languages in the use of articles. Let us suggest that abstracts and names of materials in English are without article whereas in French and German they have article, e.g. *water* but *l'eau* and *das Wasser*. Examples: *Honour must be our only guide. — L'honneur doit être notre seul guide. — Die Ehre soll unsere einige Führerin sein*. A. Biard[44] explains it by the fact that whereas the English article *the* expresses real determination, the other languages idealized it, transferred it to the unreal. Similarly the nouns expressing indefinite plurality (e.g. men, animals, flora, minerals, etc.) are used without article in English but with article in French and German. We will give examples in English, French, and German:

43 Cf. *Úvod do hovorové čínštiny* [Introduction to Colloquial Chinese] (Praha, 1967), 136 f.
44 A. Biard, *L'article défini dans les principales langues européennes*. Première partie: *L'article "the" et les caractéristiques différentielles de son emploi* (Bordeaux, 1908).

Men are mortal. — Les hommes sont mortals. — Die Menschen sind sterblich.

Plants breathe but not in the way animals do. — Les végétaux respirent, mais non à la façon des animaux. — Die Vegetabilien atmen, aber nicht wie die Tiere.

As indefinite are regarded in English those things that do not have any form, individual physiognomy, or certain demarcation. However, if in French a concrete object of individual form and material physiognomy is concerned such as *le cheval, la charrue,* or an object limited by its intellectual physiognomy in its range, extent, or duration, such as *la toise, le pied, la pouce, l'anné, le mois, le jour, l'heure, la minute,* etc., English distinguishes a certain inner and spontaneous determination of this object which is specified, representing one genus, one class or category of objects. Examples:

The horse is our noblest conquest, the plough is our most useful invention. — Le cheval est notre plus belle conquête, la charrue est notre plus utile invention.

The year is twelve months, the month is twelfth part of the year. — L'année a douze mois, le mois est la douzième partie de l'année.

However, in plural there is no article in English whereas French and German do have article: *Horses are our noblest helpmates, ploughs our most valuable implements of labour. — Les chevaux sont nos plus précieux instruments de travail. — Die Pferde sind unsere edelsten Gehülfen.* It is just this difference in the use of article when the concept of completeness or generalness is concerned that, according to Biard, forms the basic characterization of the use of article not only in English, French, and German, but also in most other principal European languages.

According to I. Poldauf[45] the French definite article is, above all, a word-generic signal (even if separable) and this is why it can

---

[45] Ivan Poldauf, "Srovnání s mateřštinou při vědeckém zkoumání jazyků" [Comparison with Mother Tongue in Scientific Investigation of Languages], *Sborník Vysoké školy pedagogické v Olomouci, Jazyk a literatura* (Praha, 1954), 67.

well be the bearer of the expression of a partitive understanding of the content of meaning. According to Poldauf, in the case of articles we are concerned with ranging with the category of determinedness, the absence of real article corresponding to "an indefinite quantity of (further) uncountable" (*water, boys*) and satisfactorily meeting even the needs of indicating partitiveness. In spite of this even here the signal of partitiveness permeates (e.g. *Betty Botter bought some butter* = *du beurre*). German stands in the middle between these languages: the article is rather word-generic but indicates even the "(further) uncountable"; partitiveness ceased to be expressed in the Middle High-German time. In Czech the expression of partitiveness by means of genitive becomes extinct (*ubývá vody* [gen.] > *voda* [nomin.] *ubývá* 'water is running low'; *té krásy* [gen.] > *ta krása* 'that beauty' [nomin.]).

According to Henry Frei[46] the opposition of affirmative and corresponding negative sentences shows (see the table) that *de* is here both partitive and indefinite and that this difference is exclusively due to the context but that this article is never definite; it is called NON-DÉFINI. Consequently, the partitive article is a syntagm with which the "signifié global" is the consequence of the combination of NON-DÉFINI with DÉFINI; it is a kind of NON-DÉFINI. This presupposes a dichotomic organization of the French article where INDÉFINI and PARTITIF are in opposition to the DÉFINI:

DÉFINI (*le, la*; *les*)

NON-DÉFINI: INDÉFINI (*un, une*; *des*)

   PARTITIF (*du, de l', de la*; *des*)

Il a du *papier*	*Il n'a pas* de *papier*
Il a un *papier*	*Il n'a pas* de *papier*
Il a des *papiers*	*Il n'a pas* de *papiers*
Il a le *papier*	*Il n'a pas* le *papier*
Il a les *papiers*	*Il n'a pas* les *papiers*

---

[46] Henry Frei, "Tranches homophones (à propos de l'article partitif du français)", *Word* 16: 3 (1960, 317-322).

This organization is confirmed by the fact that impersonal verb tolerates with it both the INDÉFINI and the PARTITIF but excludes from this position the DÉFINI: *Il est arrivé* une *lettre*, des *lettres*, du *courrier*. The third criterion, the choice of the representatives *en* or *le* and the impossibility of interchanging them mutually is the principal line of demarcation between the INDÉFINI and PARTITIF on one hand and the *défini* on the other:

Il a du *papier*	*Il* en *a*
Il a un *papier*	*Il* en *a un*
Il a des *papiers*	*Il* en *a*
Il a le *papier*	*Il* l'a
Il a les *papiers*	*Il* les a

PARTITIF and INDÉFINI are neutralized in plural — they are distinguished only in context.

We will also consider the French article from the point of view of its value. Its basic role is morphological and determinative. Compare the following examples:[47]

un *programme de restauration économique*; le *programme* d'une *restauration économique*; le *programme* de la restauration économique. Or: *j'aime à aller* en automobile; *j'aime à voyager dans* une *automobile Peugeot*; *j'aime à voyager dans* l'automobile de mon oncle, *elle est très douce*.

By means of article it is possible to indicate a number of fine differences. Cf., e.g., *c'est l'œvre* du fou; *c'est l'œvre* d'un fou; *c'est* une *œvre* d'une fou *qui s'appelait Michel*; une *œvre* de fou.

Italian has the definite article for masc. sing. *il* and *lo*, for femin. *la*, e.g. *il padre* 'the father'; *la madre* 'the mother'. The article *lo* is used before words of masculine gender beginning with *s* followed by a consonant (the so-called *s impura*, "covered *s*"), e.g. *lo sguardo* 'the look', *lo sbaglio* 'the mistake'. *Lo* is further used with words of masculine gender that begin with *z*, e.g. *lo zio* 'the uncle', *lo zelo* 'the zeal'. If a word begins with a vowel, the articles *lo* and *la*, owing to the encounter of two vowels, have the form *l'*,

47   Ferdinand Brunot, *La pensée et la langue* (Paris, 1936), 167.

e.g. *l'anno* 'the year', *l' erba* 'the herb'. Plural of *il* is *i*, of *lo (l')* is *gli* before a vowel, a *z* and a covered *s*; plural of *la* is *le*.[48] Examples: *il cane* 'the dog' — *i cani* 'the dogs'; *l'amico* 'the friend' — *gli amici* 'the friends'; *la sorella* 'the sister' — *le sorelle* 'the sisters'.

The indefinite article for masculine gender is *un* and *uno* before words with a covered *s* or *z*, for the feminine gender *una*, e.g. *un padre* 'a father', *un amico* 'a friend', *una madre* 'a mother', *uno specchio* 'a mirror', *uno zio* 'an uncle'. The vowel of the indefinite article may be elided only with words of feminine gender, e.g. *un' amica* 'a (she) friend' instead of *una amica* but *un amico*, *un uomo*.

The Italian article has some specific features which differentiate it from the article in English and German as well as in other languages. We will quote at least the most important ones[49]. The article is used:

1. After the verb *avere*, when special bodily characteristics are given, e.g. *Francesca ha i denti bianchi, gli occhi azzurri, i capelli biondi e le labbra vermiglie.* — *Francesca has white teeth, blue eyes, fair hair and red lips.* — *Franziska hat weisse Zähne, blaue Augen, blonde Haare, rote Lippen.*
   Questo ragazzo ha la testa grossa. — *This boy has a big head.* — *Dieser Knabe hat einen dicken Kopf.*
2. Before *di cui, cui*:
   L'uomo, la (di) cui riputazione è perduta, è sfortunato. The man whose reputation is lost, is unfortunate. — *Der Mann, dessen guter Ruf verloren ist, ist unglücklich.*
3. Before words that in English and German stand without article but in spite of it can be conceived in a partitive sense, e.g. *L'occupazione è il miglior rimedio contro la noia.* — *Occupation is the best remedy against boredom.* — *(Die) Beschäftigung ist das beste Mittel gegen Langweile.*
4. Before the names of continents, lands, provinces, etc., if the

---

[48] The vowel of the articles *gli* and *le* can be elided before an identical vowel of the following word, e.g. *gl'Inglesi* 'the English', *l'erbe* 'the herb'.
[49] According to Carl Marquard Sauer, *Italienische Konversationsgrammatik* (Heidelberg, 1919), 227 f.

whole concept or its certain part is meant: *L'Austria Superiore* — *Upper Austria* — *Oberösterreich.*

I fiumi della Germania — *The rivers of Germany* — *Die Flüsse Deutschlands.*

However, when they have the function of adjectives in genitive, the definite article is usually dropped:

L'ambasciatore di Francia — *The French ambassador* — *Der französische Gesandte.*

Il console d'Italia — *The Italian consul* — *Der italienische Konsul.*

5. Before proper names of well-known poets and artists, e.g. *il Tasso, il Rossini,* etc.

6. Before the names of artistic works, e.g. *Il Giulio Cesare di Shakespeare* — *Julius Caesar by Shakespeare* — *Julius Cäsar von Shakespeare.*

   Il Mosè di Michelangelo — *Moses by Michelangelo* — *Moses von Michelangelo*; *La Lucia di Donizetti,* etc. However, if a Christian name precedes, the article is dropped: *Dante Alighieri, Michelangelo Buonarotti,* etc.

7. Before the names of some towns: *Il Cairo, la Spezia, la Bastia, la Mecca.*

   Compare, however: *la Rocella* — *La Rochelle*; *l'Aia* — *den Haag* — *the Hague.*

8. Before words designating some rank or title and before the words *signore, signora* and *signorina,* it they are not used in addressing, e.g.

   Il conte Pallavicini — *Count Pallavicini* — *Graf Pallavicini*; *Il signor Travetti* — *Mr. Travetti* — *Herr Travetti.*

9. In many sayings such as:

   Studiare il francese, l'italiano, etc. — *To study French, Italian* — *Französisch, Italienisch lernen.*

   Suonare il pianoforte — *To play piano* — *Klavier spielen*; *Essere il benvenuto* — *To be welcome* — *Willkommen sein.*

   Giuocare al bigliardo, all carte, etc. — *To play billiards, at cards* — *Billiard, Karten spielen.*

   La settimana scorsa, l'anno scorso, etc. — *Last week, last year* — *Vergangene Woche, vergangenes Jahr.*

On the other hand, there are cases when in Italian there is no article contrary to English and German. We quote some of them:

1. Before cardinal numerals following the names of rulers: *Carlo Decimo* — *Charles the Tenth* — *Karl der Zehnte*; *Enrico Quarto* — *Henry the Fourth* — *Heinrich IV*.
   Similarly there is no article before the adjective *magno* with a name: *Alessandro Magno* — *Alexander the Great* — *Alexander der Grosse*.
   Compare: *San Carlo* — *Saint Charles* — *der heilige Karl*.
2. After the verbs *essere, divenire, diventare, rendersi, fare, nascere, morire, parere, sembrare*; *essere creduto, riputato*; *ritornare, essere dichiarato, proclamare, mostrarsi*, etc., if a noun designating rank, office, nation, state, etc. follows them, e.g. *Luigi Napoleone venne eletto imperatore* — *Louis Napoleon was elected emperor* — *Ludwig Napoleon wurde zum Kaiser erwählt*.
   Davide fu proclamato re d'Israele. — *David was proclaimed King of Israel*. — *David wurde zum Könige von Israel ausgerufen*.
3. In quoting frequented places, e.g. *Andare in giardino* — *To go to the garden* — *In den Garten gehen*.
   In agreement with Italian is mostly English but not German in the following cases:
   Andare a scuola, a teatro, a casa — *To go to school, to the theatre, home* — *In die Schule, ins Theater, nach Hause gehen*.

The partitive article in Italian is *di* which merges with the definite article into the forms *del, dello, della, dei, degli, delle*. Examples: *il vino* 'the vine' — *del vino* 'some vine'. *Io vedo gli uomini* 'I see the people' — *Io vedo degli uomini* 'I see some people'.

Compare with French:

Ha mangiato del *pane* — *Il a mangé* du *pain* — *He ate bread*. *Ei sono* degli *uomini che* ... — *Il y a* des *gens qui* ... — *There are people who* ...

On the whole, there is great freedom in using or omitting the article in expressing partitiveness. However, it is necessary to note that, as a rule, the article is omitted when the sentence is negative, e.g. *egli non ha denaro* 'he has no money'; or *non abbiamo fiori* 'we have no flowers'.

The partitive article has its own declination, that is to say, special forms for genitive, dative and accusative. As nominative, the merger *di* with definite article or a mere noun is used. In dative, *a* or *ad* precede the nominative form but this is a comparatively rare case. Examples: *tu pensi sempre a (del) denaro, a (del) vino, a (dei) libri* — 'You always think of money, wine, books'. Genitive, on the other hand, is far more frequent but also simpler, as the article is dropped and *di* is added to the noun itself: nomin. *(della) carta*, gen. *di carta*; nomin. *(del) vino*, gen. *di vino*. This case occurs when a noun without article is governed by a determining noun, e.g. *Una bottiglia di vino* — *A bottle of wine* — *Eine Flasche Wein. Un pezzo di carne* — *A piece of meat* — *Ein Stück Fleisch.*

By means of this genitive form there are often expressed German and English material adjectives, e.g. *un anello d'oro* — *a golden ring* — *ein goldner Ring.*

This genitive form stands also after adverbs of quantity such as *niente* 'nothing', *qualche cosa* 'something', etc., e.g. *niente di buono* — *nothing good* — *nichts Gutes*; *qualche cosa di bello* — *something beautiful* — *etwas Schönes.*

In other languages the function of the partitive article is expressed either by periphrasis (*a bit of, part of, a little*, etc.) or by a noun without article, for example in Spanish *ha comido pan* 'he ate bread'.

To this group belongs also the language of the Isles of Marquises.[50] In this language the definite article is *te* in singular, e.g. *te énata* 'the man', *te tau* or *na* in plural: *te énata* 'the men'.

The indefinite article in singular is *e, he, á*, e.g. *e énata* or *he énata* 'a man', the article *á* being used before simple units (unités simples), e.g. *á tahi* 'one', *á úá* 'two', etc.

The use of the indefinite article *he* is necessary after the ex-

---

[50] Cf. R. I. Dordillon, *Grammaire et Dictionnaire de la Langue des Iles Marquises* (Paris, 1931), 7-10, 17.

pressions *i óto, i taá, i úna, i pataá, ua, ma, ma úna, io*, etc., for example *i óto he faé* 'in the house', *i taá he vai* 'by water', *i úna he fenna* 'on the ground', *i pataá he úa* 'by the pit', *ua he henua* 'on earth', *ma he aánui* 'by train', *ma ína he poti* 'on a boat', *io he one* 'on the table', etc.

The indefinite article in plural is *mon, na, naho*, e.g. *mon énata* 'men', *na hakaíki* 'chiefs'.

Declension of articles:

Sg. Nom. *te, he*
    Gen. *no te, na te, a te, to te, ta te*
    Dat. *i te*
    Acc. *te, i te*
    Voc. *e, e te*
    Abl. *no te, mei te, na te, e, e te, i te*
Pl. Nom. *na, te tau, te huaá, mou, naho, ta*
    Gen. *no na, na na, a na, o na, to na, ta na, no te tau, to te tau, na te tau, ta te tau*
    Dat. *i na, i te tau, i mou*
    Acc. *na, te tau, te huaá, i te tau, i te huaá*
    Voc. *e na, e te tau, e mou*
    Abl. *no na mei na, no te tau, mei te tau, e te tau, i te tau*

The definite article *te* substantivizes the verb or verbal adjective, e.g. *e kai* 'to eat' — *te kai* 'the eater'.

The definite article *te* preceding the verb *e* 'to be' expresses the negation of the verb. When it is repeated twice it substantivizes the verb and confers on it a negative meaning.

The partitive article is *titahi mea, ona, tona, mou, na*, e.g. *á tuú mai titahi mea pake* 'give me tobacco', or *á hano i te mea vai* 'go to look for (some) water'.

Article is not used:

1. before proper names of persons,
2. before place names,
3. before the names of rivers and mountains,
4. before the names of constellations and stars,

5. before the words *tai* (designating a part of the sea between parts of land or a part of land marking off the sea) and *uta* (part of a valley marking off a mountain),
6. before the names of days and months,
7. before the names of peoples and tribes,
8. before the words *vaho* ('outside'), *óto* ('the inside', 'interior'), *úna* ('on the top'), *áo* ('the bottom').

B. ONE MEMBER OF THE CATEGORY OF DETERMINEDNESS VS. INDETERMINEDNESS IS EXPRESSED BY AN INDEPENDENT WORD, THE OTHER MEMBER IS PROCLITIC OR ENCLITIC

This type is represented in the first place by the Germanic languages Danish, Norwegian, and Swedish.

In Danish the definite article in singular has the enclitic form *-en* for the common gender and *-et* for the neuter gender, e.g. *Hest*en 'the horse', *Hus*et 'the house', in plural there is a common ending *-ene (Hest*ene, *Hus*ene*)*. The indefinite article has the form of an independent word: *en* for the common gender (e.g. *en Mand* 'a man') and *et* for the neuter gender (e.g. *et Hus* 'a horse'). With an attributive adjective the definite article is an independent word: *den, det* in singular, *de* in plural and the adjective ends in *-e* in both genders and numbers, e.g. *den gode Hest,* plural *de gode Heste*; *det røde Hus,* plural *de røde Huse.*

The adjective with an indefinite article has no ending: *en sort Hest* 'a black horse' — *den sorte Hest* 'the black horse'. In the neuter gender the adjective has the ending *-t, -t,* e.g. *et langt Haar* 'the long hair'.

The principle rules of the use of articles in Danish:[51]

1. Personal names in singular have no article. If a name is accompanied by an attribute it is preceded by the demonstrative pronoun *den, det, de* in the function of article, e.g. *den rare Christian* 'dear C.' Also as a surname: *Pepin den Lille* 'Pepin the Small'.

---

[51]   Cf. Palle Spore, *La langue danoise* (Copenhague, 1965), chapter 9.

Personal names in plural have the definite article when they designate the whole family, e.g. *Hansen* — *Hansenerne* 'the Hansens' — 'les Hansen'.

Personal name can become common name and in that case it has the article, e.g. *mæcen* — *mæcenen* 'the maecenas'.

2. The names of towns are, as a rule, without article, as well as the names of countries, mountains, islands, rivers, and lakes. Exceptions:

   (a) The names of countries ending in a stressed *-i* have the article, e.g. *Tyrkiet, Algeriet, Normandiet.*

   (b) The names of mountains ending in *-bjerg* have the article: *Himmelbjerget, Oliebjerget.*

   (c) If the name expresses a plurality (archipelago, mountain chain) by means of a noun in plural, the article is obligatory, e.g. *Azorerne* — *les Açores, Balearerne* — *les Baléares, Alperne* — *the Alps* — *les Alpes.*

   (d) Some important and long known rivers usually have the article: *Elben* 'the Elbe' — 'l'Elbe'; *Nilen, Rhinen, Seinen, Themsen* ('the Thames' — 'la Tamise'). Without article: *Donau* 'the Danube' — 'le Danube', *Maas* 'the Maas' — 'la Meuse'. Also three Danish lakes are without article: *Tissø, Arresø, Mossø.*

3. Definite article is used with common names to designate a familiar thing, for example, *toget er forsinket* 'the train is overdue'.

4. The definite article is used, generally in singular, with nouns designating a genus (comp. the generic article in French), e.g. *hunden er et klogt dyr* 'the dog is a clever animal'; *hunden* 'the dog' does not mean a particular dog but dog in general, as a genus. Plural is less frequently used, but it is possible to say *hundene er kloge dyr.* However, the form without article is preferred: *hunde er kloge dyr.* Nouns designating a substance or abstract nouns (or words that are not used in plural) do not take article: *smør er et vigtigt næringsmiddel* 'butter is an important foodstuff'.

The indefinite article is used with indefinite, indetermined nouns, e.g. *en mand* 'a man', *et hus* 'a house'. If the noun is attributive and the subject is determined, there is usually no article: *han er ikke murer* 'he is no mason'. If the subject is indetermined, the indefinite article is used, e.g. *det er* en *dreng* 'that is a boy'.

The indefinite article can be used with a personal name either to indicate a member of a family (e.g. *han er en typisk Goldschmidt* 'he is a typical Goldschmidt') or to indicate that the personal name is used as a common name (e.g. *en macen* 'a maecenas').

Nouns are used without article in the following principal cases:

1. With the words expressing quantity, e.g. *mange heste* 'many horses', *fem biler* 'five autos'. Without article are, of course, the nouns determined by demonstrative and possessive pronouns and by a genitive, e.g. *disse heste* 'these horses', *min bog* 'my book', *hans kone* 'his wife' *mendens hat* 'the man's hat'.

2. In addressing: *hør her, kaere ven* 'listen, dear friend'.

3. If the attribute of a noun is a superlative or ordinal numeral, the article is omitted, e.g. *sidste gang sagde han ...* 'last he said ...' — 'la derniere fois, il a dit ...'; *med største fornøjelse* 'with much pleasure' — 'avec beaucoup de plaisir'; *han bor på første sal* 'he lives on the first floor' — 'il habite au premier étage'.

4. To indicate in singular an indetermined quantity of a substance or, in plural, an indetermined number of countable material (in French the partitive article is used), e.g. *jeg glemte at købe konvolutter* 'I have forgotten to buy envelopes' — 'j'ai oublié d'acheter des envelopes'. If, however, the name of a substance is of an enumerative character, it has the article, e.g. *en øl* 'a (bottle of) beer'. In *en udmærket vin* 'an excellent wine' — 'un vin excellent' the article indicates which kind of wine is concerned.

5. In a number of expressions in which the noun is either governed by a verb or by a prepositional complement, e.g. *købe hus* 'to buy a house' — 'acheter une maison', *ryge pibe* 'to smoke a pipe' — 'fumer la pipe', *gå i skole* 'to go to school' — 'aller à

l'école', *lide af gigt* 'to suffer from rheumatism' — 'suffrir de rheumatismes', *få mæslinger* 'to catch measles' — 'attraper la rougeole', etc.

6. With a noun in apposition to a pronoun of the first or second person, to a personal name, or to a numeral, e.g. *jeg fjols* 'imbécile que je suis', *I franskmænd* 'vous autres Français', *kong Frederik* 'le roi Frédéric', *side* 10 'page 10'.

7. If a noun is an attribute of a determined subject, especially in telegraphic style, e.g. in newspaper headlines: *Dreng forsvundet i jolle* 'Boy disappeared in a jolly boat' — 'Garçon disparu en yole'.

Similarly in Swedish[52] the definite article in singular, common gender, is *-en* (when the noun ends in a consonant) and *-n* (when the noun ends in a vowel), e.g. *månad* 'month' — *månaden* 'the month'; *blomma* 'flower' — *blomman* 'the flowers'. Neuter nouns in singular have the ending *-et* if they end in a consonant or stressed vowel, or *-t* if they end in an unstressed vowel, e.g. *smultron* 'strawberry' — *smultronet* 'the strawberry'; *bo* 'abode' — *boet* 'the abode', *öga* 'eye' — *ögat* 'the eye'.

In plural the nouns of common gender have the ending *-na*[53], e.g. *gossar* 'boys' — *gossarna* 'the boys', *flickor* 'girls' — *flickorna* 'the girls'. Neuter nouns have the ending *-a*, if their plural ending is *-n* (e.g. *förhållanden* 'circumstances' — *förhållandena* 'the circumstances' and the ending *-en* if their plural is identical with singular (e.g. *namn* 'names' — *namnen* 'the names'). Neuters of foreign origin with plural in *-er* have the article always in *-na*, e.g. *partier* 'parties' — *partierna* 'the parties'.

The indefinite article, like in Danish, is an independent word in Swedish: for the common gender it is *en*, and for the neuter it is *ett*, e.g. *fader* 'father' — *en fader* 'a father', *moder* 'mother' — *en moder* 'a mother', *barn* 'child' — *ett barn* 'a child'.

---

[52] Cf. Edward Theodor Walter /-Lund/, *Schwedische Konversationsgrammatik* (Heidelberg, 1916).

[53] For masculine nouns also the ending *-ne* is used; however, the ending *-na* is steadily increasing in use.

Similar to German, Swedish has the indefinite or strong declension of adjectives accompanying a noun and the definite or weak declension:

1. For the common gender in singular the adjective is in the basic form: *en god man* 'a good man', *en god flicka* 'a good girl'.
2. For the neuter gender in singular the adjective takes the ending *-t*: *ett snällt barn* 'a well-behaved child'.
3. In plural the form of the adjective is *-a* for all genders, e.g. *goda män* 'good men', *goda flicker* 'good girls', *goda barn* 'good children'.

Definite declension

The definite declension has, as a rule, the ending *-a* in singular and plural of all genders. Nouns that have natural masculine gender have in the higher style often *-e*[54]. Examples: *den goda mannen*, pl. *de goda männen*; *den goda flickan*, pl. *de goda flickorna*; *det goda barnet*, pl. *de goda barnen*.

Participles in *-ad* and superlatives in *-ast* have the ending *-e* instead of *-a*: *det älskade barnet*, pl. *de älskade barnen*; *den vackraste flickan*, pl. *de vackraste flickorna*.

Instead of enumerating all the rules of the use of the definite article in Swedish we will give here some cases when the use of definite article in Swedish differs from that in German. It is in the following cases:

1. After the demonstrative pronoun *den (det, de) här* 'this', *den (det, de) där* 'that', *den (det, de) der* (demonstrative), e.g.
   Den mannen var det ej 'Der Mann war es nicht'.
   Den här flickan är vacker 'Dieses Mädchen ist hübsch'.
   Det där barnet är sjukt 'Jenes Kind ist krank'.
2. In inscriptions, indications of parts of books, e.g. *förra delen*, *senare delen* 'erster Teil, zweiter Teil' — 'the first part, the second part'; *fjärde uppträdet, scenen* 'vierter Auftritt, vierte Szene' —

---

[54]   This *-e* is necessary (a) if an adjective stands without any noun, e.g. *den gode*, (b) if an adjective follows a noun, e.g. *Karl den Store*, (c) with an exclamation or festive address, e.g. *Store gud! Gode herrar och svenske män!*

'the fourth scene'; *första lektionen* 'erste Lektion' — 'the first lesson'. But: *Detta ord förekommer i första lektionen* 'Dieses Wort kommt in der ersten Lektion vor' — 'This word appears in the first lesson'.

3. In some special expressions, e.g.:

till det yttre '(schön) von Gesicht' — 'a pretty face'
till utseendet 'von Ansehen' — 'by sight'
av naturen 'von Natur' — 'of nature'
av hjärtat (hjärtans) gärna 'vom Herzen gern' — 'with all one's heart'
lägga på hjärtat 'sich (etwas) zu Herzen nehmen' — 'to take (a thing) to heart'
mot aftonen 'gegen Abend' — 'by the evening'
över natten 'über Nacht' — 'overnight'
om dagen, natten 'bei Tage, bei Nacht' — 'in the day, night'
till åren 'an Jahren' — 'by years'

The definite article is not used in Swedish in contrast to German and mostly in accordance with English in the following cases:

1. With the names of materials and with abstracts in general meaning, especially when they are linked with prepositions, e.g. *Jag föredrager vatten (öl) framför mjölk* 'Ich ziehe der Milch das Wasser (Bier) vor'. — 'I prefer water (beer) to milk'. *Sanning är det bästa ting* 'Die Wahrheit ist das beste' — 'Truth is the best'. *Han är skyldig till högförräderi* 'Er ist der Hochverrats schuldig'. — 'He is guilty of treason'.

2. With personal names, e.g. *Där hava vi Fredrik* 'Da ist (der) Friedrich'. — 'Here is (the) Frederic'.

3. With dates in answer to the question 'when', e.g. *Han dog år 1970* 'Er starb im Jahre 1970' — 'He died in the year 1970'.

4. With adverbial expressions formed from a noun and preceding a preposition, e.g. *i begrepp* 'im Begriffe' — 'on the point of', *i gång* 'im Gange' — 'on the go (at work)', *i stånd* 'imstande' — 'able to, capable of', *på allvar* 'seriously', *på spel* 'at stake', *till sjös* 'zur See' — 'at sea', *i nödfall* 'im Notfall' — 'in case of need', *i stort* 'ins (im) Grosse(n)' — 'in (the) large', etc.

5. If a genitive precedes a noun, e.g. *konungens slott* 'das Schloss des Königs' — 'the King's castle'.

In many cases there is the definite article in German whereas in Swedish there is the indefinite article and *vice versa*, e.g. 'zum Teil' — 'partially' — *till en del* vs. *nu är han rika karlen* 'jetzt ist er ein reicher Mann' — 'now he is a rich man' or *Hon är nu en gång kära barnet* 'sie ist nun einmal liebes Kind im Hause' — 'now she is again the sweet child at home'.

Titles ending in more than one consonant or vowel or composed with *-råd* have the definite article, e.g. *skalden Topelius* 'der Dichter Topelius' — 'the poet Topelius', *målaren Andersson* 'der Maler Andersson' — 'the painter Andersson', *statsrådet Wennerberg* 'der Staatsrat Wenneberg' — 'the Privy Counsellor Wenneberg'.

Titles ending in a simple consonant and the words *furste* 'Fürst' — 'prince', *greve* 'Graf' — 'count', *herre* 'Herr' — 'Mr.', *konung* 'König' — 'king', *prins* 'Prinz' — 'prince', and often also *landshövding* 'Landshauptmann' — 'governor' and *löjtnant* 'Leutnant' — 'lieutenant' are without article, e.g. *greve Posse, professor Möller, konung Oskar I,* etc. Female titles such as *drottning, fru, fröken, madam,* etc. have no article.

The indefinite article is much rarer in Swedish than it is in German. In contrast to German, in Swedish the indefinite article is dropped before nouns indicating state, trade, nationality, and relation of one person to another, if these nouns have the function of a predicate, e.g.:
han är vetenskapsman 'er ist ein Gelehrter' — 'he is a scientist', *han blir skomakare* 'er wird (ein) Schuhmacher — 'he becomes shoemaker', *hon är svenska* 'sie ist eine Schwedin' — 'she is a Swede', *han är bror till herr A.* 'er ist ein Bruder des Herrn A.' — 'he is brother of Mr. A.', *han är vän till doktorn* 'er ist ein Freund des Doktors' — 'he is the doctor's friend'.

If, however, a nearer determination is added to the noun, the indefinite article is used, like in German: *han är en duktig vetenskapsman* 'er ist ein tüchtiger Gelehrter' — 'he is an excellent scientist'.

Further the indefinite article is omitted before a predicative noun if the latter is linked with a preposition, e.g. *Konung Vilhelm valdes till kejsare* 'König Wilhelm wurde zum Kaiser gewählt' — 'King William was elected emperor'.

There is no article before the predicative adjective, if it expresses genus, e.g. *Vinkeln är rät* 'der Winkel ist ein rechter' — 'the angle is right'.

Finally there is no article before a noun belonging to a predicate as complement (object) in certain expressions such as *få brev* 'einen Brief bekommen' — 'to receive a letter', *söka plats* 'einen Platz suchen' — 'to look for a place', *ordet stavas med stort A* 'das Wort wird mit einem grossen A geschrieben' — 'the word is written with a capital A'. As we see, even English has the indefinite article in these cases, like German.

In the other cases the use of indefinite article is, on the whole, in agreement with that in German.

Of Romance languages it is only Rumanian that has an enclitic article. The indefinite article in Rumanian is an independent word: *un* for masculine (e.g. *un prieten* 'a friend'), *o* for feminine gender (e.g. *o casă* 'a house'), in plural either the indefinite pronoun *nişte* is used for both genders in the function of article, or indefiniteness is expressed by the noun itself (thus *prieteni* or *nişte prieteni* 'friends'). The article is declined: *un, unui, unui, un; o, nişte, unor, nişte*.

The definite article in Rumanian is enclitic: -/u/l, -le for masculine, -a for feminine gender in singular, -i for masculine, -le for feminine gender in plural (e.g. *bou-l* 'the ox', *domn-ul* 'the master', *frate-le* 'the brother', *casa* 'the house', plural *boii, domnii, fraţii, casele*). The definite article too is declined: masc., sing., nom. -/u/l, -le, gen., dat. -/u/lui, accus. -/u/l, -le, voc. -/u/le, -e, -; fem., sing., nom. -a, gen., dat. -i, accus. -a, voc. -; pl. masc. nom. -i, gen., dat. -lor, accus. -i, voc. -, -lor; pl. fem. nom. -le, gen., dat. -lor, accus. -le, voc. -, -lor. In contradistinction to Danish and Swedish in Rumanian the definite article may be put even after the adjective, e.g. *marele poet* 'the great poet'. In addition to the enclitic definite article Rumanian has two more auxiliary articles, *cel* and *cea*, which serve as emphasis of the adjective following a noun, especially in apposition (e.g. *poetul cel mare* 'the great poet'), in declension of numerals (e.g. *cele patru cărti* 'the four books'), and in the formation of superlative (*poetul cel mai mare = cel mai mare poet* 'the greatest poet').

Rumanian has further the so-called ARTICOL POSESIV which has the forms *al, a*. It is used (a) before genitive so far as it does not directly precede a word with a postpositive (enclitic) article (e.g. *marea operă a poetului* 'the great work of the poet'), (b) before possessive pronouns and adjectives, if the enclitic article does not directly precede (e.g. *casele sint ale mele* 'the houses are mine'), (c) before the genitive of interrogative and relative pronouns (e.g. *omul a cărni nevastă e bolnavă* 'the man whose wife is ill'), and (d) before ordinal numerals (e.g. *etaiul al doilea* 'the second floor').

The function of Rumanian articles does not lack problems. There is, for instance, the problem of the relation between various forms of the Rumanian article and the question of accumulating articles, that is to say the use of two or more articles with one noun, e.g. *omul cel bun, calul bun al omului*. Recently attention has been devoted to these problems by V. Š. Lebanidze[55] who has tried to elucidate some problems of articles in Rumanian.

To start with, Lebanidze proves against C. Pop that the article *cel, cea* is postpositive. The current opinion (even of C. Pop) is that in cases like *omul cel bun* or *casa cea frumoasă* the first article makes the noun definite whereas the other article emphasizes the adjective. Lebanidze further argues: if the use of *cel* depended upon the adjective, that is to say if it meant an emphatic stressing of the adjective, then *cel* could be used in any cases in which the necessity of such a stressing of the attributive function of the adjective appears: however, one cannot say *un om cel bun* or *o casă cea frumoasă*. The emphatic stressing of the adjective cannot be regarded, according to Lebanidze, as a function of the article. The function of the article *cel* is the determination of the noun.

[55] Cf. V. Š. Lebanidze, *Osobennosti artikl'a v rumynskom jazyke* [Peculiarities of article in Rumanian] (Tbilisi, 1966).

This is the case of a 'dual article'; *cel* is a constant part of this dual article and so far as it follows not only the noun but also the enclitic definite article we have full right to regard it as postpositive.

Similar is Lebanidze's opinion on the possessive article *al*. As a nominal determinant *al* has a double use:

1. It stands before the possessive pronoun:
   (a) *un prieten* al *meu*
   (b) *aceste fabrici* ale *noastre*
2. It stands before the noun in genitive:
   (a) *o symfonie* a *maestrului*
   (b) *calul bun* al *omului*

So far as *al* is regarded as a postpositive article, it is necessary to assume that the position of this article is determined in relation to the following possessive pronoun; consequently, it is its determinative. There would be no such article, argues Lebanidze, if there were no possessive pronoun. Thus, in Lebanidze's opinion, in both cases the article *al* is dependent on the preceding noun and not on the following possessive pronoun; consequently, it is postpositive. In our opinion, we cannot avoid referring to the fact that if Lebanidze is right, in the expression *un prieten al meu* the noun would have both the indefinite article *un* and the possessive article *al*, and in the expression *aceste fabrici ale noastre* there would likewise be two indicators, *aceste* and *ale*.

As far as the other variant of the use of *al* is concerned, Lebanidze's argument is similar to that in the preceding case. If *al* is regarded as a prepositive article, it must be assumed that it refers to the second noun which is in genitive. If there were no such noun there would also be no article of the kind mentioned. If *al* is a determinant of the second noun, why is it not used in all those cases where the noun in genitive functions in the quality of determinedness? Lebanidze comes to the conclusion that (a) in the construction *o simfonie a maestrului* the article *al* refers not to the following noun attribute in genitive *(maestrului)* but to the first noun *(simfonie)* with a specific, grammatical form (that means such a noun as is accompanied by the prepositive indefinite article and postpositive noun article in genitive): the article *al* is the determinant of that noun: it is a postpositive article; (b) in the construction *calul bun al omului* the article *al* refers not to the following noun attribute in genitive *(omului)* but to the first noun *(calul)* with a specific grammatical form (i.e. such a noun that accompanies the postpositive definite article, the postpositive adjective and the postpositive noun attribute in genitive); the article *al* is therefore the determinant of that noun, it is a postpositive article.

Again, an objection could be raised that the first noun would have two articles in this conception. A more serious objection seems to be the argument that in the cases quoted above the article agrees not with the noun in genitive before which it stands but with the first noun.

Lebanidze further regards the problem of article as a part of a wider problem of the word order in Rumanian sentence. He starts from L. Tesnière's suggestion[56] according to which the criterion of typological classification of languages is the order of words in sentence and distinguishes 'ordre structural' and 'ordre linéaire'. Structural is such an order of words according to which connexions between words are formed, whereas linear order is such in which words are placed in sentences. In those cases when two words occur mutually in a structural connection, two variants of their placement in linear order are possible:

1. the directing word precedes the subordinate one, e.g. *cheval blanc* in French,
2. the subordinate word precedes the directing one, e.g. *white horse* in English.

Tesnière regards the subordinate word as a knot or centre of the structural order. In agreement with this, the first variant of the arrangement of words with linear order appears to him as a centrifugal order, the second variant as centripetal order. Hence also

---

[56] Cf. L. Tesnière, *Éléments de syntax structurelle* (Paris, 1959).

the principle classification of languages into centrifugal and centripetal (LANGUES CENTRIFUGES, LANGUES CENTRIPÈTES). Tesnière further distinguishes strongly centrifugal and strongly centripetal languages, and weakly centrifugal and weakly centripetal languages. All Romance languages are centrifugal. Rumanian is a strongly centrifugal language. From this point of view Lebanidze shows that the right representative of the word order in Rumanian is not the linear order *calul cel bun* (with an absolute centrifugal force) but the order *un cal al omului* (where centrifugal force apparently predominates over the centripetal force). Postpositiveness (centrifugal force) in the system of articles absolutely predominates.

A. Hansen[57] regards article as a morpheme expressing various aspects of the noun, that is to say,

1. the incentive (introductive) aspect:
   noun + indefinite article
2. the relative (continuative) aspect:
   noun + definite article
3. the predicative aspect:
   noun + zero article.

According to Lebanidze the relative aspect is theoretically conditioned by the incentive aspect which is its starting point: *calul* means that there already was *un cal* or the form *calul* is called forth by the form *un cal*.

In Romance languages the definite article has the following basic functions:

1. It has the role of a relative actualizer, that is to say it expresses the idea of the determination of the noun.
2. Grammatically it shapes the noun.
3. So far as it arose from the demonstrative pronoun it has a deictic function. Thus in Romance languages the definite article has to a greater or smaller degree a deictic function.

---

[57] A. Hansen, *Artikel systemet i rumaensk* (København, 1952).

Lebanidze asks whether the Rumanian article fulfills those three functions and argues:

1. There is no doubt that the definite article in Rumanian plays the role of a relative actualizer; this is testified by the occurrence of the indefinite article (i.e. the incentive actualizer) and the fact of contrastiveness of these two actualizers.
2. There is no doubt that the definite article shapes the noun grammatically: it implies reference to gender and number of the noun.
3. The question of the deictic function of the article needs a discussion.

The definite article in Rumanian is different from the analogical article in other Romance languages not only by its postpositiveness. R. G. Piotrovskij[58] writes: "Here the postpositive article has no more the quality of an independent word. Moreover, from the part of the noun it is subjected to phonetic-orthographic aggluti-nation *(lup-ul)* as well as to phase *(cas-a < casă + a)*. In the functional relation the Rumanian postpositive article preserves the feature of an ancillary component of analytical-morphological form as mobile in relation to a certain word, e.g. *omul bun* but *bunul om*, or *casa fratelui* but in toponymics *Dealul lui frate ...*" According to Lebanidze the deictic function of the definite article in Romance languages represents not a grammatical but an expressively-stylistic function which has been preserved without regard to grammaticalness.

Consequently, we can sum up: in those cases when a noun has no need to express the deictic function, the definite article, without any regard to a high degree of grammaticalness, can fulfil (even minimally), beside its basic grammatical function, the deictic function as well. In those cases when the speaker wants to separate the noun within the limits of the full deictic function of the Ro-mance definite article, the Rumanian article with its "greater gram-

---

[58]   R. G. Piotrovskij, "Eščo raz ob analitičeskoj forme slova [Once more on the analytical form of the word]", *Izvestija AN SSSR, Otdel lit. i jazyka* XVI (Moskva, 1957).

maticalness" is not sufficient; its deictic function needs strengthening, that is to say, "activization".

The deictic function of the article *cel* can be clearly seen in the construction of the type *cei doi oameni* which is translated by S. Pop as "(ces) les deux hommes". So far as in the expression *omul cel bun* the deictic function is actualized by *cel* which is already present (even if in a minimal extent) in the definite article, we can say that within the limits of the dual article it plays the role of the deictic reactualizer. So far as the function of the dual article is concerned in its entirety it can be determined as a relatively deictic actualization.

The characterization of the article *al* as regards the semantic content has much in common with the characterization of *cel*: 1. *Cel* is usually connected with the definite article, *al* can accompany the noun in presence of both the definite and the indefinite article: un *prieten* al *meu* — *cal*ul *bun* al *omului*. 2. *Al* can also accompany a noun if it has a determinative with full deictic load, that is to say, the demonstrative pronoun: aceste *fabrici* ale *noastre*. Lebanidze concludes by giving the following scheme of actualization of Rumanian nouns by means of a system of articles:

1. Inceptive actualization: noun + indefinite article.
2. Relative actualization: noun + definite article.
3. Relatively-deictic actualization (with a moment of deictic reactualization): noun + definite article + *cel*.
4. Deictic-inceptive actualization: noun + indefinite article + article *al*.
5. Deictic-relative actualization: noun + definite article + article *al*.

In giving this rather detailed survey of Lebanidze's interesting work we want only to give the reader an insight into the complicated problems of Rumanian articles. So far, the problem of articles in Rumanian is by no means solved and we can only expect the results of further investigation which will contribute not only to the solution of the problem of Rumanian articles but also to the general theory of articles as well.

Armenian[59] has an enclitic definite article which has a double form: 1. -ə which is added to words ending in a consonant or diphthong *ai*, *oi*; 2. -*n* which is added to words with a final vowel or mute *j*. If a word is followed by another word with an initial vowel both -ə and -*n* may be used as definite article. The indefinite article in East Armenian is the prepositive *mi*, in West Armenian the postpositive *mə*.

Kashmiri, an Iranian language, expresses the category of determinedness vs. indeterminedness by an enclitic indefinite article -*ā* or -*āh*, e.g. *kath* 'narration', *kathā* or *kathāh* 'a narration'. In the function of definite articles are used demonstrative pronouns that have more or less original meaning. The Dardic language Tirakhi has the enclitic indefinite article -*i*, e.g. *xarāb badani* 'a bad boy', the definite article is in the form of the demonstrative pronoun *le* or *lā* (e.g. *la parana kurəras zin* 'the saddle of the white horse', *lā gaṇa putər jusā xum gā* 'the elder son became angry'), and of the demonstrative pronoun *lema* before the names of towns.

In Turkish languages this type is represented by Uzbek.[60] In this language the category of determinedness vs. indeterminedness is expressed by three forms: neutral, indefinite, and definite. The neutral form is characterized, similar to other languages, by the absence of article, e.g. *ot haivon dir* 'the horse is an animal', in Czech 'kůň je zvíře' (without article). Plural: *kaşlar uçadi* 'birds fly', in Czech 'ptáci létají' (without article). The indefinite article is expressed by means of *bir* which has a double meaning: that of the numeral 'one' and that of the indefinite article, e.g. *bir ot* 'a horse'. The definite article is expressed by means of the possessive suffix of the 3rd person singular -/s/i. Definiteness is further expressed in Uzbek by some other means, for example by demonstrative pronouns, by an adjective in -*dagi*, by an adjective in superlative, by lexical meaning, etc.

In Kurdish the indefinite article has a double form, -ək and -nə,

---

[59] Cf. Artasches Abeghian, *Neuarmenische Grammatik* (Berlin-Leipzig, 1936), 61.
[60] Cf. A. N. Kononov, *Grammatika sovremennogo uzbekskogo jazyka* (Moskva-Leningrad, 1960).

both enclitic. The indefinite article *ǝk* has its origin in the numeral *jek* 'one' and the indefinite article *nǝ* comes from the indefinite pronoun *hʮnǝ* 'some, several'. *ǝ* of the article -*ǝk* is dropped, if the word ends in a vowel. For example, *xort* 'young man', *xortǝk hat* 'a young man came'; *č'ʮra* 'lamp', *mʮn č'ʮrak k'ʮri* 'I have bought a lamp'. In a nominal complex the indefinite article means 'one of', e.g. *Hevalǝki mʮn hat* 'One of my comrades came'. In a word complex masculine nouns after the indefinite article have the izaphat ending -*i*, feminine nouns -*ǝ*, e.g. *xortǝki bǝdew* 'a (some) boy', *kǝvʮrǝki mǝzʮn* 'a (some) large stone'; *žʮnǝkǝ kŏrmandža* 'a (some) Kurdish woman'. The forms of determining words within a nominal complex depend on the forms of the determined word, that is to say, if the determined word has the indefinite article *ǝk* and the izaphat form *ǝ*, the determining words within the complex also have the formant *ǝ*, e.g. *qizǝkǝ bǝdǝwǝ mǝzʮn* 'a (some) grown-up beautiful girl'; *šǝvǝkǝ dʮ režǝ tari* 'a (some) long dark night'. On the other hand, *xortǝki bʮlʮndi bǝdǝw* 'a (some) beautiful tall youth'; *xaniki fʮrǝji gǝrm* 'a (some) warm spacious house'.

The indefinite article *nǝ (hʮnǝ)* is used both enclitically and proclitically and indicates plural. The form *nǝ* is used enclitically in connection with the noun which occurs with a nominal complex, the form *hʮnǝ* is used prepositionally. For example, *xort* 'a youth', *xortnǝ bǝdǝw hatʮn* 'beautiful young men came'; *žʮn* 'woman', *žʮnnǝ ȓʮnd dʮlizʮn* 'beautiful women dance'; *mal* 'house', *malnǝ mʮzʮn mʮn ditʮn* 'I saw big houses'.

If the determined word (the first member of the complex) stands with the form of the indefinite article *nǝ*, then in the form of the plural of determining words within the complex the indicator of plurality is *ǝ*. For example *xortnǝ bǝdǝwǝ n'ak* 'some beautiful good young men'; *kǝč'ʮknǝ nazǝ ȓʮnd* 'some sweet beautiful girls'; *k'ʮtebnǝ sʮȝǝ qalʮn* 'some thick red books'.

In the same meaning is used the indefinite article *hʮnǝ* before a noun which always occurs in the direct case, e.g. *mʮn hʮnǝ k'ʮteb k'ʮrin* 'I have bought some books'; *hʮnǝ qiz hatʮn* 'some girls came'.

The prepositive and enclitic indefinite articles are often used side by side. In that case they emphasize the indefiniteness of the name more expressively: *mьn hьn k'ьtebnə məzьn k'ьřin* 'I have bought several (some) larger books'; *hьnə xortnə bədəw* 'some beautiful young men'.

The indefinite article does not occur with proper names, numerals, pronouns, adjectives, abstract nouns and collective nouns.

The function of the definite article have in Kurdish the demonstrative pronouns *əv, əw* in singular and *əvan, əwan* in plural. When they stand before nouns and have the indicator of determinedness *a (ha)* these demonstrative pronouns fulfil the function of the definite article. The forms of the definite article distinguish in singular the direct and oblique case, and feminine and masculine gender; the plural lacks this difference. The forms of the definite article agree with the forms of nouns in gender, number, and case. The full form of the direct case of the definite articles *əva, əwa* requires that it is followed by a noun in the full form of the direct case (with the formant *a, ha*). Its oblique forms agree with the oblique forms of nouns: in singular *e* with feminine nouns, *i* with masculine nouns, in plural *a (ana)* with both feminine and masculine nouns. Examples:

1. *əva žьna hat* 'this woman came';
   əwa xorta ču 'this young man left'.
2. *əvi xorti got* 'this young man said';
   tő əvi xani dьbini 'you see the wall'.
3. *əvanv žьna (žьnana) hatьn* 'the women came';
   əwana xorta (xortana) got 'the young men said'.

The position of the definite article before a nominal complex does not affect the izaphat construction, e.g. *əva qiza bədəw hat* 'the beautiful girl came'; *mьn əwa k'ьteba qalьn k'ьři* 'I have bought the thick book'; *əwa kəč'ka řьnd baš hin dьbə* 'the beautiful girl learns well'; *əva xorte bədəw hat* 'the nice young man came'.

The definite article is used before all nouns (both concrete and abstract) including proper names to indicate objects or persons mentioned already before and to indicate a certain object which is just spoken about.

Last but not least it is necessary to mention the fact that in the declension of nouns there are certain changes according to whether the noun has the indefinite or definite article. Nouns with the indefinite article *ǝk* are declined only in singular whereas nouns with the definite article *ǝva* and *ǝwa* are declined both in singular and in plural.

The nouns with the article *ǝk* differ from the nouns without article by lacking the vocative singular and lacking the declension in plural. Masculine nouns with the article *ǝk* in oblique case accept the indicator *i* in the case when the form of their oblique case does not differ from the form of the direct case. On the other hand, the declension of feminine nouns with the article *ǝk* does not differ from the declension without article. The form of the oblique case of nouns with the article *ǝk* gives the possibility of determining the gender of nouns; *e* belongs to the nouns of feminine gender, *i* to the nouns of masculine gender.

Nouns with definite article accept in the direct case, independently of gender, the ending *a* or *ha* (in dialects) in singular and *a (ha)* or *ana* in plural.

The forms of the oblique case in singular with the definite article merge with the forms of the oblique case of nouns with the indefinite article *ǝk*, that is to say, they have the ending *e* (declension I) or *i* (declension II). The form of the oblique case in plural agrees with the form of the direct case in plural.

Among Indonesian languages this type is represented by the language of Roti (one of the islands opposite New Guinea) which has the indefinite article *esa* used quite regularly, similarly as the indefinite article in German. The definite article in Rotinese has three forms: for singular the form *a*, for plural the form *la* after vowels and *ala* after consonants; it stands after the noun. Rotinese has no personal article; proper names of persons are without article.[61]

[61] Cf. a very detailed study of Rotinese articles in J. C. G. Jonker's *Rotti-neesche spraakkunst* (Leiden, 1915), 381-391.

New Makassar (in Celebes) has personal articles *i, pusi* (rarer is *pun* which is used above all in poetry). Further it has the definite enclitic article *a* which is not dropped when a demonstrative pronoun is added to the noun.

In Assamese,[62] determinedness is expressed by means of various particles of which the particle *to* expresses the most common meaning of determinedness. The enclitic particle of determinedness is added before the case endings of the noun. In a certain form nouns are in singular only. In plural the function of a certain form is expressed by syntactic means, especially by means of demonstrative pronouns which are put before the noun. The particles of determinedness express not only determinedness, familiarity of the speaker with the given object, but also its outer appearance, animation, and other marks. That all differentiates these particles from the definite article for instance in English and from the demonstrative enclitic *-s* used in a number of Finno-Ugric languages (e.g. in Erza-Mordvin). Let us characterize these particles:

1. *kɔn* is a diminutive particle;
2. *kɔni* is a particle expressing a higher degree of diminutiveness than *kɔn*;
3. *khɔn, khɔni* (a diminutive form) is a particle used to indicate broad and flat objects;
4. *gɔs, gɔsi* (a diminutive form) is a particle used to indicate long, flexible objects;
5. *gɔraki* is a particle used with nouns designating people and having an aspect of seriousness and respectfulness;
6. *got* is a particle mostly indicating animate nouns;
7. *sota, soti* (a diminutive form) is a particle indicating oblong, flat, and split objects;
8. *zɔn, zɔna* (a form of respect), *zɔni* (feminine form) is a particle designating people;
9. *to* is a particle used with all nouns designating certain, concrete objects independent of their form;

---

[62]   Cf. V. D. Babakaev, *Assamskij jazyk* (Moskva, 1961), 55-59.

10. *tãr, tãri* (diminutive form) is a particle indicating oblong objects connected into bundles;

11. *dal, dali* (diminutive form) is a particle indicating oblong, round and hard objects;

12. *pat* is a particle designating oblong, narrow, and flat objects;

13. *phæra* is a particle designating material nouns, loose objects etc., pointing to a limited quantity of material in question.

Thus the most usable is the particle *to* which in grammatical respect is nearest to the definite article. As it is possible, according to Babakaev, to connect a word having the determinative particle with a prepositive demonstrative pronoun (e.g. *ei manuhzɔn* 'this man-the'), we are of the opinion that evidently another function is concerned here than that of the demonstrative pronoun, that is to say not the function of indication. However, in any case these particles defy any comparison with other ways of expressing the category of determinedness in other languages.

The indefinite article in Assamese is either the particle *e* connected with one of the particles of determinedness, this connection occurring before nouns (e.g. *ezɔn manuk* 'a man'), or the enclitic particle of indeterminedness *ek* with collective nouns (e.g. *mahek* 'approximately a month').

C. BOTH (OR MORE) MEMBERS OF THE CATEGORY OF DETERMINEDNESS VS. INDETERMINEDNESS ARE EITHER ENCLITIC OR PROCLITIC

1. *One article is proclitic, the other enclitic*

A typical representative of this subgroup is Arabic which has the proclitic definite article *al*, the *l* of which is assimilated to the consonant of the following word if that consonant is any of the following sounds: the emphatic *ţ, ḑ, ṣ, ẓ* and the corresponding non-emphatic *t, d, s, z*, further the dentals *t, d*, and the consonants *š, r, l, n* (e.g. *al-baitu* 'the house' but *at-tādžiru* 'the merchant').

The indefinite article in Arabic is -/u/n (the so-called "nunation"[63]), e.g. *baitun* 'a house'. The indefinite, as well as the definite article, is unchangeable in gender, number, and case; it occurs in singular only. No nunation have the so-called "diptots", for example *āhar*[u] 'another', further the forms of the regular plural masc. and the forms of dual. The meaning of articles in Arabic is similar to that in European languages.

In one of the Caucasian languages, Abazinian (in the Tapant dialect)[64], the function of the definite article is contained in the possessive proclitic particle of the 3rd person sing. of the class of non-rational beings and things *a-* which is similar to the function of articles in such European languages as English, French, or German. According to Genko there is no doubt that in this case

---

[63] The so-called "nunation" or "mimation" is a specific feature of Semitic languages. It consists of the ending -*m(a)* or, in other languages, -*n(a/i)* added to the forms of the status rectus. This ending seems to have originally a determinative function of a certain definite article (cf. J. Kuryłowicz, "La mimation et l'article en arabe", *Archiv orientální* XVIII, 1/2 [1950]) and therefore it was always lacking in the status constructus and status pronominalis (as here the noun was always determined in another way), as well as in the absolute form (status indeterminatus and praedicativus which were indefinite by their function). Later, however, the determinative function of the mimation/ nunation became extinct (as early as in Old Akkadian where all forms of status rectus in singular are automatically followed by mimation, with the exception of some proper names). With regard to the obliteration of the determinative function of mimation/nunation Old Arabic and Southern Peripheral developed a new definite article so that the forms with mimation/nunation began to be regarded as indefinite. At the same time mimation/nunation was impossible in status constructus and pronominalis. Thus a rule developed according to which any noun which is in any way determined (by article, or by another noun, or by a possessive pronoun) has no mimation/nunation whereas any noun not determined in such a way possesses it. In other Semitic languages mimation/nunation has either gradually disappeared (as for example in Ak- kadian) or has been preserved without a special semantic function in plural of the status absolutus (in languages of northern central group). In the other Semito-Hamitic languages there are no — or only very dubious — traces of mimation/nunation in singular. It is, however, probable that such forms of plural as the Berber -*ən*, or the Chad -*en*, -*una*, and probably also the Berber -*in* as well as the Berber remnant of dual, -*in*, are derived from the forms with nunation (cf. I. M. Diakonoff, *Semito-Hamitic Languages* [Moscow, 1965], 61-63).

[64] Cf. A. N. Genko, *Abazinskij jazyk* (Moskva, 1955), 101 f., 118 f., 125 f.

the function of the possessive pronoun is considerably weakened and is manifested only in contrast to the other possessive pronouns. In the use of this particle in the function of definite article it is possible to observe differences between the Tapant and Škaravan dialects on one hand and the Transcaucasian Abkhaz dialects on the other hand. In the Abazinian language the addition of the particle *a-* characterizes an object known to the speaker or known from the context of speech. The forms without *a-* are rather frequent; for example, on the question how a certain object or phenomenon is called the answer is the basis of a word preserving the meaning of singular. Quite different situation is in Abkhazian. It is possible to say that in Abkhazian a noun with the particle *a-* appears as a normal form which does not express determinedness any more.[65] Thus, e.g. *tšy* means in the Abazinian language 'a horse' (that has not yet been spoken of), in Abkhazian it is an expression of a more abstract, collective concept 'horse generally' and may be translated both by singular and by plural, e.g. *tšy symam* 'I have no horse' (one or more).

The enclitic morpheme *-kI* expresses in Abkhazian: (a) singleness, e.g. *tšykI* 'one (single) horse' (in contrast to the collective case *tšy* 'horse [generally], horses'), and (b) indefiniteness, e.g. *tšykI* 'a (unknown, not mentioned before) horse' (in contrast to the definite case *atšy* 'the [known] horse'). In Abazinian, on the other hand, the morpheme *-kI* expresses merely singleness, consequently *tšykI* 'one (single) horse', indefiniteness being expressed by the simple basic form, thus *tšy* 'horse (some)', definiteness by the morpheme *a-*, e.g. *a-tšy* 'the (definite) horse'.

Determinedness or indeterminedness is expressed even in the attributive linking of a noun with an adjective, e.g. *tšdŷu* '(some) big horse', *atšdŷu* 'the (certain) big horse'.

The American Indian language Nahuatl has the determined article in the suffix *-tl*, *-tli* which disappears in plural or after a

---

[65] Of a contrary opinion is Robert Bleichsteiner ("Die kaukasische Sprachgruppe", *Anthropos* 32 [1937], 65) who quotes examples of reading: *a-bla* 'the eye', *bla-k'ə* 'an eye', but *bla* 'eye', does not, according to Bleichsteiner, occur independently.

possessive pronoun. According to Frédéric Müller it is a suffix of individualization which is concerned here, e.g. *koa-tl* 'the serpent', *kalli* (instead of *ka-tli*) 'the horse'. The indefinite article is represented by the proclitic *no-*, e.g. *no-kal* 'a horse'.

Hermann Nekes who wrote a detailed grammar of the Bantu language Yaoundé (Jaunde),[66] speaks about a demonstrative proclitic particle *é* which is said to serve as a nearer determination of the noun and is regarded as an article. Some nouns are connected with the article permanently, e.g. *ési̯á* 'father', *ésoa'* 'your father', *ésa'ngá* 'aunt'. The plural prefix precedes the article, e.g. *ékôkòo'* 'a large fish', plural *bẹékôkòo'*. Nekes does not write why he regards this demonstrative particle as an article but from its use we can conclude that it is really a sort of article. It follows from the fact that the demonstrative pronoun *ńo'* 'this' has a demonstrative meaning only in the case when it is added to a noun with an article, e.g. *é mode ńo'* 'this man'. Without article, *ńo'* has the meaning of a local determination or of a pronominal copula 'here (it) is', 'it is'. On the contrary another pronoun, *-tě* 'that (one), the mentioned' never has an article.

2. *Both articles are enclitic or proclitic*

In the Elamic language[67] the names of persons in singular have the enclitic article *-k*, if the name is definite and *-r*, if the name is indefinite. According to E. Reiner the form with *-k* is a form of *"locutive"*, connecting the name with the speaker (e.g. *rutu hani-k u-r-e* 'my dear wife' means that the wife belongs to the speaker), whereas the form with *-r* is the form of "non-locutive" connected with the third person.

In the Khāmtī language[68] the indefinite article is formed by

[66] Hermann Nekes, *Lehrbuch der Jaunde-Sprache* (= *Lehrbücher des Seminars für orientalische Sprachen zu Berlin*, Band XXVI) (Berlin, 1911). Jaunde is a Bantu language spoken in southern Cameroon, its area reaching beyond the boundaries of Cameroon and ending in Gabun on the river Ogowe.

[67] Cf. I. M. D'jakonov, *Jazyki drevnej perednej Azii* (Moskva, 1967), 96.

[68] It belongs to the Siamese-Chinese language family and is spoken in the eastern part of the Lakhimpur District, between Nishmi and Singpho, south

adding *ā-lǔng* 'one' after the noun, e.g. *kōn ā-lüng* 'a certain man'. The function of the definite article is expressed by the pronoun *nai* 'this', e.g. *mū khan* 'pigs', *mū nai khan* 'the pigs'. Plural is indicated by prefixing or suffixing the particle *khan*; if a pronoun or definite article is added to a word, *khan* is suffixed. It is hard to decide whether genuine article is concerned here.

In the Mayāng language[69] the indefinite article is *āgō, āgot* following the noun it qualifies. For example, *mānū āgō* 'a man'. Sometimes it combines with the noun, e.g. *gorāgot* for *gorā āgot* 'on a horse'. The demonstrative pronoun *augō (autā* or *aukhonā)* is used for the definite article, for example *bāyok khulā augoi* 'the younger brother', *rājā ōgoi* 'the king', *pūtōk ōgō* 'the son', *sāruk autā* 'the share'. Like the indefinite article it follows the noun it belongs to. When a noun with an article is declined, the declensional suffixes are added to the article, not to the noun; e.g. *mānu āgor* 'of a man'. However, it remains to ascertain whether the demonstrative used as definite article has really assumed the function of a genuine definite article.

According to Grierson, in Kurmālī Thār, Eastern Magahī dialect of Bihārī, the pleonastic suffix *ṭā, ṭāi*, or *ṭāy* is very common and sometimes is used in the function of the definite article, e.g. *chhāwā-ṭā* 'the child', *bēṭā-ṭāy* 'the son'. As indefinite article the suffix *-ek* is used, e.g. *thar-ek* 'a little'.

Both articles are proclitic in Oubykh.[70] As the definite article Oubykh uses the deictic *a* which is put before the noun and the adjective and makes them definite, e.f. *a-c⁰ ä* 'the house'. This article has much wider use than in French and also because it can relate not only to one word but to a group of words as well, e.g. *a-c⁰ä-s⁰-dǝxǝ* 'le *(a-)* maître *(dǝxǝ)* — (de-) (la-) petite *(s⁰)* maison *(c⁰ä)*'. Before an epithetic adjective preceding a noun the use of *a-* is facultative, e.g. *yedänä a-nǝs⁰ǝ-nǝ a-pc⁰'ǝ qǝ-nǝ zä-p*

---

of Brahmaputra. Cf. G. A. Grierson, *Linguistic Survey of India* 2 (Calcutta, 1904), 141-147.

[69] According to G. A. Grierson (cf. *Linguistic Survey of India*, vol. J, 419-421) Mayāng is a mongrel form of Assamese spoken by the tribe of Mayāng in the State of Manipur.

[70] Cf. Georges Dumézil, *La langue des Oubykhs* (Paris, 1931), 13-16.

ʻxädiku ʻune fille tres belle *(nəsᵒə)*, pure *(pcᵒʼəqə)*ʼ, but *λäƂ-nə xeyšqa-nə zä-tʻitʻ* ʻun homme puissant *(λäƂ)*, riche *(xcyšqa)*ʼ. Here is concerned an indefinite noun which is preceded by an indefinite article *zä* ʻaʼ.

Before an epithetic adjective which is followed by a noun of manner and forms a component with it, the article *a-* is normally not used: *a-tʻitʻ-giζä* ʻthe great manʼ. However, we can decompose this expression and repeat (or add) the article before an adjective, e.g. *a-pʻ xädiku a-nüsᵒə* ʻthe pretty girl (whom...)ʼ.

The use of the article *a-* before an attribute is governed by the following rule: if the attribute is a noun which is preceded neither by an adjective nor by a possessive prefix, it has no article; if the attribute is an adjective (or adverb) or a noun which is preceded by an adjective or possessive pronoun, the article has the priority of use:

1. Attribute = noun not preceded by an adjective or possessive prefix:
   Ƃaβa-nə a-w-Ƃ-ôtʻ ʻtu le-vends en-merchandiseʼ — ʻYou are selling it like goodsʼ.
   sofu γedänä tʻitʻ-šewa-yetʼ ʻSofu était tres homme-fortʼ — ʻSofu was a very strong manʼ.
2. Attribute = adjective, adverb, or noun preceded by an adjective or possessive prefix: *poλə-məsᵒä a-yedä* ʻquatre-jours, (cʼest) beaucoup!ʼ — ʻfour days, thatʼs too much!ʼ
   a-caca a-pλə-xəxə-n a-š-qə-n ʻla broche toute rouge devenue ...ʼ — ʻthe whole broach turned red ...ʼ
   a-məzə a-cäcä-yetʼ ʻlʼenfant était petitʼ — ʻthe child was smallʼ.
   a-si-nikʼ ä-nə a-lä-gi-πôtʻ ʻelle-restera comme-mon-amieʼ — ʻshe will remain my friendʼ.

As indefinite article in singular the word *zä* ʻoneʼ is used, often strengthened by the suffix *gwarə (gwärä, gwärə, gwara, gworə ...)* ʻa certainʼ, e.g. *zä-tʻ itʻ* or *zä-tʻ itʻ-gwarə* ʻa (certain) manʼ. To achieve emphasis, *zä* before *gwarə* or before a nominal epithet can be repeated several times: *zä-gwičaqa zä-gwara* ʻa certain wordʼ. Or: *zä-çi-zä-Ƃyä-s zä-tʻ itʻ-gwara* ʻun certain homme assis-sur-un-chevalʼ — ʻa certain man sitting-on-horsebackʼ.

In plural, indefiniteness is either not expressed or is indicated by such forms as *zä-žva* (or *zä-ž'ö, zä-zᵒu*) 'un troupe' — 'a group', *zä-k'up* 'id.', *za-k'ä-jä* 'quelques' — 'some'; *t'ít'-na* 'des hommes' (or in collect. sing. *t'ít'* 'de[s] homme[s], on'), *zä-t'ít'-žva* or *zä-k' up-t'it* 'un groupe, une troupe d'hommes' — 'a group of people', *masᵒä-zawlä* 'plusieurs jours' — 'more days', *sᵒä-zawlä* 'plusieurs années' — 'more years'.

After numerals the nouns (indicating persons) can be preceded by the particle *zäywa (zäyo-, zäyaw-)*, which means 'unity', e.g. *šä-zäyojiλä* 'trois unités de freres' — 'three brothers'.

The expletive use of *zä* 'one' before other numerals is frequent: *zätqoa zä-šä* 'un-deux un-trois', i.e. 'deux ou trois' — 'one-two one-three', i.e. 'two or three'.

A great number of nouns are without articles, especially in expressions formed — according to the Turkish and Persian usage — with the verbs *i-š* 'do' and *π* 'give' and in abstract expressions. Words of foreign origin (Turkish, Arabic, Georgian, etc.) are often without article. Examples: *Xasa i-š* 'faire délibération' — 'to think over' *,gúnah i-š* 'faire péché' — 'commit sin', *zäyä i-š* 'faire guerre' — 'make war', *gucafə i-š* 'faire doute, douter' — 'to doubt'; *gučaqa π* 'donner parole, promettre' — 'to give word, to promise', *salam π* 'donner salut, saluer' — 'to greet'.

Among Indonesian languages, Kupangese has enclitic definite and indefinite article: *lusa la* 'the stag' — *lusa mesa* 'a stag'. Rotinese has the enclitic definite article in singular *a*, in plural *la* after vowels and *ala* after consonants, the indefinite article is *esa* 'one' which is used quite regularly, like in German.

In Nama, a Hotentot language[71] belonging to the family of Hamitic languages we find an enclitic definite and indefinite article. The definite article is *-b, -s*. The enclitics also express gender, that is to say *-b* expresses the masculine, *-s* the feminine gender. The ending *-i* which expresses *genus commune* had originally the function of an indefinite article and had nothing in common with the differentiation of gender. However, the function of the indefinite

---

[71] Cf. Carl Meinhof, *Lehrbuch der Nama-Sprache* (Berlin, 1909), 48-49.

article has been preserved till the present day. It may be affixed to any noun, masculine or feminine, e.g. *khóib* 'the man' — *khoïï* 'a man'; *taras* 'the woman' — *taraï* 'a woman'. Nouns of masculine gender ending in a consonant have instead of *-b* the article *-i*: *ómi* 'the house', *xámi* 'the lion'. Nouns are in certain cases also used without article.

In some class languages of Sudan the expression of determinedness or/and indeterminedness is closely connected with noun classes. Thus the Temne language[72] does not distinguish a definite and indefinite form of nouns in all classes. The definite form is mostly designated by the vowel *a* with a high pitch. However, there is, according to Westermann, no sufficiently clear and consequent evidence so that we may be able to make a definite decision. It is often uncertain whether a definite or indefinite form is concerned.

In Temne class 1 designates by the prefix *ù-* an indefinite form, by the prefix *ɔ́-* with a high pitch a definite form with nouns designating people, certain animals and individual things. These prefixes are in relation to the personal pronoun 3rd pers. sg. *ɔ-* so that *ɔ́-bài* virtually means 'he the king'.

Class 4 which has the indefinite prefix *a-* and the definite *á +* nasal cons., comprises nouns of class 1 pl. designating people, e.g. *à-bài* 'kings' — *áŋ-bài* 'the kings'. The prefix *áŋ-* is in relation to the personal pronoun 3rd pers. pl. *aŋ* (without a certain tone); high pitch is, consequently, characteristic of the definite form.

In Sherbro *a-* forms plural of nouns designating people. This plural prefix of the indefinite form of class 1 of nouns is in a close relation to the personal pronoun 3rd pers. pl. which is *aŋ* in subjective and *ŋa* in objective case side by side with the form *a*. Definite forms of nouns are expressed by the suffix *-lɛ*, e.g. *na* 'cow' — *na-lɛ* 'the cow'; *ve* 'bird' — *ve-lɛ* 'the bird'.

[72] Cf. Diedrich Westermann, *Nominalklassen in westafrikanischen Klassensprachen und in Bantusprachen* (= *Mitteilungen des Seminars für orientalische Sprachen an der Friedrich-Wilhelms-Universität zu Berlin* XXXVIII) Berlin, 1935), 1-13.

In class 5 the definite form is the same as in class 4, e.g. *áŋ-bàmp* 'the bird', *áŋ-tɔ̀n* 'the dog'.

Class 6 which has the indefinite prefix *ɛ̀-* and definite *ɛ̀-* with a high pitch, comprises nouns of class 5 in plural, e.g. *ɛ̀-reka* 'books' — *ɛ́-reka* 'the books'.

In class 8 the definite form of nouns designating things, which in singular have *ŋ-* and in plural *m-*, is represented by the prefix *a-*, e.g. *m-ump* 'narrations' — *a-m-ump* 'the narrations', *m-es* 'names' — *a-m-es* 'the names'.

Class 9 which has the prefix *ŋ-*, expresses the definite form by a prefixed *a-*, e.g. *ŋ-es* 'name' — *a-ŋ-es* 'the name'.

There is no agreement whether the prefix *ra-* in class 10 means a definite form. According to Westermann the definite form has the prefix *r-* (used before stems beginning with a vowel); in this case an *a-* is prefixed, e.g. *a-r-im* 'the word', *a-r-oŋ* 'the street'; this supports the assumption that *ra-* is a definite form, *rə-* an indefinite form.

In class 13 the definite *ka-* stands against the indefinite *kə*, whereas no definite counterpart is given against the indefinite *k-*.

Class 15 with prefixes *tə-*, *t-*, comprising plurals of most nouns of class 13 but also of class 10 and 1, has in the definite form the prefix *ta-*, e.g. *tə-lɛn* 'horns' — *ta-lɛn* 'the horns'.

In the Nyangbo language the function of the article may be contained in nominal suffixes *-nɔ*, *-na* which have a mildly demonstrative meaning and are used both in singular and in plural, e.g. *kɛ-lɛ́-nɔ* 'the wind', *ba-nu-nɔ* 'the people'.

3. *The definite article (enclitic or proclitic) only*

Among European languages the enclitic definite article is found in Bulgarian and Macedonian. It is used not only with nouns but also with adjectives, possessive pronouns and ordinal numerals. In Bulgarian it has the following forms:

1. Singular: in the masculine gender there are used the full forms *-ăt* and *-jat* and the short forms *-a* and *-ja*, e.g. *čovek* 'man' — *čovekăt, čoveka* 'the man'; *prijatel* 'friend' — *prijateljat* 'the

friend'. Nouns ending in a consonant mostly have the article -ăt and -a, e.g. vlak 'train' — vlakăt, vlaka 'the train'.

Nouns of masculine gender have the article -ta, e.g. ulica 'street' — ulicata 'the street', sestra 'sister' — sestrata 'the sister'.

Nouns of neutre gender have the article -to, e.g. dete 'child' — deteto 'the child', more 'sea' — moreto 'the sea'.

2. Plural: the nouns of masculine, feminine and neuter gender ending in -i or -e have the article -te, or the article -ta if they end in -a or -ja. For example, ženi 'women' — ženite 'the women', gradove 'towns' — gradovete 'the towns'; măže 'men' — măžete 'the men', deca 'children' — decata 'the children'. It is interesting to observe that the article of feminine nouns ending in a consonant is always stressed: dlan 'palm (of the hand)' — dlantá, radost 'joy' — radosttá.

Adjectives have the same article as nouns: in singular masc. it is -jat, -ja, feminine -ta, neuter -to and plural of all genders -te. The full form of the article is used only in nominative, in the other cases the article is reduced. Further it is necessary to point out to the fact that in linking an adjective with a noun the article is added only to the adjective whereas the noun is without article, for example mladijat măž 'the young man'. If the adjective is preceded by a possessive pronoun (or ordinal numeral), the article is attached to that pronoun (or numeral) and both the adjective and the noun are without article, e.e. mojat dobăr prijatel 'my good friend', părvijat uspešen opit 'the first successful attempt'.

In Macedonian and to a limited extent also in some Bulgarian dialects the enclitic definite article has three forms:[73]

1. Sing. masc. -ot, fem. -ta, neut. -to
   pl. masc./femin. -te,   neut. -ta

---

[73] Cf. R. G. A. de Bray, Guide to Slavonic Languages (London, 1951), 267-269. Cf. also K. Horálek, Úvod do studia slovanských jazyků [Introduction to the Study of Slavic Languages] (Praha, 1955), 241-244, as well as Blaže Koneski, Gramatika na makedonskiot literaturen jazik [Grammar of the Macedonian Literary Language] (Skopje, 1967), 225-236.

For example, *volot* 'the ox', pl. *voloite*; *mečkata* 'the bear', pl. *mečkite*; *seloto* 'the village', pl. *selata*. Masc. nouns in *-izam* drop *-a-* in using the definite article but words of foreign origin ending in *-ur* keep that *-a-*. For example, *romantizam* 'romanticism', with article *romantizmot*; *centar* 'centre', with article *centarot*.

Feminine nouns in *-st*, in using the definite article *-ta*, drop one *t*, e.g. *radost* 'joy', *radosta* 'the joy'. All other feminine nouns keep the *-ta*, e.g. *prolet* 'spring', with article *proletta*, *smrt* 'death', *smrtta*. Voicefullness of a voiced consonant before the article is not affected in spelling: *zapoved* 'order' — *zapovedta*.

This form of article expresses a direct reference (the Czech demonstrative pronoun *tento* 'this').

2. Sing. masc. *-ov*, fem. *-va*, neut. *-vo*
   pl. masc./fem. *-ve*, neut. *-va*
   This form indicates, according to de Bray, someone or something who or which occurs near the speaker (according to Horálek a demonstrative meaning is prevailing here).

3. Sing. masc. *-on*, fem. *-na*, neut. *-no*
   pl. masc./fem. *-ne*, neut. *-na*
   This form expresses a reference to a more distant person or thing (the Czech *onen* 'that').

Masculine nouns in *-a* accept the feminine article, e.g. *sudja* 'judge' — *sudjata* 'the judge'.

Some nouns can be either of masculine or feminine gender, in accordance with the article used:
pesokot or *pesokta* 'the sand'
lojot or *lojta* 'the tallow'
potot or *potta* 'the sweat'
žarot or *žarta* 'the red-hot coal'
životot or *životta* 'the life'.

The definite article may be affixed to an attributive adjective instead of a noun, e.g. *beliot vol* 'the white ox', *arnata kniga* 'the good book', *beloto pile* 'the white chicken'.

If two or more adjectives precede a noun, the article stands only with the first adjective, if no special emphasis is expressed, e.g. *brzata planinska reka* 'the fast-flowing mountain river'.

Certain geographical names are used with article, e.g. *Oxridsko (to)Ezero* 'Lake Ohrid'; *Alpite* 'the Alps'.

Article is not used in adverbial expressions such as *na pazar* 'to market', *na prolet* 'in spring', *so glava* 'with one's head'.

In India the Nagpuriâ language, belonging to the Bihārī group, and spoken in the north and east of Jashpur, sometimes uses the suffix *har* to express the idea of definiteness, e.g. *beṭā-har* 'the son'.

Oriyā, one of the four languages (together with Bengali, Bihari, and Assamese) making up the Eastern group of Indo-Aryan languages (according to Grierson, Linguistic Survey of India, vol. 5, part 2), uses as definite article the suffixes *ṭā* and *ṭi*, the first one being used with irrational beings and things, the second one with rational beings, e.g. *ghōṛā-ṭā* 'the horse', *pilā-ṭi* 'the child'.

In Chhattisgarhi (spoken in Raipur and Bilaspur) *har* is added to a noun as definite article, e.g. *gar* 'a neck', *gar-har* 'the neck'. In Halabi (a dialect of Marathi) the word *bītā* 'a person' is sometimes used as a kind of definite article, e.g. *bāp-bītā* 'the father'.

According to I. M. D'jakonov[74] the enclitic article plays an important part in the Khurrit and Urart languages: the particle *-nə* expresses that the name with which it is used appears definite. For example, *Haldi-nə uštabə* 'God Khaldi has appeared'. In plural this particle has the form *-na*, e.g. *tiwe-na* '(certain) words'.

The definite enclitic article can also be found in Hebrew and Aramaic; it is the original *hā* (a demonstrative element).[75]

In Aramaic this article was suffixed and created the so-called STATUS DETERMINATUS (or EMPHATICUS). In nominative singular the *h* was elided so that the article is *-ậ* in singular, *-ậ* in plural. The determinative meaning of this article which has been preserved in western Aramaic, became extinct in eastern Aramaic dialects (in Syrian, Babylonian, Talmud and in the Manda dialect) and

---

[74]   I. M. D'jakonov, *Jazyki drevnej perednej Azii* (Moskva, 1967), 137-139.
[75]   According to some scholars the Aramaic article is admitted to be connected with the demonstrative *'ā*, different from *hā*.

the status determinatus became the normal form of noun. According to another opinion the determining meaning of this article in western Aramaic is secondary, it is rather regarded as an old accusative ending. However, neither of these explanations are generally accepted.[76] Examples from the Biblical Aramaic: ʾᵉlåh (absolute form) 'God, a God' — ʾᵉlåhå 'the God'; ʾeṣbəʿån (absol.) 'fingers' — ʾeṣbəʿåtå 'the fingers'.

In Modern Hebrew the definite article is also ha- (before unstressed h, ʿ and before ḥ it is he-) which is unchanged both in masculine and in feminine gender and in all numbers (singular, plural, and dual). If the definite noun is followed by an attributive adjective, the adjective must also have the definite article, e.g. bajt 'house', ḳaṭan 'small' — habajt haḳaṭan 'the small house'. Indeterminedness of the noun is expressed by the absence of the definite article, e.g. bajt ḳaṭan 'a small house'. If the noun is determined and the following adjective is without definite article, the adjective has the function of a predicate, e.g. habajt hajafe 'the nice house' — habajt jafe 'the house is nice' (cf. Vladimír Sadek, Novohebrejština, Praha 1970, 7-8).

The enclitic definite article exists in Hamitic languages Hausa, Shilh, Somali, and Galla. In Hausa the function of the masculine definite article is performed by the enclitic morpheme -na, the feminine definite article is -ta. These forms are shortened to -n and -t (-r, -l) and also used to form genitive.[77] In Shilh the enclitic stressed definite article is -ya, after consonants -a, e.g. a-gźyu 'a head' — a-gayu-ya 'the head', plural i-guya 'heads' — i-guya-ya 'the heads'; ergeza 'the man'.[78] In Somali the article does not differ in number[79] but it differs in gender according to the ending

---

[76] Cf. Hans Bauer and Pontus Leander, Grammatik des biblisch-Aramäischen (Halle, 1927), 84-85.

[77] Cf. Carl Meinhof, Die Sprachen der Hamiten (Hamburg, 1912), 80. On the other hand, A. Seidel (Togo-Sprachen [Dresden, Leipzig, 1904] 79) asserts that Hausa has no article.

[78] Cf. C. Meinhof, Die Sprachen der Hamiten, 110.

[79] According to L. Reinisch, whereas C. Meinhof (Die Sprachen der Hamiten) quotes the plural kŭa, kŭi, kŭo. Meinhof also does not differ article from demonstrative when he writes: "Die einfachste Form des Demonstrativs ist der Artikel".

of the noun to which it is affixed. Thus in the masculine gender there are the following variants: 1. *ka, ki, ku, (ko)*, 2. *ga, gi, gu, (go)*, 3. *ha, hi, hu, (ho)*, 4. *a, i, u, (o)*, in the feminine gender: 1. *ta, ti, tu, (to)*, 2. *da, di, du, (do)*. The variants 1 - 4 of masculine gender and 1 - 2 of feminine gender respectively are different according to the ending of the noun. The vowel is changed according to whether an object close to the speaker *(a)*, remote *(i)*, or very far *(u, o)* is spoken of. For example, *nin-ka, nin-ki* 'the man', *faras-ka, faras-ki* 'the horse', *bur-ta* 'the hill', *ori-da* 'the woman'. When a noun is linked with an adjective the article is only with the noun, e.g. *ninka yar* 'the little man' (man-the little).[80]

In Galla the definite article for masculine is *-tsha*, for feminine *-tti*, e.g. *garba* 'a slave' — *garbitsha* 'the slave' — *garbi-tti* 'the female slave'.

The Sudanese language Tegele spoken in Kordofan[81] has only an enclitic definite article. In this language the plural of nouns is formed by the suffix *-an* with the variants *-ẹn, -in, -ọn, -un, -n*. To this suffix the article *-dẹ, -dẹn* may be attached, e.g. *ẹlẹk*, pl. *ēlẹk-ẹn-dẹ* 'the king'; *um* 'man', pl. *um-in-de* 'the men'; *iki* 'sheep' (sg.), pl. *iki-n-den* 'the sheep' (pl.).

The suffix *-de* indicating the definite article occurs also in the Sudanese dialect Katla (spoken in the territory south-west of El-Obeid), e.g. *mumwiṅ-dẹ* 'the elephants'; *gurŝal-dẹ* 'the men'.

One of the most important Togo languages, Ewe,[82] has a postpositive definite article of identical form in singular and in plural, *a* (seldom *la*), e.g. *amẹa* 'the man' — *amẹawo* 'the men'. The article is also affixed to a noun which is accompanied by a possessive pronoun, e.g. *eṅkua* 'his-eye-the'.

Some Cushitic languages attach the definite article *-ti* to feminine nouns.[83]

[80] Cf. L. Reinisch, "Die Somali Sprache, III", *Südarabische Expedition* V: 1 (Wien, 1903), 50-53.
[81] Cf. Carl Meinhof, "Sprachstudien im egyptischen Sudan", *Zeitschrift für Kolonialsprachen*, VII, 113.
[82] Cf. A. Seidel, *Togo-Sprachen* (Dresden, Leipzig, 1904), 3, 16.
[83] Cf. Joseph H. Greenberg, "The Languages of Africa", *IJAL* 29 (1963), No. 1, Part II, 47.

Also the Hamitic language Masai[84] has the masculine article in singular *ol-*, in plural *il-*, the feminine article in singular *en-*, in plural *il-*, the feminine article in singular *en-*, in plural *in-*; for example, *ol-kaldes* 'the ape', plural *il-kaldes-in* 'the apes'; *en-gias* 'the work', plural *in-gias-in* 'the works'. Thus the article is linked here with the expression of the function of gender. In addition, with the masculine gender is linked the concept of largeness, with the feminine gender the concept of smallness and weakness.

In Bedauye the article differs in gender and number. In masculine gender the subject form of the article in singular is *wū, ū,* in plural *yā, ā,* the object form is *wō, ō* in singular, and *yē, (yi), ē (i)* in plural. In the feminine gender the subject form of the article is *tū* in singular, *tā* in plural, the object form is *tō* in singular, *tē (te)* in plural. It is interesting to find that in Bedauye there is no special relative pronoun but that either the article is used instead of it or it is omitted at all. In Hausa there is a masculine definite *-na (-n)*, feminine *-ta (-t, -r, -l)*.

Santali[85] uses as a definite article but also to form abstract nouns the enclitic suffix *-tăt'*, e.g. *dare-tăt'*, 'the tree', *maran-tăt'* 'the greatness'. Likewise the dialects of Santali, for example Karmali or Kalha, Mahle. Korwa, another dialect of Kherwari, has the article *-tō* or *-tū*, e.g. *apā-tō* 'the father', *hopon-tū* 'the son'. The noun can have both the article and the pronoun: *apa-te-e* 'father-the-he'.

Tibetan has for the masculine gender the forms of enclitic definite article *pa, pô, pho, bo,* for the feminine gender *ma, mo,* e.g. *mi-bo* 'the man', *mi-mo* 'the woman'.

Among Indonesian languages, the enclitic definite article can be found in Bimanese (e.g. *wai ede* 'the woman'). Sawunese has the enclitic definite Sachartikel *ne* in singular, *he* in plural, New Makassarean has, beside personal articles *i, pun* also the enclitic

---

[84] Cf. C. Meinhof, *Die Sprachen der Hamiten*, 195.
[85] A dialect of the Khervārī language, the most important of all the languages of the Munda group spoken approximately by 1 3/4 mil. people in India in the area about 300 miles from Ganges in the north as far as Baitarani in the south. Cf. Grierson, vol. 4, 30-41.

definite article *a* which does not drop if a demonstrative pronoun is added. Buginese has, beside personal articles *la*, *i* also the enclitic definite Sachartikel *e*, e.g. *aruṅ e* 'the king'.

4. Only Indefinite Article (Enclitic, Proclitic)

This subtype is represented especially by literary Persian[86], Tajik and Afghan. However, these languages do not represent the pure type C 4 as, in addition to the enclitic article, they also have an independent article arising from the numeral 'one'. Consequently, they belong partly to type A III.

Persian can form the indefinite article in three ways: (a) by means of the enclitic particle *-ī*, e.g. *ketāb-ī* 'a book', (b) by means of the numeral *yek* 'one', e.g. *yek ketāb*, (c) by combining both preceding expedients, e.g. *yek ketāb-ī*. Similarly in plural: (a) *ketābhā-ī*, (b) *yek ketābhā*, (c) *yek ketābhā-ī* 'books'.[87] The first way is used in colloquial language. Interesting is the position of the indefinite article with a further determined noun. If the noun follows a qualified adjective, two constructions are possible:

(a) the enclitic particle is affixed to the noun, that is to say, to the end of the whole group: *ketāb-e kamyāb-ī* 'a rare book';
(b) the enclitic particle is affixed to the noun and the adjective is without izaphat: *ketāb-ī kamyāb*. If the noun is determined by another noun, a qualifying one, the article *-ī* is attached

---

[86] The literary Persian language has no definite article but the colloquial language uses in the function of definite article the stressed suffix *-e*; it occurs only in singular and is facultative (e.g. *pasar* 'young man' — *pasare* 'the young man'). It may be cumulated with a demonstrative pronoun, e.g. *īn pasare* 'the (this) young man' (= whom we are speaking about). The preposition *az* is used as a certain kind of partitive article, e.g. *čerā az īn zabānhā harf mīzanand ke ...* 'pourquoi parlent-ils de telles langues, qui ...' (literally: de ces langues qui ...). Or: *az īn qabīl čīzhā* 'des choses de ce genre' (literally: de ce genre de choses). For details cf. G. Lazard, *Grammaire du persan contemporain*(Paris, 1957).

[87] The function of the indefinite article in singular and plural is, however, not identical. The indefinite article in singular means indefiniteness and at the same time unity: *ketāb* 'book' — *ketāb-ī*, *yek ketāb-/ī/* 'a book' (= whatsoever). The indefinite article in plural means only indeterminedness: *ketābhā-ī*, *jek ketābhā/-ī/* 'des livres, certains livres'.

to the end of the group: *tādž-e zar-ī* 'une couronne d'or' — 'a golden crown'. The indefinite article *yek* can precede the whole group: *yek ketāb-e kamyāb-ī* 'a rare book', *yek tādž-e zar* 'une couronne d'or' — 'a golden crown'.

Tajik[88] expresses indeterminedness or singularity of the object by means of the unstressed suffix *-e*, e.g. *odam-e* 'a (certain) man', *sol-e* 'a (certain) year'. In the role of indefinite article is also used the numeral *jak* 'one', e.g. *jak kampir bud, du pisar došt* 'there once was an old woman; she had two sons'; *kī guft? — Jak odam* 'who told you? — A man'.

The suffix *-e* is also used, if the noun is followed by an attributive subordinate sentence which modifies it. In such a case its function can be defined as a selective one, that is to say one definite object is selected out of a number of similar objects so that later (in the subordinate sentence) one of its characteristic features might be designated and thereby concretized, e.g. *duxtare, ki xozir in džo bud, dar nazdikī az Todžikiston omad* 'the girl who was just here, recently came from Tajikistan'. Adjectives usually do not have *-e*. In the attributive izaphat construction *-e* is admittedly added to adjectives (so far as it is added to the last word) but semantically it refers not to the adjective but rather to the whole construction, e.g. *daraxti balande* 'a (certain) tall tree'. However, if the adjective extends its function into a phrase, if it substitutes the omitted noun (substitutive use of adjectives), the adjective assumes all grammatical characteristics of nouns, i.e. the category of number and determinedness vs. indeterminedness, e.g. *nazdikoni vaj dar kišlok mondand* 'his relatives stayed in the village'.

Though Tajik possesses no definite article it can, at least to a limited extent, in a certain case express determinedness by means of flexion (cf. type E 1).

To this type belongs partly also the language of the Afghan Khasars (Yakaulang dialect).[89] In addition to the numeral *yak* 'one' (e.g. *yak kitōp* 'a book', *yak bōča* 'a boy') the indetermined-

---

[88] Cf. V. S. Rastorgueva, "A Short Sketch of Tajik Grammar", *IJAL* 29: 4, Part II (The Hague, 1963), 19-21.
[89] Cf. V. A. Jefimov, *Jazyk afganskix Xazara* (Moskva, 1965), 27.

ness or singularity of an object is expressed in this language by
means of *yak* + unstressed *-i* (identical with the izaphat *-i*), e.g.
*yak rŭz da dašt rōfta budum, didum, ki da yak jō-i zimi čarčuqur
šuda* ... 'When I came to the steppe (and) saw that on one place
the ground (is) turned ...' Without *yak*, *-i* is used only very rarely,
e.g. *tawassut-i ar kudam az i ōr sē-i mŭ zimin-a mōla kada mitani* 'By
means of each of these three (machines) we can harrow the ground'.

In some cases the indefinite article *-i* may be added not only
to nouns but also to other *nomina* (e.g. to adjectives) which are
subjected to substantivization, e.g. *dit, ki qatčučō-i az i jak siyō-i
kaṭa xaṵ kada* 'Simurgh saw that something large, black was
sleeping with its young ones'.

Similar to Tajik, determinedness can, to a limited extent, be
expressed by flexion (cf. type E I).

In Beludji[90] the category of indeterminedness (singularity) is
expressed by means of an unstressed *-ē*, e.g. *aspē* 'a horse', *dāstē*
'a hand'.

There are many languages in which the function of the indefinite
article is performed by the numeral 'one'. It is difficult to determine when a numeral and when an article is concerned. Perhaps
in those languages in which it is used very regularly a certain
tendency toward the function of an article may be admitted,
especially when the numeral 'one' is modified in some way as it
is, for example, in the Brāhūī language[91] where a shortened form
of the numeral *asī* 'one', *-as*, is suffixed to the noun, e.g. *bandagh-as*
'a man', *bandaghas-e* 'to a man'. In this case one can evidently
speak about an article.

In the dialect of Braj Bhākhā or Antarvēdī[92] the enclitic particle *ē* is used as indefinite article: *jānē-kau* 'of a certain man',
naukarē 'a servant'.

[90] Cf. *Jazyki narodov SSSR* I., 329.
[91] Cf. G. A. Grierson, *Linguistic Survey of India* 4 (Calcutta, 1906), 622.
This language is spoken in the provinces of Sarawan and Jhalawan in Ba-
luchistan.
[92] Spoken, according to Grierson (vol. 9, part 1), in the southern part of
Agra, in the larger part of Bharapur, in Dholpur and Karauli, in the western
part of Gwalior, and in the east of Jaipur.

In the Indonesian language Fordate[93] (Ambon-Timor group) the indefinite article is represented by the postpositive numeral *isaa* 'one', e.g. *tomat'isaa* 'a man', in plural by the indefinite numeral *bokoe*. If a noun is determined by situation etc., it expresses determinedness. If it is not determined, it has the indefinite article (both in singular and in plural). Consequently, *tomatta nmaa* means 'the man comes' and not 'a man comes', whereas *tomat'isaa nmaa* means 'a man comes'. In plural, *tomatta rmaa* means not 'some men came' but 'the men came'.

D. LANGUAGES IN WHICH THE CATEGORY OF DETERMINEDNESS VS. INDETERMINEDNESS IS INHERENT IN THE NOUN ITSELF OR IN ANOTHER WORD CATEGORY

Raoul de la Grasserie (cf. op. cit. p. 320) speaks in this case about a latent article. As example may be given modern Persian[94] where the singular of nouns can designate:

1. Indetermined quantity, e.g. *pul dāram* 'j'ai de l'argent' — 'I have money'; *ketāb hast* 'Es gibt ein Buch' — 'There is a book'.
2. determined unity, e.g. *zan* 'the woman'. Colloquial speech uses here the definite article in the form of a stressed enclitic *-e*, e.g. *zan-e*; this suffix may be cumulated with a demonstrative: *in zane* 'this woman'.

The plural of nouns may designate, according to situation:

1. Determined plurality, e.g. *zanān* or *zanhā* 'the (mentioned) woman'.
2. Indetermined plurality, e.g. *zanhā* "des femmes" — 'some women' (a certain number of women).

From this follows that the noun in Persian has, both in singular and in plural, a double value: it is either definite or indefinite. *Ketāb* means 'livre, un livre, le livre (en question)' — 'book, a

---

[93] Cf. P. Drabbe, "Spraakkunst der Fordaatsche taal", *VBG* 67: 1 (1926), 7.
[94] Cf. Gilbert Lazard, *Grammaire du persan contemporain* (Paris, 1957), 58-61.

book, the book (in question)'; *ketāb-hā* means 'livres, des livres, les livres (en question)' — '(some) books, the books (in question)'.

To make things clear we must add that Persian has an indefinite but not a definite article. It is interesting to observe that for the expression of the function of the indefinite article Persian has three expedients as we have already mentioned in pp. 162 f. Thus we can conclude that indeterminedness is a marked feature of the opposition determinedness vs. indeterminedness whereas determinedness which is inherent in simple noun forms is an unmarked feature of that opposition. In other languages there are different situations: there are languages in which the word stem is regarded as marked, in other languages as unmarked. Or, determination can occur in plural in opposition to singular, or *vice versa*, in singular in opposition to plural.

In Albanian the word stem serves as indetermined singular whereas the indetermined plural has a postpositive indetermined article, e.g. *mal* 'a mountain' — *male* 'mountains'. The postpositive definite article is both in singular and in plural, e.g. *mali* 'the mountain' — *malet* 'the mountains'. Consequently, Albanian must be classed with type E I as there is a differentiation of the nominative and accusative singular of determined nouns whereas indetermined nouns lack that differentiation. The situation in Albanian is further complicated by the so-called deictic article.

We have quoted three Balkan languages, Bulgarian, Rumanian and Albanian, as having at least one enclitic article. All three languages have an enclitic definite article, they differ only in the form of the indefinite article: Rumanian has an independent indefinite article, Albanian has an enclitic definite article and Bulgarian has no indefinite article. This likeness and geographical situation offer a comparison of these three languages: it was done by D. Michov[95] and in our opinion it will be useful to mention here at least his conclusions:

---

[95]   D. Michov, "Die Anwendung des bestimmten Artikels im Rumänischen, verglichen mit der im Albanesischen und Bulgarischen", *XIV Jahresbericht des Instituts für rumänische Sprache zu Leipzig* (Leipzig, 1908), 108-110.

1. In Albanian the article is used with all proper names, in Rumanian with feminine proper names and with all geographical names, whereas Bulgarian lacks the article in all these cases.
2. A more frequent use of generic article in Rumanian, its limited use in Bulgarian.
3. Article is used with words in titles in Rumanian, omitted in Albanian and Bulgarian.
4. Omission of article with absolute nouns after a preposition (except *cu*) in Rumanian, whereas in Albanian the article is omitted only after certain prepositions and after nouns determined by an attribute; generally there is liking for forms without article after prepositions. In Bulgarian the article can be used with an absolute *nomen* after all prepositions but there is a still greater liking for articleless forms after prepositions.
5. Prepositive article exists in Rumanian and Albanian but not in Bulgarian.
6. Predominance of the determinative significance of attributive complement in Rumanian as well as the originally only determinative significance of possessive pronoun, ordinal numeral and superlative which require a regular use of article. Likewise in Albanian where, however, the article with a noun, but not independent article, may be dropped.

   A different situation is in Bulgarian where the qualificatory significance seems to be more common. The more frequent is, however, the omission of article with an attributively determined *nomen*, especially with proper names and compound geographical designations.
7. The use of article in Rumanian and Bulgarian with nouns to which the article relates and which precede a demonstrative pronoun, and omission of article if a noun follows a demonstrative pronoun. In Albanian the use of article with *nomina* followed by a demonstrative pronoun.
8. In Rumanian, as well as in Albanian, the use of article with a *nomen* standing in certain idioms when addressing but always the omission of article in Bulgarian.

9. Predominance of articulated forms in Rumanian which is explained from the determinative significance (cf. point 6) of the attributive complement, whereas in Bulgarian absolute forms predominate.

10. Predominance of articulated forms in Rumanian and Albanian in titles and inscriptions and non-verbal expressions, in Bulgarian mostly absolute forms being used.

11. The effort to use always the article with the subject *nomen* in Rumanian especially when it is closely determined, a less frequent use of article in Albanian, nearly only articleless form in Bulgarian (with the exception of the cases when a quite definite person or thing is concerned).

12. Nearly exclusive use of the article with the forms following adverbs of comparison in Rumanian, the use of absolute forms in Albanian and Bulgarian.

13. The deictic significance of article is very rare in Bulgarian.

14. Also the possessive meaning of article which explains the lack of article with absolute family names in Bulgarian whereas in Rumanian and Albanian article is always used.

15. A frequent occurrence of the distributive significance of article in Rumanian and Albanian (the formation of adverbs of time) but only an insignificant use of this kind of article in Bulgarian.

16. Liking for the forms with article as common forms in Rumanian, whereas in Albanian and Bulgarian there is nearly no evidence of their use.

17. Liking for the use of article in Bulgarian as means of expressing feeling.

In Azerbaijani the simple form of nouns also implies indetermination (in nominative and accusative) but besides, it is possible to use the indefinite article *bir*. To express determination either a special form is used (if the direct object is to be expressed it is the definite case of the object -/n/U), or it is understood from the context and from the absence of special indefinite words such as *bir* (cf. types A III and E I). *Bir* in the function of indefinite article is unstressed whereas in the function of the numeral 'one' it is not only stressed but also followed (as the other numerals) by classificators or units of measure or count.[96]

The latent article with proper names can be regarded as nearly universal. If we say 'Charles was there', we mean a definite, concrete person. Only comparatively rare in languages is the use of article with proper names. This is, for example, in Albanian, where proper names have the article but lose it in vocative or in connection with the indication of the situation or employment of the person in question. Here the indication has the definite article and forms with the name a unit, e.g. *Lek kovači* 'the smith Alexander'.

A simple situation is in the Dravidian language Kurukh[97] where in the case of masculine nouns there are two bases: a simple one used to express indeterminedness and the basis with the suffix *-as* expressing determinedness, e.g. *āl* 'a man' — *āl-as* 'the man'. Both bases are inflected in exactly the same way.

E. LANGUAGES IN WHICH THE CATEGORY OF DETERMINEDNESS VS. INDETERMINEDNESS IS EXPRESSED BY FLEXION

I. The Category of Determinedness vs. Indeterminedness Is Expressed by the Flexion of Nouns

This way of expressing determinedness or indeterminedness is fairly frequent among languages of the world. Thus, e.g., in many Altaic languages accusative designates a certain, definite object, whereas for an indetermined object the basic form with a zero suffix, i.e. nominative, is used.

Let us discuss the situation in Turkish. The definite accusative in Turkish has the suffix *-i/ı/ü/u*, e.g. *bahçeyi gördüm* 'I saw the garden'. For the indefinite accusative, on the other hand, there is no ending but instead the indefinite article *bir* is used, e.g. *bir*

---

[96] Cf. Fred W. Householder Jr. and Mansour Lofti, *Basic Course in Azerbaijani* (= *Uralic and Altaic Series*, 45) (Indiana University Publications, Bloomington — The Hague, 1965), 26.

[97] Cf. G. A. Grierson, *Linguistic Survey of India*, vol. 4, 412. Kurukh is a Dravidian language spoken by about 1/2 mil. people in Bengal.

bahçe gŏrdŭm 'I saw a garden'. Similarly in the other Turkish languages. Let us quote, for example, Uzbek where the definite article has the ending *-ni*, e.g. *paxta* 'cotton' — *paxtani* 'the cotton' (accus.); *dost* 'friend' — *dostni* 'the friend' (accus.); *ot* 'horse' — *otlar* 'horses' — *otlarni* 'the horses' (accus. pl.). It is interesting to observe that in colloquial speech the determinative suffix is sometimes combined with the possessive suffix of the 3rd person singular *-si*, e.g. *ota* 'father' — *otasin* '(his) father' (accus.). In Kirgiz the object of the transitive verb is in general case (i.e. nominative has a zero ending and equals accusative), if it is indefinite or general. Cf. *bir alma jedim* 'I ate an apple' (= any apple) — *bir almanĭ jedim* 'I ate the apple' (= a specific apple) — *almanĭ jedim* 'I ate the apple'; or: *čay ičtim* 'I drank tea' — *čaydĭ ičtim* 'I drank the tea'. The forms in *-nĭ* and *-dĭ* are definite accusative forms. A noun in general case without the modificator *bir* may be either definite or indefinite according to the context but, as a rule, it is definite. If it occurs with the modificator *bir*, the construction is always indefinite. On the other hand, if a noun has the object suffix *-ni* and is not accompanied by the word *bir*, the construction is definite. Compare:

> *bir kara at aldĭm* 'I bought a black horse'
> *kara atnĭ aldĭm* 'I bought the black horse'
> *kara at aldĭm* 'I bought (the, a) black horse'.

In Chuvash the so-called objective relational morpheme combines most dative and accusative features of other languages or the function of direct and oblique object (hence its name). In Chuvash that suffix is *-/n/a*, e.g. *arman* 'mill' — *armana* 'to a mill', 'the mill' (accus.); *alăk* 'door' — *alăka* 'to a door, the door' (accus.); *ĕne* 'cox' — *ĕnene* 'to a cow, the cow' (accus.). If the object is general or unspecified, the zero suffix is used, if it is specified and definite, the case with the corresponding suffix is used. Indefinite accusative is then homonymous with the so-called absolute case.

In Tatar, indeterminedness is expressed by the numeral *ber* 'one', determinedness by the demonstrative pronoun *tege* 'the'. Nouns designating an indetermined object are used in the indefinite case, determined objects are designated by nouns in accusative case.

Another language possessing a determinative declension of nouns is Mordvin. Raoul de la Grasserie (op. cit. pp. 316-317) gives a complete paradigm of two declensions: determined and indetermined. The indicator of determination in singular is *t*, in plural *mä*; *ava* 'woman' has the following declension:

	singular	
	indetermined	determined
nomin.	*ava*	*ava-š*
gen.	*ava-ng*	*ava-t*
incessive	*ava-sa*	*ava-te-sa*
elative	*ava-sta*	*ava-te-sta*
illative	*ava-s*	*ava-t-s*
ablative	*ava-da*	*ava-te-tzda*
adlative	*ava-ŭ*	*ava-te-ŭ*
abessive	*ava-ftima*	*ava-te-ftima*
translative	*ava-ks*	*ava-te-ks*

	plural	
	indetermined	determined
nomin.	*ava-t*	*ava-t-nd*
gen.	*ava-t-nen*	*ava-te-nen*
incessive	*ava-sa-t*	*ava-te-nene-sa*
elative	*ava-sta-t*	*ava-te-nene-sta*
illative	*ava-s-t*	*ava-t-nene-s*
ablative	*ava-t-da*	*ava-t-nene-zda*
adlative	*ava-to-ŭ*	
abessive	*ava-to-ftima*	
translative	*ava-ko-t*	

The indicator *nä*, plural *næ* is a demonstrative pronoun.

In the Erza language[98] there are also two declensions of nouns: the basic and the definite declension. The basic declension of the word *kudo* '(a) house':

---

[98] Cf.. *Jazyki narodov SSSR III*, 180.

	Singular
nom.	*kudo*
gen.	*kudoň*
dat.	*kudoneň*
abl.	*kudodo*
iness.	*kudoso*
el.	*kudosto*
ill.	*kudos*
prol.	*kudova*
compar.	*kudoška*
abess.	*kudovtomo*
transl.	*kudoks*

The definite declension of the word *kudo-s* 'the house':

	singular	plural
nom.	*kudos'*	*kudotne*
gen.	*kudont'*	*kudotneň*
dat.	*kudonteň*	*kudotneneň*
abl.	*kudodont'*	*kudotnede*
iness.	*kudosont'*	*kudotnese*
el.	*kudostont'*	*kudotneste*
ill.	*kudonteň*	*kudotneneň (-tnes)*
prol.	*kudovant'*	*kudotneva*
compar.	*kudoškant'*	*kudotneška*
abess.	*kudovtomont'*	*kudotnevteme*

In the Drakin dialect of Erza-Mordvin[99] as well as in the Mokša literary language[100] the so-called determinative declension has three cases, nominative, genitive, and dative, both in singular and in plural. The singular suffixes have their origin in demonstrative pronouns, the plural suffixes are composed of two components: of the plural indicator and of the indicator of determination which is represented by the demonstrative pronoun *ne* 'this, these':

    alaša '(a) horse'.

[99] A. V. Jakuškin, *Osobennosti morfologii drakinskogo dialekta erzja-mor-dovskogo jazyka* (Saransk, 1959).
[100] Cf. *Jazyki narodov SSSR III*, 203-204.

determinative declension

	singular	plural
nom.	*alašas'* 'the horse'	*alašatne* 'the horses'
gen.	*alašat'*	*alašatneň*
dat.	*alašati*	*alašatnendi*

According to the opinion of some scholars the Finno-Ugric primitive language had the accusative suffix *-m* which has been preserved in a number of Finno-Ugric languages, e.g. in the abovementioned Mordvin, further in Cheremis, Finnic *(-m > -n)* and in Lapp. Beside Volga Finnic languages it has been preserved in a number of Vogul dialects as well. It also occurs in nearly all Samoyed languages and therefore it is regarded as Uralic. The question of the determinative declension is subject of N. Sebestyén's paper.[101] The determinative declension has in morphological respect one feature common to these languages: as the basic word in all cases occurs the simple form of nouns having the possessive suffix of the 3rd pers. sing. and used in a determinative sense. As a concrete case the Samoyed language of Nenets can be named: there the noun forms provided with possessive suffixes (especially 3rd pers. sing.) can, according to the context, express either the possessor or the definite article. Thus, for example, the word *hal'eda* means not only 'his fish' but also 'the fish' (the possessive suffix being here *-da*).[102] From that follows that in Nenets three determinative declensions can be distinguished: 1. nominative forms and identical unmarked accusative forms, 2. accusative forms with the suffix *-m*, and 3. the dative form. It is significant that the determinative word forms of this kind occur only in certain sentence types: 1. in imperative sentences whose predicate is the imperative form of the verb; 2. in exhortative and optative sentences whose predicate is the form of the precative or optative

[101] N. Sebestyén, "Zur Frage der determinierenden Deklination im Yuraksamojedischen", *Acta linguistica academiae scientiarum hungaricae* X (1960), fasc. 1-2, 55-93.
[102] Cf. Péter Hajdú, *The Samoyed Peoples and Languages* (= *Uralic and Altaic Series* 14) (Indiana University Publications, Bloomington - The Hague, 1963).

of the verb; 3. in sentences expressing a wish, or intention, and whose predicate is the conditional of the verb; 4. in sentences expressing a wish, intention, fulfilled request, sometimes also a need, and whose predicate is the indicative form of the verb. The author then tries to solve the question of the essence of the demonstrative declension, the characteristic features of the basic development of those three categories and that which differentiates them from the corresponding forms of the possessive declension. In her opinion the essence of the determinative declension is intelligible on the grounds of a syntactic relation of the determinated nominal forms to the predicative verb: in all three categories the forms documented in the text express, by their relation to the predicative verb, some *desideratum*. Such relations may often express, as the author shows, the fact that the wished-for object has just come over into the ownership of the person designated by the morphological element, or that a certain wished-for state has just set in. In a similar way Edit Vertés[103] points to the syntactic relation of determination to the predicate. That is to say, she emphasizes that in those Finno-Ugric languages which do not have in all their dialects the accusative suffix, there is another possibility of turning the attention of the hearer to the definiteness of the accusative object: the predicate may point to the definiteness of an accusative complement by its being expressed in objective (not subjective) conjugation. Even in Hungarian it is just the objective conjugation which in the first place points to the determinedness of the accusative object, as the accusative suffix of both the definite and indefinite object is -*t*. In Vogul,[104] Ostyak, and

---

[103] Cf. Edit. Vertés, "Beiträge zur Frage des finnisch-ugrischen bezeichneten Akkusativobjekts", *Acta linguistica academiae scientiarum hungaricae* X (1960), fasc. 1-2, 180-194.

[104] In Vogul (Mansi) the category of determinedness vs. indeterminedness of nouns is expressed in a very complicated way so that this language should be classed either with some special group or with several groups simultaneously. That is to say, in this language the determinedness vs. indeterminedness is expressed both by means of cases and by means of verb conjugation and in some cases by means of ancillary words. Determinedness of the word-subject of an action is expressed by the form of additive, determinedness of the word-object of an action is expressed by the form of instrumental but it may

Mordvin the objective conjugation is also used when the accusative object is definite. That the possessive suffix does not always indicate possession only but very strongly intervenes in the area of genuine determination is testified — as also shown by Edit Vertés in the above mentioned paper — by the fact that possessive suffixes with names do often so little indicate the possessive relation that there can even be a number of possessive suffixes which do not belong to the same person. Kellgren[105] writes that in Finnic the possessive suffix points to genuine possessiveness only by means of the genitive, otherwise it has only a determinative function. Thus *hän otti miekkansa* has the approximate meaning 'he took the sword'. If the possessivity is to be emphasized it is necessary to use, in addition to the suffixed pronoun, the possessive pronoun (genitive personal pronoun) too: 'it is his sword, it belongs to him': *se on hänen miekkansa*, not only *se on miekkansa*. 'He took a sword' means *hän otti miekkan*. There are still more languages in which the possessive suffix is also article. To give at least one such language, we will mention Armenian (cf. p. 142).

In Tungus there are two accusatives: one with the ending -*a*, -*ja* which in many cases is used partitively (e.g. *mō* 'wood' — the partitive accusative *mōja*), and another determinative with the suffix -*wa* whose labial is dependent on the preceding sound so that we have the forms -*wa*, -*ma*, -*ba*, or -*pa*, e.g. *hunāt* 'the girl', accus. *hunātpa*, pl. *hunilba*, *hunilwa*.[106]

In Paleosibirian languages Aljator and Koryak there is a double declension of nouns.[107] To declension I (basic) belong the nouns

---

also be grammatically without any form if it is expressed by the objective form of the verb conjugation. In some cases the expression of definite vs. indefinite subject or object of an action is realized by means of articles. The definite article *анъ* is used with nouns already mentioned before, in the first mention of the object the indefinite article *akv* is used. Cp. also E. I. Rombandeeva, "Mansijskij jazyk", *Jazyki narodov SSSR* III, 347.

[105] Kellgren, *Grundzüge der finnischen Sprache*, 74.

[106] Cf. G. J. Ramstedt, *Einführung in die altaische Sprachwissenschaft* I (Helsinki, 1952), 30.

[107] Cf. *Jazyki narodov SSSR* V, 271, 274, 294, 296. The Aljutors live on the northeastern coast of the peninsula Kamchatka, the Koryak language belongs to the Chukchee-Kamchatkan group of Paleosibirian languages.

designating non-man and nouns designating an indefinite man, declension II (demonstrative, determinative) designates a definite, concrete man. The names of men (as for example in Koryak *appa* 'papa', *v'av'a* 'mama' etc. which always mean something definite) and proper names of people are declined only according to declension II. The second declension differs from the first one by the presence of the suffix -*na*-.

Of Caucasian languages we will mention here the West Circassian (Adygei), and East Circassian (Kabardian). In Adygei[108] the definite form of nouns is expressed by the morphemes -*r* and -*m*, whereas the indefinite form has a zero indicator: *une* '(a) house' — *une-r* 'the house'. The category of determinedness vs. indeterminedness is not expressed in nouns that have a generic meaning. The morphemes -*r*, -*m* do not express determinedness in nouns expressing an abstract concept, in proper nouns and also in the nouns designating unique objects (*tyge* 'sun', *maze* 'moon', etc.). The category of determinedness vs. indeterminedness is missing in plural; however, it is expressed by the context.

In Kabardian[109] there are two forms of nouns: definite and indefinite. The indicators of definiteness are, like in Adygei, the morphemes -*r* and -*m*. Indefiniteness is expressed by the absence of affixes. Nouns in definite form have three cases: nominative *(-r)*, ergative case *(-m)*, and instrumental *(-čIe)*. Nouns in indefinite form have only the endings of the instrumental case.

To this group may also be added the expression of determinedness and indeterminedness by means of different nominal-verbal forms in Turkish though it could also be classed with subtype III of this group which includes the expression of the category of determinedness by means of verbal forms. As is well known, Turkish is a strongly nominal language. Definite and indefinite forms occur in Turkish in the present, past, and future participle. Examples:

(a) indefinite present participle:

---

108   Cf. *Jazyki narodov SSSR* IV, 148-149.
109   Cf. *Jazyki narodov SSSR* IV, 168.

sőylemek 'to tell, speak': *çok sőyler bir adam* (aorist stem) 'a much speaking man';
(b) definite present participle:
gelen adam 'the coming man';
(c) indefinite past participle:
çok gőrműş bir adam (aorist stem) 'a man who has seen much';
(d) definite past participle:
gelmiş olan vapur 'the steamer that has come';
(e) indefinite future participle:
Italya'ya uçacak bir tayyare 'a plane which will go to Italy'.
— *Almanya'dan gelecek posta* (future stem), 'the post that will come from Germany';
(f) definite future participle:
gelecek olan vapurdan bir haberiniz var mı? 'Have you any news about the steamer that will come?'

In colloquial speech only two participles are usually used: the definite present participle for the present and past action and indefinite future participle for the future tense (both definite and indefinite).

Let us once more return to the expression of determinedness and indeterminedness of the object in accusative. This phenomenon is namely not limited to Uralic and Altaic languages only. It can be found in Iranian languages as well. Such is the case of Modern Persian where the definite object is expressed by the postposition *-rā* whereas the indefinite object is expressed without this postposition. For example, *īn bāghrā mībīnam* 'I see this garden', but *bādaz šām čāī va qahve jā ābe ğau mījāvarand* 'After supper they serve tea, coffee, or beer'.

The Iranian language Vaygalī belonging to the group of Kafir (i.e. West-Dardic) languages which is spoken in the area of Nuristan in Afghanistan expresses determination by placing the noun (direct object) in oblique case which has the endings *-ä, -ə* (after a consonant), *-ō* (after *-ä*) and *-ē* (after *-ī*) and the plural *-ã̃, -ũ̃, -ẽ̃*. The noun in nominative expresses the function of a direct indefinite object: *narī ãw yām* 'I am eating bread'. Besides, indefiniteness is expressed by the proclitic article *e* and the numeral *ew*, *ĕk* 'one'. The noun in an oblique case has the function of direct object, if it expresses a definite, determinated object, e.g. *gurō grằtilom* 'I bind the horse'. Likewise in Prasun, belonging to the same group of languages, the category of determinedness is expressed by means of the direct or oblique case of the noun in the function of the direct object in dependence on its concrete or abstract meaning; even here the indefinite article (*ate[k/g]*, oblique case *ategiš*) is used. Similar conditions are in central Dardic languages Gavar, Tirakhi and Khovar.[110] However, these languages have, in addition, the indefinite and definite article (see type A I, B, A I). The language of the Afghan Khazars (cf. V. A. Jefimov, op. cit. sub *[89]*, pp. 72-73) has a double object: definite and indefinite. The definite object is expressed by the enclitic *-a/-ra*, the indefinite object without that enclitic.

In some Slavic languages the vocative suffix seems to express determinedness, e.g. in Czech *člověk* 'man' — vocative *člověče!*, *žena* 'woman', — voc. *ženo!*, in Serbo-Croatian *momak* 'young man' — voc. *momče!*, *žena* 'woman' — voc. *ženo!*, in Polish *wuj* 'uncle' — voc. *wuju!*, *panna* 'virgin, young lady' — voc. *panno!* However, we cannot but express strong doubts about that. It can be argued that vocative is beyond sentence construction, that it stands on a level different from that of other cases. In addition, it has also a different emotive flavour. Rather different is the situation in Bulgarian which has the postpositive article in all cases except vocative. Does it mean that in Bulgarian the vocative itself implies determinedness so that it needs no more the postpositive article? If it is so then it explains and confirms the determinedness of vocative in other Slavic languages. After all, we can name even other languages, e.g. German and English in which nouns used in addressing have no article. In Old Slavonic the opposition of determinedness and indeterminedness is manifested in the nouns of masculine gender in the contradiction of *o*-stem and *u*-stem doublets. The *u*-stem forms express indeterminedness.

---

[110] D. I. Edel'man, *Dardskie jazyki* (Moskva, 1965).

Thus, for example, the form *rabovi* corresponds with the Greek form τωδουλω, whereas the form *rabu* is a translation of the Greek δουλω. The opposition of determinedness and indeterminedness in Old Slavonic is also expressed in adjectives (by complex flexion).

II. The Category of Determinedness vs. Indeterminedness Is Expressed by the Flexion of Adjectives

In the preceding chapter we have mentioned the fact that in Old Slavonic the opposition of determinedness and indeterminedness is expressed by a complex flexion of adjectives. One of the most clean-cut representatives of this group is Serbo-Croatian. In this language adjectives have double forms: definite and indefinite. Definite adjectives have in nominative sing. masc. the ending *-i*, femin. *-a*, neut. *-o* after a hard consonant and *-e* after a soft consonant. For example, *dobri, dobra, dobro* (masc., femin., neut.) 'good'; *lijepi, lijepa, lijepo* 'beautiful'. Indefinite adjectives end in masculine gender in a consonant, in feminine in *-a*, in neuter in *-o* after a hard consonant and in *-e* after a soft consonant, e.g. *dobor, dobra, dobro*; *lijep, lijepa, lijepo*. As it may be seen, not all forms are different. Besides nominative sing. masc. there are different forms of genitive, dative, accusative, and locative masc., of genitive, dative, and locative sing. neut., whereas feminine gender and plural of all genders have identical forms of both definite and indefinite adjectives in all cases. Like indefinite adjectives are also declined the possessive adjectives in *-ov, -ev, -ljev*, and *-in*, e.g. *bratov, bratova, bratovo* 'of the brother, brother's, brotherly' (masc., femin., neut.), *očev, očeva, očevo* 'of the father, father's', *sestrin, sestrina, sestrino* 'of the sister, sister's' (masc., femin., neut.), etc. All adjectives do not possess both forms: some have only the definite, some only the indefinite form. The above mentioned adjectives in *-ov, -ev, -ljev*, and *-in* have only the indefinite form, whereas adjectives in *-ji, -čki, -ski*, and *-ški* have only the definite form, e.g. *dječji* 'child's, children's', *junački* 'heroic', *hrvatski* 'Croatian', as well as adjectives indicating place and time, e.g. *desni* 'genuine', *prednji* 'front' (adj.), *današnji* 'today's', etc.

According to de Braye in modern colloquial speech the use of indefinite adjectives becomes rather limited. Most frequently they are used predicatively in nominative.

In Slovenian the difference between indefinite and definite adjectives is limited to nominative and accusative singular masc. nouns, e.g. *dragi sin* 'the dear son', *novi klobuk* 'the new hat' — *drag sin* 'a dear son', *nov klobuk* 'a new hat'. In the other genders and numbers the opposition of definite and indefinite adjectives is neutralized, e.g. *draga sestra* means according to the context either 'the dear sister' or 'a dear sister'. In Slovenian, as well as in Serbo-Croatian, the adjective, if used predicatively, has indefinite forms. According to de Braye[111] in Slovenian most adjectives differentiate the definite forms from indefinite ones by intonation.

In Old English and in Old Germanic languages adjectives were declined in two different ways which are usually called "strong" and "weak" or "pronominal" and "nominal" or "indefinite" and "definite" declension. Adjectives were declined according to the nominal or weak declension when the noun, by which it was qualified, was definite, i.e. when it was connected with a definite article, or with a demonstrative or possessive pronoun. However, if the noun was without article, the adjective was declined according to the pronominal or strong declension. The two declensions have the following forms in Old English:

Indefinite (Pronominal or Strong) Declension

	Singular			Plural
	Masc.	Femin.	Neut.	
Nom.	*blind*	*blind*	*blind*	*blinde*
Gen.	*blindes*	*blindre*	*blindes*	*blindra*
Dat.	{ *blindum* / *blinde*	*blindre*	{ *blindum* / *blinde*	*blindum*
Accus.	*blindne*	*blinde*	*blind*	*blinde*

[111] R. G. A. de Braye, *Guide to Slavonic Languages* (London, 1951), 401.

Definite (Nominal or Weak) Declension

| | Singular | | | Plural |
	Masc.	Femin.	Neut.	
Nom.	*blinda*	*blinde*	*blinde*	*blindan*
Gen.	*blindan*	*blindan*	*blindan*	*blindra*
Dat.	*blindan*	*blindan*	*blindan*	*blindum*
Accus.	*blindan*	*blindan*	*blinde*	*blindan*

Thus, for example, 'a blind man' is in Old English *blind man*, 'the blind man' is *(se) blinda man*. Even when the Anglo-Saxon *se* cannot be regarded as an article but as a demonstrative pronoun, there is no doubt that the opposition of determinedness and indeterminedness is just inherent in the different declension of adjectives.

There are traces of the differentiation of determinedness and indeterminedness in the flexion of adjectives in Czech, e.g. *vévodův* 'the duke's' (adj.) in opposition to *vévody* (genitive of noun, indefinite) 'of a duke'. However, this difference seems to lose ground in the present-day language.

The problem of the so-called nominal determination is, in our opinion, very interesting just for its relation to the determination expressed by an independent definite article. Heinz Wissemann has devoted a thorough attention to this problem.[112] According to him the so-called "Bestimmtheitsform" in Lithuanian (i.e. definite forms of adjective) is a certain kind of determination[113] but in

---

[112] Heinz Wissemann, "Zur nominalen Determination", *Indogermanische Forschungen* 63: 1 (1957), 61-78.

[113] Another opinion regards the complex adjective in Lithuanian as an expression of emphasis. A. Valeckiene (*Kalba in literatūra* 2 [1957], 161 f.) accepts both opinions: the complex adjective in Lithuanian expresses both determination and emphasis. Pavel Trost ("O složeném adjektivu balto-slovanském" [On the complex adjective in Balto-Slavic], *Bulletin Ústavu ruského jazyka a literatury* X, 35-38) points out to the fact that the use of complex adjectives in Lithuanian does not square with the use of the (definite) article in languages possessing article. According to Trost, the complex adjective in Lithuanian is either determinative but not qualificative, or anaphoric. "It goes without saying", writes Trost (p. 37), "that in languages possessing

quite another way than in languages which possess art icle. Syntag as a whole is not determinated. In cases when languages possessing article determine by means of article a complex consisting of an attribute and a name to which it belongs, Lithuanian has mostly the indefinite form. An important complement of the concept of a kind of article has been proposed by Gamillscheg who has coined the term "Gelenkspartikel". Gamillscheg's starting point is Greek where article serving as a linking of noun and attributive complement has mostly the function of "Gelenkspartikel". This "Gelenkspartikel" can easily assume a genuine function of article, for instance the function of anaphoric article. Gamillscheg shows, for example, that the Latin pronoun *ille* has the function of the "Gelenkspartikel". Wissemann deducts from a certain evidence that the Lithuanian definite form has the function of a genuine "Gelenkspartikel". Similarly as the function of the Latin *ille*, the pronominal element of the definite form in Lithuanian makes the adjective psychologically independent, declining the attention from the whole complex to both parts. The author shows that even in Old Bulgarian there is a certain tendency in expression which leads to the "Gelenkspartikel". A strong favour of asyndeton and of forming "Gelenkspartikel" in Bulgarian and Slavic has evidently its origin in the same tendency. Wissemann further comes to the conclusion that a certain form of an independently standing adjective in Lithuanian and in Old Bulgarian mostly has the function of anaphoric article. It is true that in Old Bulgarian the "Gelenkspartikel" has functionally changed into anaphoric article but it has come out of use. The further Slavic development shows the full loss of the function of the pronominal element of definite forms as the means of expression of nominal determination — it becomes a genuine flexive ending.

Further it is necessary to stress with P. Trost (cf. op. cit. sub

---

article the determinative adjective need not be linked with the definite article but can be used with either the definite or the indefinite (zero) article. However, Lithuanian expressions having a compound (determinative) adjective often correspond to German compounds (e.g. *aukštoji mokykla* $=$ *Hochschule,* i.e. *die Hochschule* or *eine Hochschule*)".

[113], p. 37) the double use of compound adjectives in Lithuanian: when the adjective differentiates a couple of objects (classes or individuals) and when the adjective has a substantival validity. In the first case the adjective is, according to Trost, undoubtedly strongly determinative. The other case is rather obscure: the compound adjective does not determine the noun but substitutes it; such a use seems to have been separated from the anaphoric function, not *vice versa*.

Different from Lithuanian is the situation in Latvian where the identification of the compound adjective with definite article is being accepted as correct (cf. Trost, op. cit. p. 38). Whereas in languages possessing article the article with a possessive pronoun is suppressed, in Latvian the compound adjective is linked with the possessive pronoun. The situation, in Trost's opinion, refutes every doubt about the fact that the Old Slavic compound adjective expresses determination in the sense of definite article.

III. *The Category of Determinedness vs. Indeterminedness Is Expressed in Verbal Forms*

To this subtype belongs, in the first place, the Hungarian language which, however, as we have already seen, belongs to subtype AI as well (cf. p. 82 f.). This language possesses three kinds of conjugation[114]: 1. subjective, 2. middle or *-ik* conjugation used with certain verbal roots instead of subjective conjugation, and 3. objective conjugation. The subjective form (or its functional equivalent, the middle conjugation with words that require it instead of subjective conjugation) is used when a vaguely defined object of action is concerned, whereas the objective form (with an expressed object or without it) indicates the existence of a direct object.

The subjective conjugation is used, according to Hall, when

1. the verb has an intransitive meaning, e.g. *megyek* 'I go';
2. when a specific direct object is not intended, e.g. *mit csinálsz?* *nézek* 'what are you doing? I am looking';

[114] Cf. Robert A. Hall Jr., *An Analytical Grammar of the Hungarian Language* (= *Language Monograph* 18) (Baltimore, 1938), 49, 90 ff.

3. the direct object is present but does not indicate a sharply defined object, e.g. *képeket nézek* 'I am looking at pictures (in general)';
4. the direct object is a pronoun which does not indicate any specific object, that is the interrogative pronoun or indefinite pronoun (with some exceptions), e.g. *mit olvasol? semmit sem olvasok* 'What are you reading? I am reading nothing';
5. the direct object is a personal pronoun or *mindnyáj-* of the first or second person sing. or plur., e.g. *Szeretsz-e minket? Mindnyájatokat szeretek* 'Do you like us? I like all of you'.

The objective conjugation is used when

1. no direct object is specified but is understood, e.g. *eszed* 'you eat it', *nézed-e a képet? nézem* 'Are you looking at the picture? I am looking at it';
2. if the direct object is indicated as clearly defined:
   (a) by the use of a proper name, e.g. *láto-d-e Palio bácsit?* 'Do you see Uncle Paul?'
   (b) with a noun by the presence of definite article, personal possessive suffix, attributively used demonstrative, or indefinite or interrogative pronoun designating a specific object or all-inclusive meaning (cf. *[c]*), e.g. *olvasom a hirlapot* 'I am reading the newspaper'; *eladom a künyvcimet* 'I sell my books'; *ezt a kőnyvet már régen olvastam* 'I read this book long ago'; *melyik hirlapot olvasod?* 'What newspaper are you reading?';
   (c) when the direct object is a personal pronoun or *mindnyáj-* in the third person sing. or plur., a reflexive pronoun, reciprocal pronoun, personal possessive pronoun, demonstrative pronoun or one of the indefinite and interrogative pronouns which designate a specific object or have all-inclusive meaning (*melyik* 'which?', *mind* 'every', *valamennyi* 'all whatsoever' and all indefinite pronouns ending in *-ik*), e.g. *ismerem őket* 'I know them'; *mindnyájukat szeretem* 'I like all of them'; *megőlte magát* 'he killed himself'; *szeressétek egymást* 'love one another'; *Jánoséit adtam vissza, az*

enyéimet tartottam meg 'I gave back John's, but kept my own'; *ezt olvasom* 'I am reading this'; *melyiket akarod? valamennyit akarom* 'which do you want? I want all of them';

3. when the direct object of the verb is a sentence introduced by a relative pronoun or *hogy* 'that', e.g. *nem tudom, hogy mit akaraz* 'I do not know what you want'.

Thus in Hungarian the formal expression of the category of determinedness covers the whole syntactic complex and as formal expedient is used the determinant with the noun and the determinant with the verb. Essentially, however, the category of determinedness is inherent in the noun itself, not in the objective conjugation which does not determine by itself. This can be concluded from the fact that the proper name is linked with the verb in an objective conjugation. This seems to be a case of congruence.

As we have already mentioned, the definite declension is used with a definite accusative object in Vogul, Ostyak, and Mordvin. In the Samoyed languages such as Nenets, Selkup, Nganasan, and Enets there exists an indefinite tense which expresses an action in which the hearer does not take part, for example in the Selkup language: *Kup tüŋa* 'the man came'.[115] Likewise in Dogrib, an American language of the Athapaskan group as well as in Apache and Chipewyan the category of determinedness is expressed by verbal forms, that is by prefixes.[116]

The category of determinedness vs. indeterminedness is in a limited way connected with the verb in Welsh. In negative sentences as well as in interrogative and conditional sentences the verb *oes* 'to be' (and not *y mae* or *yw*) is used with indefinite nouns (see examples in type A II).

---

[115] Cf. *Jazyki narodov SSSR* III, 407, 421.
[116] Cf. W. Davidson, *A Preliminary Analysis of Active Verbs in Dogrib* (= *Studies in the Athapaskan Languages*, University of California Publications in Linguistics 29) (Berkeley and Los Angeles, 1963), 48-55.

F. DETERMINEDNESS VS. INDETERMINEDNESS IS EXPRESSED
BY STRESS OR INTONATION

To this type belongs Ossetic[117] where determinedness is expressed
by shifting the stress to the first syllable, if it is normally on the
second syllable. For example, *bælás* '(a) tree' — *bǽlas* 'the tree';
bydýr '(a) field' — *býdyr* 'the fields'; *færǽt* '(an) ax' — *fǽræt* 'the
ax'. If an attributive adjective is added, stress is shifted one syllable
back in an expression of indeterminedness and two syllables back
in an expression of determinedness; consequently *cyrgъ færǽt* '(A)
sharp ax' — *cýrgъ færæt* 'the sharp ax'. This phenomenon is
historically connected with the past existence of the definite article *i*
which in the Digor language has been preserved up to the present
day. It is necessary to suggest that the contrast between definiteness
and indefiniteness cannot be expressed in the case of nouns that
are stressed on the first syllable.

A language belonging partly to this group is Slovene where,
according to de Braye (op. cit. sub *[111]*, p. 401), most adjectives
differentiate the definite form from the indefinite one by intonation.

Finnic, in addition to grammatical and lexical expedients uses
stress to express indeterminedness. According to L. Hakulinen[118]
indeterminedness is expressed by a stronger stress, that is by a
dynamic accent, whereas determinedness is indirectly expressed
by an unstressed word. Examples (the strongest stress is indicated
by a dot after the vowel of the first syllable): *Uu·si py·rstőtähti on
lő·ytynyt* 'There was discovered a new comet' (i.e. any comet). —
Uusi pyrstőtähti on lő·ytynyt 'A new comet was discovered'; *Maa·
njäristys Kaakkois-Euroopassa* 'An earthquake in south-eastern
Europe' (i.e. there was unexpectedly an earthquake in south-
eastern Europe). — *Maanjäristys Kaa·kkois Euroopassa(kin)* 'An
earthquake (even) in south-eastern Europe' (i.e. an earthquake has
already been in another place).

---

[117] Cf. M. I. Isaev, "Osetinskij jazyk", *Jazyki narodov SSSR* I, 241. Also
V. I. Abaev, *A Grammatical Sketch of Ossetic* (Bloomington - The Hague,
1964), 12.
[118] L. Hakulinen, *Razvitije i struktura finskogo jazyka* II (Moskva, 1955),
181-196.

G. LANGUAGES WITHOUT ARTICLE

A typology of languages based on the occurrence of the category of determinedness vs. indeterminedness cannot ignore a considerable number of languages which apparently do not express this category or express it only weakly, marginally. We will now discuss some languages in which this category is latent or missing.

Let us begin with Indo-European languages. Most of them do express the category of determinedness vs. indeterminedness. To them belong, for example, most Iranian languages, Armenian, Greek, Albanian, the Baltic languages, Germanic, Romance, and Celtic languages. It is, however, missing partly in Slavic languages and nearly completely in Indian languages.

With the exception of Bulgarian[119] and of some Russian dialects Slavic languages possess no article. Serbo-Croatian admittedly expresses the category of determinedness, however not by means of an article but by means of a special declension of nouns. According to J. Kurz, Slavic languages had and partly still have the possibility of putting demonstrative pronouns in certain cases after the nouns, frequently enclitically. This use does not, however, testify to the fact that together with it a rudimentary use of demonstrative pronoun in postposition as an article is linked. The article has developed from them only later in the Balkan environment as one of the manifestations of the tendencies of development common to Balkan languages. For primitive Slavic it is not possible to presuppose the use of demonstrative pronouns in postposition (in connections occurring in the oldest texts of that language, e.g. *rodъ sъ* 'generation this', *rabъ tъ* 'servant the', *lъstьcь onъ* 'artful [man] that', *zъlyi tъ rabъ* 'bad the servant', etc.) in

---

[119] On the origin of article in Slavic languages and especially in Bulgarian and on the chronology of its existence see especially Josef Kurz, "K otázce členu v jazycích slovanských se zvláštním zřetelem k staroslověnštině [On the problem of article in Slavic languages with a special regard to Old Slavic]", *Byzantinoslavica* VII (1938), 212-340, VIII, 172-288. A critical analysis of newer literature concerning this question is contained in Kurz's paper "K otázce chronologie existence členu v bulharském jazyce [On the question of the chronology of the existence of article in the Bulgarian language]", *Acta universitatis Carolinae* (1968), *Philologica* 1-3, 117-129.

the function of article or in a function close to the article, even in that part of primitive Slavic of which Bulgarian and Russian have developed. The postpositive article or at least its rudiments can be found even in some Russian dialects. However, it must be emphasized that in older times there was no article in Slavic, either a prepositive or a postpositive one. According to Kurz the comparison of the Bulgarian postpositive article with the post-positive use of demonstrative pronouns in Russian did not pay satisfactory attention to differences; it leads only to the statement of parallelism and agreement in the possible position of demon-strative pronouns after nouns, especially in the anaphoric function. The agreement was, however, not limited to Bulgarian and Russian but had a wider, common Slavic extension.

In Czech and in other Slavic languages (e.g. in Sorbian and Polish) nearest to the function of article is the pronoun *ten* (masc.), *ta* (femin.), *to* (neut.). Josef Zubatý writes[120] that in Czech the pronoun *ten* is often used to imitate the German article. Especially in superlative it is incorrectly used, e.g. *máme na skladě ty nejnovější vzorky* 'we have on stock the latest samples', or *růže je ta nejkrásnější květina* 'rose is the most beautiful flower', etc. However, there are also cases in which, according to Zubatý, that pronoun can or must be used, e.g. *to je* ten *sluha* 'it is the servant' (when he was already spoken of), or *to je* to *neštěstí, to je* ta *bída, že mi nikdo nechce rozumět* 'that is the bad luck, the misery that nobody wants to understand me'. The nature of the pronoun *ten* is also subject of Vilém Mathesius's paper.[121] That the weakening of the deictic meaning of that pronoun has sometimes progressed very far is, according to Mathesius, evident from the fact that in translating into a foreign language, for example into English, it is often sufficient to use the definite article for the Czech pronoun *ten*. This is especially possible in comparative expressions, in super-lative, and before differentiating relative sentences. In these cases the attributive *ten* comes in colloquial Czech near to the definite

---

[120]   Josef Zubatý, "Ten", *Naše řeč* 1 (1916), No. 10, 289-294.
[121]   Vilém Mathesius, "Přívlastkové *ten, ta, to* v hovorové češtině" [Attri-butive *ten, ta, to* in colloquial Czech], *Naše řeč* 10 1926), 39-41.

article. Of course, it is only near to it because its use can always be explained by sentential and situational connection. According to Mathesius we cannot speak about a genuine article until its use necessarily follows even from the meaning of the noun itself, be singular determinedness (individualizing article) or general determinedness (generic article) concerned. However, nothing of the kind can be ascertained, even in colloquial Czech. Another scholar who points to the weakening of the demonstrative function of the pronoun *ten* in colloquial Czech is František Oberpfalzer.[122]

Another important contribution on expressing the indefiniteness of object in Czech comes from J. Zubatý.[123] In his opinion the Czech word *jeden* is not identical with the concept of indefinite article as it expresses more than an indefinite article, in fact it adds to the "indefinite" concept a certain degree of definiteness which is not implied in the indefinite article. Neither is it identical with the German indefinite article. The German *ein* is, according to Zubatý, not only indefinite article but also a word by which the German can express the same as the Czech expresses by the word *jeden*. However, German lacks in the concept of *ein* that difference which is present in Czech if the noun stands alone or is connected with the word *jeden*. Josef Vachek writes[124] that Modern Czech has no indefinite article as an expression of fortuity and situational newness. Its semantic field is shared in Czech by the weakened numeral *jeden* 'one' and the indefinite pronoun *nějaký* 'some'. According to Vachek, the pronoun *nějaký* has a more extensive area than its approximate English equivalent *some* but, on the other hand, some meanings of the English *some* are outside its area and are expressed by the indefinite numeral *několik* and partly also by the pronominal type *kterýsi (jakýsi)*. The Czech *nějaký* has, according to Vachek, in comparison with the English *some*, in addition a part of those tasks which in English are performed by the indefinite article, as far as there is felt in

---

122 František Oberpfalzer, *Jazykozpyt* (Praha, 1932), 44.
123 Josef Zubatý, "Jeden", *Naše řeč* 2 (1918), 69-78, 106-112.
124 Josef Vachek, *Obecný zápor v angličtině a v češtině* [General negation in English and in Czech] (= *Práce z vědeckých ústavů, LI. Příspěvky k dějinám řeči a literatury anglické* 6) (Praha, 1947), 44-45.

Czech the necessity of satisfying these needs, that is to express the fact of fortuity and situational newness at all. In Vachek's opinion there is felt a need in Czech to express certain situational newness only if a surprising, situationally unforeseen newness is concerned. We have, for example, the sentence *Okolo rybníka je hráze* 'There is a mole round a pond' (= generally) but *Okolo toho rybníka je ted' nějaká hráze* 'Round the pond there is some mole now' (= it is something surprising, there was no mole there before and now they have built one there; consequently there is a substitute of article). This example shows that the pronoun *nějaký* becomes substitute of the indefinite article only when the reality it refers to is something truly new and, consequently, for the observer not quite definite so far.

A similar situation is in Polish[125]: in the Polish folk language the pronouns *ten, on* are often used in the meaning of indefinite article. According to Nitsch in Kashubian dialects the pronoun *ten* is often used in the function of article through the influence of German. Also in Sorbian[126] the pronoun *ten, ta, to* is frequently used before nouns in the meaning of the German article *der, die, das*. However, such use of the pronoun *ten* is regarded as incorrect. In other cases, when the demonstrative pronoun *ten* is used in a similar way as the German definite article (especially in the stressed position of the noun in question, before numerals, if a counted object occurs in the given quantity only, e.g. *te sedym dny tyžeńa* 'the seven days of the week') the pronoun can be regarded as a demonstrative with a weakened demonstrative meaning. The cases where, apart from the above-mentioned cases, the pronoun *ten* is used as article, can be explained as influenced by German.

If the above-mentioned Slavic languages have no article it does not mean that they are unable to express the category of determinedness vs. indeterminedness. The expedient for its expression is the position of the word in sentence which can express both

[125] Cf. T. Benni, J. Łoś, K. Nitsch, J. Rozwadowski and H. Ułaszyn, *Gramatyka języka polskiego* (W. Krakowie, 1923), 331.
[126] Cf. G. Schwela, *Lehrbuch der Niederwendischen Sprache* (Heidelberg, 1906, Cottbus, 1911), 99.

determinedness and indeterminedness as for example in Czech: *Kniha leží na stole* 'The book is on the table' and *Na stole leží kniha* 'There is a book on the table' (= On the table is a book). The free word order in Slavic languages makes possible the full use of functional sentence perspective for the aims of expressing the opposition determination vs. indetermination.

In the Ngad'a language[127] the demonstrative pronouns *kĕna* and *kĕnana* are used in conversation to designate familiar persons and things in the function of the article.

In Suahili[128] the demonstrative pronouns have an emphatic or pointing function when standing before a noun, e.g. *Wale watu wote ni wageni* 'All the (before mentioned) people are foreigners' (*wale* 'those', *watu wale* 'those people'). The normal position of demonstrative pronouns in their demonstrative function is after the governing noun.

A kind of definite article are the so-called object pronouns standing close before the verb stem, for example

Kiongozi a-li-ni-tw-ambla 'The leader has told me',
Kiongozi a-li-tw-ambla 'The leader has told us',
Tu-li-m-kuta Mwariama 'We met (him) Mwariama',
M. a-li-m-tembelea Waziri 'M. called on (him) the minister'.

The following table gives the morphemes of object pronouns:

person	before cons.	before vowel		person	before cons.	before vowel	
sg. 1.	*-NI-*	*-NI-*	'me, to me'	pl. 1.	*-TU-*	*-TW-*	'us, to us'
2.	*-KU-*	*-KW-*	'you, to you'	2.	*-WA-*	*-WA-*	'you, to you'
3.	*-M-*	*-MW-*	'him, to him, her, to her'	3.	*-WA-*	*-WA-*	'them, to them'
class 2 3rd p. sg.	*-U-*	*-U-*	'him, to him, her, to her'	class 2 3rd p. pl.	*-I-*	*-I-*	'them, to them'

[127] Cf. P. Arndt, "Grammatik der Ngad'a Sprache", *Verhandelingen van het Koninklijk Bataviaas Genootschap van Kunsten en Wetenschappen*, Bandung 72 (Ende, 1933), 16.
[128] Cf. Karel F. Růžička, *Úvod do swahelštiny* [Introduction to Suahili] (Praha, 1968), 13, 25.

In the Bira language[129] the function of article seems to be contained in the postpositive demonstrative pronoun *la* which is said to be of Sudan origin, e.g. *mbuhu la* 'the man'. The *la* is often connected with the other demonstratives with the meaning 'this'.

Demonstrative pronouns are used to designate definite objects in many other languages. Thus in the Indonesian language Suluk[130] these demonstratives are *iní* 'this, these', *yadtu, yaun* 'that, those' (postpositive), e.g. *vaai-iní* 'this house', *sekayan-yadtu* 'that (distant) boat'. A similar function have the demonstrative pronouns *ica, tica, natica, ética* in the Sika language [131] and the appositive demonstrative *nén* in the Sichule language.[132] In the Alune language[133] the numeral *sae* is occasionally used in the function of indefinite article.

The position of the word in a sentence connected with the stressed or unstressed character of the given word expresses the category of definiteness vs. indefiniteness in Finnic. According to L. Hakulinen the following cases can occur:

1. The indeterminedness of the subject or even the indeterminedness of the direct object in the case of a passive predicate is expressed by their position after the predicate and by their stronger emphasis than is that of the predicate. Examples: *Tulee* ke·vắt 'spring comes'; *Tắstắ koivuhalosta tulee* ki·rvesvarsi 'From this birch log arises an axe-handle'.

2. The determinedness of the subject or direct object (in a passive sentence) is expressed by their position before the predicate and by adding stress which so far as it reaches the maximum

---

[129] Cf. Carl Meinhof, "Die Sprache der Bira", *Zeitschrift für Eingeborenen-Sprachen* 29 (1938/39), 241-287. Bira belongs to Bantu languages spoken in the area of the Ituri springs. According to Meinhof it is a mixed language, originally a Sudan language which accepted many Bantu words from various sources as well as grammatical forms, often incomplete and corrupt.

[130] Cf. M. B. Hardaker, *An Introduction to Suluk* (Sarawak MJ 11, (1963), 143.

[131] Cf. P. Arndt, *Grammatik der Sika-Sprache* (Ende, Flores, 1931), 20.

[132] Cf. H. Kähler, "Die Sichule-Sprache auf der Insel Simalur an der Westküste von Sumatra", *Afrika und Übersee*, Beih. 27 (1955), 22.

[133] Cf. H. Niggemeyer, "Alune-Sprache. Texte, Wörterverzeichnis und Grammatik einer Sprache West-Cerame", *Zeitschrift für Ethnologie* 76, 58.

equals the stress of the predicate. Examples: Kevät *tu·lee* 'the spring comes'; Kirvesvarsi *tulee tä·stä koivuhalosta* 'The axe-handle arises from this birch log'.

3. In a sentence in which the subject or direct object (in a passive sentence) in connection with stress stands on the first place, the indeterminedness of secondary sentence members relating to the predicate is expressed by their position after the predicate and by the same stress as that of the subject or of the respective object of a passive sentence. Examples: *Ku·ka on unohtanut pihalle* ku·okan? 'Who has forgotten a hoe in the yard'; *Ha·ukka vei* ka·nan 'A hawk has snatched a hen'.

4. Determinedness of secondary sentence members relating to the predicate in the preceding sentence type is expressed by their position before the predicate and by the same stress as that of the subject or direct object of a passive sentence. Examples: *Ku·ka kuokan pihalle on unohtanut?* 'Who has forgotten the hoe in the yard?'; *Ha·ukka kanan vei* 'A hawk has snatched the hen'.

5. In a sentence in which the predicate in connection with stress stands on the first place, the indeterminedness of the subject or direct object (in a passive sentence) is expressed by their position after secondary sentence members relating to the predicate and by the same stress as that of minimum intensity resting on the predicate. Examples: *Tu·li meille* vi·eras 'There came to us a guest'; *Kuu·luiko sisälle* huu·to? 'Has a cry reached the room?'

6. Determinedness in the preceding sentence type is expressed by the position of the subject or direct object (in a passive sentence) before secondary sentence members relating to the predicate and by the stress equalling the maximum stress of the predicate. Examples: *Tu·li vieras meille* 'The guest came to us'; *Kuu·lui huuto sisälle* 'The cry has reached the room'.

7. In a sentence in which a secondary sentence member in connection with stress stands on the first place, determinedness of the subject or of the respective subject of the owner expressed by genitive, adhesive, or other case, or of the direct object

(in a passive sentence or of an impersonal verb) is expressed by their position before all secondary sentence members relating to the predicate and bearing a stress equalling the maximum stress of the first word of the sentence. Examples: *Hu·omenna* isä *matkalle lähtee* 'Tomorrow the father sets on the trip'; *Va·roiksi* vieras *koiraa lyö* 'In every case the stranger beats the dog' (a proverb); *Hu·omenna* laivan *pitäisi tulla* 'Tomorrow the boat should come'.

8. Indeterminedness in the preceding sentence type is expressed by the position of the subject or direct object (in a passive sentence) after the attribute in agreement with the case ending "*a*" and by adding to it the stress equalling the minimum stress of the first word. Examples: *Hä·neltä uutisen kuuli* va·eltava te·ini 'a wandering scholar heard the news from him'; *E·nsi vuonna maassamme näkyy* a·uringonpimennys 'Next year there will be sun's eclipse in our country'.

9. Comparison of nominative (and the accusative concordant with it) or of partitive genitive:

(a) In the case of the short form of the infinitive dependent on an impersonal construction (including the passive) or on the imperative of the verbs of 1st or 2nd person which indicates existence, statement, or interruption, determinedness can be expressed by genitive singular or plural when indeterminedness is expressed by nominative (or by the accusative concordant with it) or by partitive singular or plural. This difference is strengthened by a stronger stress on the indetermined word and also by its position after the predicate. Examples: Kirjeen *piti tulla* mi·nulle 'I was to get a letter'. — *Minulle piti tulla* ki·rje 'I was to get the letter'; Kuuman veden *tulisi olla* he·ti va·lmiina 'Hot water should be *directly ready*'. — Kuu·maa *ve·ttä tulisi olla* he·ti va·lmiina '*Hot water* should be directly ready'; Lentokentän *pitäisi tää·llä valmistua* e·nsi vuonna 'It is necessary that the aerodrome be ready here in the next year'. — *Tänne pitäisi e·nsi vuonna valmistua* le·ntokenttä 'Next year it is necessary that the aerodrome be ready'

(b) Similar is the expression of the category of determinedness vs. indeterminedness of the subject part of participle construction when the predicative part of the construction is an intransitive verb indicating existence, statement, or interruption. For example, the participle construction depending on a verb in active voice: *Huomasin* veden *valuvan katon rajasta* 'I noticed water running from the roof eaves'. — *Huomasin katon rajasta valuvan* vettä 'I noticed water running from the roof eaves'. *Näin* vieraiden *tulevan* 'I saw guests coming'. — *Näin* vierata *tulevan* 'I saw the guests coming'; *He luulivat* voimien *riittävän* 'They thought they had enough strength'. — *He luulivat* voimia *riitävän* 'They thought they had enough strength'. Participle construction dependent on a verb in passive: Railon *kerrottiin taas auennen* 'They said an unfrozen place had arisen'. — *Jäähän kerrottiin taas auenneen* railo 'They said an unfrozen place had arisen in the ice'. Hiekan *havaittiin valuneen veden mukana* 'They noticed that the sand went together with water'. — *Veden mukana haivattiin valuneen* hiekkaa 'They noticed that together with water went sand'.

10. Comparison of accusative partitive. With accusative it is in some cases possible to express determinedness of direct object, and with partitive its indeterminedness. To strengthen this opposition the word order and stress are often used in addition. However, it usually refers to words in plural only; in singular such difference may be expressed by corresponding cases only with names of materials and with collective and abstract names. Examples: *Luin* kirjat 'I have finished reading the books'. — *Luin* kirjoja 'I read books'; Marjat *jo syötiin* 'They have already eaten the strawberries'. — *Syötiin* marjoja 'They were eating strawberries'. — *Toin* vettä 'I brought some water'. — Kahvi *tarjotaan parvekkeella* 'They serve the coffee on the balcony'. — *Parvekkeella tarjotan* kahvia 'On the balcony they serve coffee'.

The difference in determinedness may appear even in such

cases as *Ostin* sakset 'I have bought a pair of scissors' (determinedness) — *Ostin* saksia 'I have bought a pair of scissors' (indeterminedness). In the first sentence the direct object may be definite as well as indefinite. As a matter of fact, this way of expressing the category of determinedness vs. indeterminedness is by far not always possible so far as the opposition of the position of the accusative and partitive of the direct object is also used for other purposes.

11. Comparison of the nominative partitive with the plural and singular of the predicate. The subject in nominative when the predicate is in plural expresses determinedness but the subject in partitive when the predicate is in singular expresses indeterminedness. At the same time the determinedness of the subject is strengthened by a relative lack of stress but the indeterminedness by a relative presence of stress. The word order is also often used for the purpose of a clearer difference, the unstressed word being preferentially put before the predicate and the stressed word after it. Examples:

(a) *Vierat* tulivat *vastaan* 'The guests came to meet...' — Vieraita tuli *vastaan* 'To meet came the guests...'; Ruoka on *pöydällä* 'The meal is on the table' — *Pöydällä* on ruokaa 'On the table there is a meal'; Hiekka valui *veden mukana* 'The sand went together with water'. — *Veden mukana* valui hiekkaa 'Together with water went sand'.

(b) Negative and interrogative sentences:
Isäntä ei ole *ta·lossa* 'The lord is not in the house'. — *Talossa* ei ole i·säntää 'In the house there is no lord'; Tu·liko pappi *mukaan?* 'Has the pastor also come (with you)? — Tuliko pa·ppia *mukaan?* 'Has together with you come the pastor?' In such sentences the partitive can have even another function and then the category of determinedness vs. indeterminedness remains unexpressed. Thus, for example, in the sentence *Täällä ei ole* i·säntää 'There is no lord (of the house) here (The house is without lord)' the last word may be conceived as definite; the partitive is expressed here by a negative form of the sentence.

Consequently, the definite, last word may be regarded as interrogative: *Oliko* lääkäriä? 'Was there the doctor?'; here the partitive adds a negative shade to the sentence, so far as the inquirer who used the partitive expects a negative answer.

12. The opposition of singular and plural of predicate. Indeterminedness of the numeral performing the role of a subject is expressed by the singular of the predicate, determinedness by the plural. Examples: *Kolme liittolaisvaltaa* oli jo ratkaissut *kantansa* 'Three allied states have already cleared up their position' (the other allies not yet). — *Kolme akselivaltaa* olivat jo ratkaisseet *kantansa* 'The three axis states have already cleared up their position' (all three states are known).

13. The opposition of unipersonality and multipersonality of predicate. The indeterminedness of a word which originally was the subject used only in plural *(plurale tantum)* or the indeterminedness of a word in plural denoting dual objects, a set of objects or a group of objects denoting a familiar wholeness is expressed by the unipersonality of an intransitive, usually locally-adverbial predicate with the meaning of existence, statement, or interruption. The determinedness of the subject in nominative plural is expressed by the multipersonality of the predicate. In addition, as means of strengthening, stress and word order are asserted: *Taskussani* on *kintaat* 'I have my gloves in my pocket'. — *Kintaat* ovat *taskussani* 'I have my gloves in my pocket'; *Lapsella* on *kullankeltaiset hiukset* 'The child has golden hair'. — *Kullankeltaiset hiukset* ovat *hänellä yhä entisellään* 'He has golden hair as before'. In some cases the meaning of the word and its linking with other words in a sentence makes the word comparatively definite, even if there was no mention about it before. For example, *Mieheltä paleltui korvat* 'The man's ears have been frozen'.

14. Declinability and indeclinability of a noun modification. In singular it is possible to express the definiteness of a noun modification which has no expression of determinedness, by means of agreement of the case with the main word, and

indeterminedness by its position, in an unchanged form, before the main word. Examples: *Luulimme häntä* isäntä *Heikki Kaasiseksi* 'We took him for Mr. Heikki Kaasiseksi'; *Halusin tavata Erkki Repolaa* yliyohtajaa 'I wanted to meet Erkki Repolaa, the principal director'. — *Halusin tavata* ylijohtaja *Erkki Repolaa*, literally, 'I wanted to meet the principal director Erkki Repolaa'.

We have given a rather detailed survey of the use of word order and stress in Finnic for expressing the opposition of determinedness vs. indeterminedness because in this case we meet evidently with the functioning of the same principle of functional sentence perspective as occurs in Czech and in many other languages.

It is interesting to observe that the position in sentence influences determinedness, similarly as in Slavic languages, also in Chinese where, for example, the subject at the beginning of a sentence is, as a rule, definite.[134] However, there are cases — though not frequent ones — when a noun in the function of subject may be preceded at the beginning of a sentence by a tonically weakened numeral (jī) plus numerative in the sense of 'one' (= some). Another important rule is that in Chinese the subject following a predicative verb is, as a rule, indefinite, e.g. *láil³ kʰ³ren* '(some) guests came'.

Though this chapter should deal with languages in which the category of determinedness vs. indeterminedness is latent or missing, we are aware that we were able to give here examples of some languages in which this category is latent but we dare not assert that there are languages in which it is missing entirely. It remains an important task of linguistics to find out whether there are languages which have no category of determinedness vs. indeterminedness at all or whether this category may safely be regarded as universal in language be it expressed in an overt or in a latent way.

---

[134] Cf. *Úvod do hovorové čínštiny*, I [Introduction to Colloquial Chinese] (Praha, 1967), 137.

CONCLUSION

There is no doubt that the expression of the category of determinedness vs. indeterminedness in different languages reveals very diverse NEEDS. We can suppose that people, irrespective of the language they speak, have in mind either certain, definite, already known objects, or uncertain, indefinite, unknown objects. This kind of differentiation of objects in the minds of people is reflected in their languages. We should therefore investigate the relation of this national category of thinking to the ways it is expressed in different languages. Does the attitude language adopts toward expressing this category, and the way it expresses it, reveal something of the way of thinking of its speakers? Do the differences in expressing determinedness and indeterminedness in language reflect an analogous differentiation in mind? These are problems for psychologists and psycholinguists.

In setting a typology of occurrence of the category of determinedness vs. indeterminedness we have established a broad scale of formal and stylistic expedients by which this category is realized in various languages. Our approach is not the only one possible and it is not exempt from problems. There are some overlappings: some languages are mentioned in two or more types or subtypes. The removal of these overlappings would, however, have increased the number of types and subtypes, and, consequently, would have made the typology more complicated, if not obscure.

We can safely assert that there is no other linguistic category that is expressed by such diverse means as the category of determinedness vs. indeterminedness. The occurrence of this category in languages is an excellent example of the usefulness of the concept of centre and periphery of language system. We have seen that in some languages the category of determinedness vs. indeterminedness is apparently in the centre of language system whereas in other languages it is more or less in its periphery. In some languages it plays only an unimportant part or even tends to disappear. Its diverse assertion in language goes not only from the centre to the periphery of the language system but also from its surface to its core.

BIBLIOGRAPHY

Abeghian, Artasches, *Neuarmenische Grammatik* (Berlin-Leipzig, 1936).

Adriani, N., "Spraakkunst der Bare'e-taal", *VBG* 70.

Arndt, P., "Grammatik der Ngad'a Sprache", *Verhandelingen van het Bataviaans Genootschap van Kunsten en Wetenschappen*, Bandung 72 (Ende, 1933).

——, *Grammatik der Sika-Sprache* (Ende, Flores, 1931).

Babakaev, V.D., *Assamskij jazyk* (Moskva, 1961).

Bauer, Hans, and Pontus Leander, *Grammatik des biblisch-Aramäischen* (Halle, 1927).

Behaghel, O., *Deutsch Syntax* I (Heidelberg, 1923).

Benni, T., F. Łoś, K. Nitsch, J. Rozwadowski, and H. Ułaszyn, *Gramatyka jazyka polskiego* (W Krakowie, 1923).

Biard, A., *L'article défini dans les principales langues européennes* (Bordeaux, 1908).

——, *L'article "the"* (Bordeaux, 1908).

Bleichsteiner, R. "Die Kaukasische Sprachgruppe", *Anthropos,* 32 (1937).

Boas, Franz, *Handbook of American Indian Languages* (Washington, 1911).

Bowen, John T., and T. J. Rhys Jones, *Teach Yourself Welsh* (London, 1960).

Brandstetter, Renward, *Der Artikel des Indonesischen verglichen mit dem des Indogermanischen* (= *Monographien zur Indonesischen Sprachforschung* X) (Lucerne, 1913).

De Braye R. G. A., *Guide to Slavonic Languages* (London, 1951).

Brøndal, V., *Ord klasserne* (Copenhagen, 1928).

Brugmann, M., *Die Demonstrativpronomina der indogermanischen Sprachen.* XXII: Band der Abhandlungen der philologisch-historischen Klasse der Königl. Sächsischen Gesellschaft der Wiss., No. VI (Leipzig, 1904).

Brunot, Ferdinand, *La pensée et la langue* (Paris, 1936).

Bühler, K., *Sprachtheorie* (Jena, 1934).

Capell, A., "Notes on the Fila Language", *Journal of the Polynesian Society* CI (Wellington, 1942).

Carnoy, A. J., "Psychologie de l'article grec", *Symbolae grammaticae in honorem Ioannis Rozwadowski* I (Cracoviae, 1927).

Caro, G., "Zur Syntax des bestimmten Artikels im Englischen", *Die Neueren Sprachen* IV, 4.

Christopherson, Paul, *The Articles. A study of their theory and use in English* (Copenhagen-London, 1939).

Collinson, William Edward, *Indication* (= *Language Monographs* 17) (Baltimore, 1937).

Davidson, W., *A Preliminary Analysis of Active Verbs in Dogrib* (= *Studies in the Athapaskun Languages, University of California Publications in Linguistics* 29) (Berkeley and Los Angeles, 1963).

Deutschbein, M., *System der neuenglischen Syntax* (Gothen, 1917).

Diakonoff, I. M., *Semito-Hamitic Languages* (Moscow, 1965).

Dinneen, Francis P., *An Introduction to General Linguistics* (New York, 1967).

Djakonov, I. M. D., *Jazyki drevnej perednij Azii* (Moskva, 1967).

Dmitrijev, N. K., *Stroj tureckogo jazyka* (Leningrad, 1939).

Dordillon, R. I., *Grammaire et Dictionnaire de la langue des Iles Marquises* (Paris, 1931).

Drabbe, P., "Spraakkunst der Fordaatsche taal", *VBG* 67:1 (1926).

Dumézil, Georges, *Le langue des Oubykhs* (Paris, 1931).

Dupuy, Eugène, and Charles Ranaivo, *Le Malgache simplifié* (Paris, 1903).

Edelman, P. I., *Dardskije jazyki* (Moskva, 1965).

Edman, L., "Über den Gebrauch des Artikels im Neuhochdeutschen" (dissertation) (Upsala, 1962).

Erben, Johannes, *Abriss der deutschen Grammatik* (Berlin, 1959).

Firbas, Jan, "On the Communicative Value of the Modern English Finite Verb", *Brno Studies in English* III (Praha, 1961).

——, "On Defining the Theme in Functional Sentence Analysis", *TLP* 1 (Praha, 1964).

——, "From Comparative Word-Order Studies", *Brno Studies in English* IV (Praha, 1964).

——, "K otázce nezákladových podmětů v současné angličitině" [On the problem of non-thematic subjects in Contemporary English], *Časopis pro moderní filologii* 39 (1957).

——, "More Thoughts on the Communicative Function of the English Verb", *Sborník prací filosofické fakulty brněnské university* (1959).

——, "Non-Thematic Subjects in Contemporary English", *TLP* 2 (Praha, 1966).

——, "Some Thoughts on the Function of Word Order in Old English and Modern English", *Sborník prací filosofické fakulty brněnské university* (1957).

——, "Thoughts on the Communicative Function of the Verb in English, German, and Czech", *Brno Studies in English* I (Praha, 1959).

Frei, Henry, "Tranches homophones (à propos de l'article partitif du français)", *Word* 1:3 (1960).

Gamillscheg, E., "Zum romanischen Artikel und Possessivpronomen", *Supplementheft XV der Zeitschrift für französische Sprache und Literatur* (1937).

Geijer, P. A., "On artikeln, dess ursprung och uppgift särskildt i franskan och andra romanska sprak", *Studier i modern Sprakvetenskap* I (Upsala, 1898).

Genko, A.N., *Abazinskij jazyk* (Moskva, 1955).

de la Grasserie, Raoul, "De l'article", *Mémoires de la Société de linguistique de Paris* IX (1896), 285-322, 381-394.

Greenberg, Joseph H., "The Languages of Africa", *IJAL* 29:1 (1963).

Grierson, G. A., *Linguistic Survey of India* 2, 4 (Calcutta, 1904/1906).

Gr'unberg, A. L., "Tatskij jazyk", *Jazyki narodov SSSR* I (Moskva, 1966).

Guillaume, G., *Le problème de l'article et sa solution dans la langue française* (Paris, 1919).

Haas, J., *Französische Syntax* (Halle, 1916).

Hajdú, Péter, *The Samoyed Peoples and Languages* (= *Uralic and Altaic Series* 14) (Bloomington - The Hague, 1963).

Hakulinen, L., *Razvitije i struktura finskogo jazyka* II (Moskva, 1955).

Hall, Robert A., Jr., *An Analytical Grammar of the Hungarian Language* (= *Language Monograph* 18) (Baltimore, 1938).

Hammerich, L. L., *Indledning til tysk grammatik* (Copenhagen, 1935).

Hample, Zdeněk, and Jaroslav Holbík, *Učebnice portugalštiny* [Textbook of Portuguese] (Praha, 1965).

Hansen, A., *Artikel systemet irumaensk* (København, 1952).

Hardaker, M. B., *An Introduction to Suluk* (Sarawak, N.J., 1963).

Hermann, Eduard, *Die Wortarten* (Berlin, 1928).

Heymann, W., "Über die Lehre vom bestimmten Artikel im Englischen", *Englishe Studien* XII.

Hill, A. A., "A Re-Examination of the English Articles", *17th Annual Round-table*, F. P. Dinneen, ed. (= *Monograph Series on Languages and Linguistics* 19) (1966).

Hjelmslev, Louis, *Principes de grammaire générale* (København, 1928).

Hodler, W., *Grundzüge einer germanischen Artikellehre* (Heidelberg, 1954).

Horálek, Karel, *Úvod do studia slovanských jazyků* [Introduction to the Study of Slavic Languages] (Praha, 1955).

Householder, F. W., Kostas Kazazis, and Andreus Koutsoudas, "Reference Grammar of Literary Dhimotiki", *IJAL* 30: 2, Part II (Bloomington-The Hague, 1964).

Il'jiš, B. A., *Sovremennyj anglijskij jazyk*, 2nd ed. (Moskva, 1948).

Jakuškin, A. V., *Osobennosti morfologii drakinskogo dialekta erzja-mordovskogo jazyka* (Saransk, 1959).

Jazyky narodov SSSR IV, V.

Jefimov, U. A., *Jazyk afganskix Xazara* (Moskva, 1965).

Jespersen, O., *Essentials of English Grammar* (London, 1933).

——, *Language* (London, 1922).

——, *A Modern English Grammar* I-III (Heidelberg, 1910-27).

——, *A Modern English Grammar on Historical Principles* VII, *Syntax* (London, 1954).

Jonker, J. C. G., *Rottineesche Spraakkunst* (Leiden, 1915).

Kähler, H., "Die Sichule-Sprache auf der Insel Simalur an der Westküste von Sumatra", *Africa und Übersee*, Beih. 27 (1955).

Kellgren, A.H.A. *Grundzüge der Finnischen Sprache* (Berlin, 1647).

Kelly, John, *A Practical Grammar of the Ancient Gaelic, or Language of the Isle of Man, Usually Called Manks* (London, 1870).

Koneski, Blaže, *Gramatika na makedonskiot literaturen jazik* [Grammar of the Macedonian Literary Language] (Skopje, 1967).

Kononov, A. N., *Grammatika sovremennogo uzbekskogo jazyka* (Moskva-Leningrad, 1960).

Krus, M., and L. I. Škarban, *Tagal'skij jazyk* (Moskva, 1966).

Krušel'nickaja, K. G., "Smyslovaja funkcija porjadka slov v sovremennom nemeckom jazyke" (dissertation) (Moskva, 1948).

Kühner, R., *Griechische Grammatik* (Hannover, 1955).

Kun, H., "Over zogenaamde Verbindingsklanken in het Tagata en wat daarmee overeenkomt in 't Kawi", *Verspreide Geschriften* XIII (The Hague, 1927).

Kuryłowicz, J., "La mimation et l'article en arabe", *Archiv orientální* XVIII; 1/2 (1950).

Kurz, J., "K otázce chronologie existence členu v bulharském jazyce [On the question of the chronology of the existence of article in the Bulgarian language]", *Acta universitatis Carolinae* (1968), *Philologica* 1-3.

——, "K otázce členu v jazycich slovanských se zvláštním zřetelem k staroslověnštině [On the problem of article in Slavic languages with a special regard to Old Slavic]", *Byzantinoslavica* VII (1938).

"Languages of the World: Indo-Pacific fascicle three", *Anthropological Linguistics* 6: 9 (Indiana University, 1964).

Lazard, G., *Grammaire du persan contemporain* (Paris, 1957).

Lebanidze, V. Š., *Osobennosti artikl'a v rumynskom jazyke* [Peculiarities of the article in Rumanian] (Tbilisi, 1966).

Lotz, John, "Grammatical Derivability", *In Honor of Anton Reichling, Lingua* 21 (Amsterdam, 1968).

Majzel, S. S., *Izafet v tureckom jazyke* (Moskva, 1957).

Marouzeau, J., *Lexique de la terminologie linguistique* (Paris, 1951).

Mathesius, Vilem, *Čeština a obecný jazykozpyt* [The Czech Language and General Linguistics] (Praha, 1947).

——, "Přívlastkové *ten, ta, to* v hovorové češtině" [Attributive *ten, ta, to* in colloquial Czech], *Naše řeč*, 10 (1926).

——, *Obsahový rozbor současné angličting na základě obecně lingvistickém* [A Function Analysis of Present-Day English on a General Linguistic Basis] (Praha, 1961).

Matthews, W. K., "The Polynesian Articles", *Lingua* 2 (Amsterdam, 1926).

Meinhof, Carl, *Lehrbuch der Numa-Sprache* (Berlin, 1909).

——, "Die Sprache der Bira", *Zeitschrift für Eingeborenen-Sprachen* 29 (1938/1939).

——, *Die Sprachen der Hamiten* (Hamburg, 1912).

——, "Sprachstudien im egyptischen Sudan", *Zeitschrift für Kolonialsprachen* VII.

Michov, D., "Die Anwendung des bestimmten Artikels im Rumänischen, verglichen mit der im Albanesischen und Bulgarischen", XIV *Jahresbericht des Instituts für rumänische Sprache zu Leipzig* (Leipzig, 1908).

Miklosich, F., *Vergleichende Grammatik der slavischen Sprachen* IV (Wien, 1968-1874).

Moskalskaja, O., *Grammatika nemeckogo jazyka* (Moskva, 1958).

Nekes, Hermann, *Lehrbuch der Jaunde-Sprache* (= *Lehrbücher des Seminars für orientalische Sprachen zu Berlin*, Band XXVI) (Berlin, 1911).

Niggemeyer, H., "Alune-Sprache. Texte., Wörterverzeichnis und Grammatik einer Sprache West-Cerame", *Zeitschrift für Ethnologie* 76.

O'Beirne, Seán, *Irish Self-Taught* (London).

Oberpfalzer, František, *Jazykozpyt* (Praha, 1932).
Paul, H., *Prinzipien der Sprachgeschichte* (Halle, 1886).
——, Deutsch Grammatik, Bd. III. (Halle. 1954).
Pekeel, Gerhard, "Grammatische Grundzüge und Wörterverzeichnis der Label-Sprache", *Zeitschrift für Eingeborenen-Sprachen* 20 (1929-1930).
Piotrovskij, R. G., "Eščo raz ob analitičeskoj forme slova [Once more on the analytical form of the word]" *Izvestija AN SSR, Otdel lit. i jazyka, XVI* (Moskva, 1957).
Postal, Paul M., "On the So-Called 'Pronouns' in English", *17th Annual Round Table* (= *Monograph Series on Languages and Linguistics 19*) (1966).
Poldauf, Ivan, "On the History of Some Problems of English Grammar before 1800", *Práce z vědeckých ústavů, LV (Příspěvky k dějinám řeči a literatury anglické — Prague Studies in English 7)* (Praha, 1948).
——, *Mluvnice současné angličtiny* I [Grammar of Contemporary English] (Praha, 1968).
——, "Srovnání s mateřštinou při vědeckém zkoumání jazyků [Comparison with Mother Tongue in Scientific Investigation of Languages]", *Sborník Vysoké školy pedagogické v Olomouci, Jazyk a literatura* (Praha, 1954).
Poutsma, H., *A Grammar of Late Modern English* II (Groningen, 1914).
Ramstedt, G. J., *Einführung in die altaische Sprachwissenschaft* I (Helsinki, 1952).
Rastorgueva, V. S. "A Short Sketch of Tajik Grammar", *IJAL* 29: 4 (1963).
Ray, S. H., *Sketch of Aniwa Grammar* (London, 1888).
Reinisch, L., "Die Somali Sprache, III", *Südarabische Expedition* V: 1 (Wien, 1903).
Robbins, Beverly L., *The Definite Article in English Transformations* (The Hague, 1968).
Rombandeeva, E. I., "Mansijskij jazyk", *Jazyki narodov SSSR* III.
Růžička, Karel F., *Úvod do swahelštiny* [Introduction to Swahili] (Praha, 1968).
Sadek, Vladimir, *Novohebrejština* [New Hebrew] (Praha, 1970)
Sauer, C. M. *Italienische Konversationsgrammatik* (Heidelberg, 1919).
Sauer, C. M., and H. Rupert, *Spanische Konversationsgrammatik* (Heidelberg, 1941).
Schwela, G., *Lehrbuch der Niederwendischen Sprache* (Heidelberg, 1906, Cottbus, 1911).
Schwyzer, E., *Zeitschrift für vergleichende Sprachforschung* 63 (1936).
Sebestyén, N., "Zur Frage der determinierenden Deklination in Yurak-samojedischen", *Acta linguistica academiae scientiarum hungaricae* X (1960).
Seidel, A., *Togo-Sprachen* (Dresden, Leipzig, 1904).
Sørensen, Holger Steen, *Word Classes in Modern English* (Copenhagen, 1958).
Spore, Palle, *La langue danois* (Copenhagen, 1965).
Stresemann, E., *Die Paulohi-Sprache, Ein Boitrag zur Kenntniss der Amboinischen Sprachengruppe* (The Hague, 1918).
Sweet, Henry, *A New English Grammar, Logical and Historical II — Syntax* (Oxford, 1898).
Teselkin, A. S., *Javanskij jazyk* (Moskva, 1961).
Tesnière, L., *Éléments de syntax structurele* (Paris, 1959).

Thomas, Owen, *Transformational Grammar and the Teacher of English* (New York, 1967).

Trnka, B., *Rozbor nynější spisovné angličtiny*, II *(Morfologie slovních druhů)* [An Analysis of Present-Day Literary English, II, Morphology of Word Classes] (Praha, 1962).

Trost, Pavel, "Německé vlivy na slovanské jazyky [German influence upon Slavic Languages]", *Československé přednášky pro V. mezinárodní sjezd slavistů v Sofii* (Praha, 1963).

——, "O složeném adjektivu baltoslovanském [On the complex adjective in Balto-Slavic"], *Bulletin Ústavu ruského jazyka a lituratury* X.

Uhlenbeck, E. M., "Bibliography", *Current Trends in Linguistics* 2, *Linguistics in East Asia and South East Asia* (The Hague, 1967).

Úvod do hovorové činštiny [Introduction to Colloquial Chinese] (Praha, 1967).

Vachek, Josef, *Obecný zápor v angličtině a v češtině* [General Negation in English and in Czech] (= *Práce z vědeckých ústavů*, LI. *Příspěvky k dějinám řeči a literatury anglické* 6) (Praha, 1947).

Valeckiene, A., *Kalba in literatūra* 2 (1957).

Vanoverbergh, Morice, "Notes on Iloko", *Anthropos* 23 (1928).

Vertés, Edit, "Beiträge zur Frage des finnisch-ugrischen bezeichneten Akkusativobjekts", *Acta linguistica academiae scientiarum hungaricae* X (1960).

Wacke, K., "Formenlehre der Ono-Sprache (Neuguinea)", *Zeitschrift für Eingeborenen-Sprachen* 21 (1930/1931).

Walter/-Lund/, Edward Theodor, *Schwedische Konversationsgrammatik* (Heidelberg, 1916).

Westermann, D., *Die Gola-Sprache in Liberia* (Hamburg, 1921).

——, Nominalklassen in westafrikanschen Klassensprachen und in Bantusprachen (= *Mitteilungen des Seminars für Orientalische Sprachen an der Friedrich-Wilhelms-Universität zu Berlin* XXXVIII) (Berlin, 1935).

Wisseman, Heinz, "Zur nominalen Determination", *Indogermanische Forschungen* 63 : 1 (1957).

Zakijev, M. Z., "Tatarskij jazyk", *Jazyki narodov SSSR* II (Moskva, 1966).

Zubatý, J., "Jeden", *Naše řeč* 2 (1918).

——, "Ten", *Naše řeč* 1 (1917), 10.

INDEX OF LANGUAGES

INDEX OF NAMES